# HOW TO GROW PEOPLE INTO SELF-STARTERS

## Thomas K. Connellan

THE ACHIEVEMENT INSTITUTE, INC., Ann Arbor, Michigan

# HOW TO GROW PEOPLE INTO SELF-STARTERS

Library of Congress Cataloging in Publication Data

   Connellan, Thomas K.
      How to Grow People Into Self-Starters

      Includes Index
      1.  Management      2.  Success

I Title

Library of Congress Catalog Number: 80-65657

ISBN: 0-936452-00-5

Distributed by:
Performance Press
2 Northwick
Ann Arbor, Michigan 48105

Printed in The United States of America

# Contents

## Graphing Techniques     165

*The Simpler the Better — 166,  Graph Goals and Goal Areas — 168, Bar and Cumulative Graphs — 172,  Graphs + Positive Reinforcement = Progress — 173,  Good Graphs Foster Healthy Competition — 173, Explanations Are in Order — 173.*

## Counseling Techniques     175

*Prediscussion — 176,  Discussion — 179,  After the Discussion — 190.*

## What To Do Now     193

*Commitment Is Key — 193,  You Set the Tone — 194,  Not a Program — 194  5-90-5 — 195,  Push Versus Pull — 195  Right to Fail — 196  Be Prepared for Success — 196,  Grow Risk Takers — 198,  Don't Be Afraid to Be Tough — 199,  Remember the Top Performer — 200,  Avoid Culture Shock — 200,  Using SSM with Other Developmental Efforts to Grow People — 201,  Don't Try to Grow People Too Fast — 203.*

# Acknowledgements

No publication of this type is complete without giving credit where credit is due.

Robert Rosenthal, George Odiorne and B. F. Skinner have all contributed greatly to the theoretical basis for the Self-Starting Mechanism. People who helped clarify my thoughts and experiences about various parts of the Self-Starting Mechanism include Les Richards, Roger Elle, Albert W. Schrader, Herbert Cohen, Robert Lorber, Fred Chaney, John Hohn, John Gunkler and Ron Zemke. Rick Nachman, John Klug, Joseph Sugarman, Joan Chester and J. C. King all made significant inputs which helped in the development of the manual.

Carlene Dettleff, Susan Jones, Cathy Arcure, Judy Stopke and the staff at Total Type and Graphics all helped with the preparation and final reading of the manuscript. Sandra, and my daughter, Avis, tolerated my irrational behavior during the preparation of this manuscript. The support and suggestions offered by Mike Casey, Pamela Dodd, and Toni Cameron all contributed to the revised edition.

To all these individuals, a very special thank you for their help in making this manual possible.

# Introduction

This manual is designed to help you be a better manager than you already are. It's my guess you're already a good manager or you probably wouldn't be reading these materials. It's been my experience that people who could use something like this the most never read it.

As the title suggests, this manual is specifically designed to help you develop Self-Starters. Self-Starters are an important part of any winning team. They are the individuals who on their own can seek out, identify and solve problems. They are the people who consistently have high performance over a long period of time. Self-Starters accept responsibility for their own actions; they inspire others to action. In short, a Self-Starter is the type of individual who has the get up and go, to stick to a job and get it done right.

There are two types of information in this manual to help you develop Self-Starters. Some publications only tell you why something works. They don't tell you how to do it. This type of publication leaves you agreeing with the idea, but not knowing what to do about it. Other publications tell you what to do, but not why it works. These leave you with something that seems to work, but since you don't know why it works, you can only use it in one particular situation. Moreover, because you don't know why it works for you, you don't know how to teach it to others or improve upon it.

I've written this manual to show you both why something works and what to do about it. Armed with both types of information, you'll have some specific techniques that you'll find work for you regularly and you can also adapt these techniques to your own organization and your own managerial style. You can coach others in the use of the Self-Starting Mechanism. Most importantly, you can use the information to improve and refine what is here.

What you have is the combined experience of my work with small, medium, and large-sized organizations. With insurance companies, financial institutions, manufacturing firms, retailers, health care organizations, wholesalers/distributors, contractors, pharmaceutical firms and the government. With presidents of multimillion dollar companies and supervisors in a company with less than $200,000 in sales.

I learned a great deal from all of these individuals. Many times, I've learned at least as much from them as I have given. Sometimes we made mistakes in improving employee productivity, but we learned from those mistakes and those mistakes are all "written out" of this manual. It's not perfect, of course; there's always room to learn. I hope you use this manual to do just that—to learn.

To maximize the benefit you get from the information in this manual, look through the key learning points in the appendix before you read each chapter. Review them again when you finish a chapter. As you read through a chapter, make notes in the margin on how you can specifically apply the techniques to your own type of situation. Jot down people's names next to tools and techniques you think they might be able to use more appropriately than you. Make it a point to identify those particular techniques you would like to discuss with some of your subordinates or colleagues.

"Oh, sure," you say, "getting me to write notes in the margin is just a way of making sure that I don't pass the book along for somebody else to read. That way you'll make you'll make more money on royalties."

Actually, that's not true. What I know is, that if as you go through the manual, you make notes in the margin on ways in which you can use the techniques, jot down ideas on how you and others can capitalize on the use of the Self-Starting Mechanism, it will work for you. It'll make your job easier; it'll make your company money, and it'll improve the performance of the people who work for you. When you find that the Self-Starting Mechanism works for you, you'll tell other people how valuable the information in this manual is. They'll all buy a copy for themselves and that's the way I'll make more in royalties. I know from experience that the more you make notes on how you can use this manual for yourself, the more benefits you'll get from it, and the more benefits you get from it, the more people you'll tell to buy a copy of their own. Besides there's no reason that somebody can't read or shouldn't read a manual where you've made notes in the margin. It just means they can't make their own notes and they won't get as much benefit from it.

Other ways in which you can maximize your learning from this manual is to use the question check lists. When you have a question about employee performance, turn to the appendix to see if it is listed there. Once you have the question, turn to the proper chapter to find out the answer. (You can also use the key learning points as your own personal check list to make sure that you're doing the things that you'd like to do.)

Most of all, improve on what you find in this manual. There is a lot of valuable information here. People have used the Self-Starting Mechanism to improve sales, improve profit, reduce absenteeism, reduce the error rate, improve the amount of cross-selling of services done by tellers, reduce the quantity of rejects, reduce the scrap rate, reduce the rework rate, improve quality, reduce the amount of unreported scrap and improve on a host of other performance indicators. The information in this manual has been worth thousands and in some cases millions of dollars to individual companies. If you use the Self-Starting Mechanism, you'll find similar results, but don't stop there. Keep on testing and improving upon what you find. Best of luck.

—TOM CONNELLAN

# HOW TO GROW PEOPLE INTO SELF-STARTERS

# The Need for Self-Starters

In today's highly competitive world, more and more organizations are turning to performance-based management technologies to maximize the return from their human assets. In particular, they are looking for tools, techniques, and systems that will help develop Self-Starters. And who exactly are Self-Starters? They're the people who can not only carry out assigned tasks well but can also, on their own, seek out, identify, and solve problems. Ever-increasing numbers of companies, managers, and developmental specialists are seeking ways to improve the performance of their department, plant, or company—and with good reason.

Consider, for a moment, these sobering facts:

1. Absenteeism is estimated to cost American industry in excess of $9 billion a year. That's 36,000 times the salary of the President of the United States or enough to fly first class from New York to San Francisco 25,000,000 times or to build 180,000 new houses; with $9 billion, you could buy 36,000,000,000 bottles of pop, a 346,000,000 year subscription to *Fortune*, or 5,625,000,000 pounds of hamburger.

2. A recent Gallop poll suggests that 50% of all wage earners could accomplish more each day if they tried. Thirty percent of these wage earners said their increases could be 20% or more. (My personal observation is that these estimates are low. Improvements greatly in excess of 20% are possible, and substantially more than 30% of the wage earners could accomplish more if they desired to do so and if the work climate was conducive. Many people often respond conservatively to surveys of this type because they're afraid either of secret coding on the questionnaires or of standards tightening up if too many negative answers come in.) What this really means is that improvement in American productivity, which has fallen to a recent low of only .4%, could be substantially

improved. It means that if everyone were as productive as he or she could be our organizations could run more effectively and efficiently with less employees; thus, many of these people could be more gainfully employed elsewhere.

3. Somewhere between 70% and 80% of each gross national product dollar goes to some form of worker compensation. If we take an average of 75%, this means that for an $8,000 car, $6,000 goes toward labor dollars at either the auto company, the tire company, the parts plant, the steel mill, the iron mine, or the dealership.

4. In 1950, it took seven Japanese or three German workers to match the industrial output of one American. Today two Japanese or 1.3 Germans can do as well.

5. In a 25-year period, from 1950 to 1975, after-tax profits declined from 9% to less than 5%.

Consider, too, these less dire but nonetheless troubling facts:

- At least once a day, everyone in a management position slams down some object and mutters, "If you want something done right, you've got to do it yourself."

- The vice president of one company is reputed to order soap for the washrooms himself because he can't find someone to do it right.

- Most organizations are like ducks. From the outside, they're calm and serene, moving steadily ahead through the water. Up close, however, you see a different view: the ducks' feet are paddling furiously just to keep the creatures afloat.

Small wonder, then, that both individual managers and entire organizational structures are looking for techniques that will help them restore productivity to a desired level. Interestingly, the solutions being sought are neither technological nor engineering solutions; they are *people* solutions. While great technological breakthroughs have helped improve individual plant, hospital, corporate, and national productivity, the ability of people to match that gain has fallen behind. As one divisional manager of a $200 million operation told me, "Our total profits are going up, but our profit percentage is going down. If we look at what we put into technological improvements and what we get back from those improvements, the return is becoming less and less. It's imperative for our management team to build the kind of climate where human productivity can improve without clubbing people over the head and without always relying upon technological systems."

Consider these paradoxes. We have sophisticated territory management techniques for salespeople, but we can't get the salespeople to submit their field sales-call reports on time. We have medical equipment that can save, prolong, or even revive life, but we can't count on the medical technician being there to run the equipment. We have cars that are safer, more economical to run, and stronger than ever before, but the cost of excessive and unnecessary sick leave in the auto industry has been estimated as high as $200 per car. Our sophisticated computers can spew forth regression analysis, mailing lists, computer labels, interconnect charges, long-distance telecommunication networks, and schedules with complex procedures (like building an automobile with 13,000 parts), but we're still stymied by problems of human error. Finally, financial institutions with telecommunication systems that transact business across the country almost instantaneously still have trouble developing the type of climate that encourages people to balance accounts correctly and cross sell services.

These examples and countless others illustrate the problems we have with our human performance systems. While our technical systems are good—even great—our human systems generally have failed to elicit the type of behavior we need from our employees.

The crux of the problem, I believe, is that many people perform below their potential. Some individuals perform well below their potential, and others perform only slightly below their potential. And some, of course, perform up to potential. Let's presume that the population of employees within the company we have to work with represents a "normal distribution" in terms of potential. For the purpose of illustration, let's say that the potential available to us ranges from 0 to 10, with 10 being the high point on the scale and 0 being the low point. A normal distribution would look something like figure 1-1.

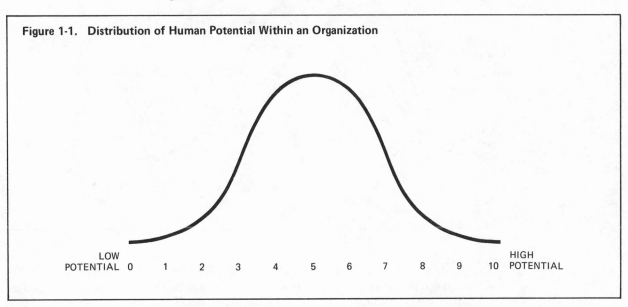

Figure 1-1. Distribution of Human Potential Within an Organization

LOW POTENTIAL  0  1  2  3  4  5  6  7  8  9  10  HIGH POTENTIAL

As you can see, there are very few 0's and very few 10's. If we were talking about intelligence here, it would mean that there are few natural geniuses, and correspondingly, few morons. But in terms of performance potential, it suggests that there are some people (the 0's, 1's, and 2's) who don't have very much potential for performance within the organization. Obviously, there aren't very many such people. The diagram also suggests that some people (the 8's, 9's, and 10's) have a tremendous potential for performance within the organization. The normal distribution also suggests that the bulk of the population lies somewhere between 3 and 7 (the 3's, 4's, 5's, 6's, and 7's); and these are the people who have solid potential for performance within the organization. Most of the people with whom we must deal will lie within this central range (3, 4, 5, 6, and 7).

As I look at different organizations, talk with practicing managers, and conduct Achievement Climate Surveys for organizations, I find that many people are performing below their potential, either consciously or unconsciously. A distribution for actual performance might look something like figure 1-2. Here we can see that, in the statistician's terms, the curve is skewed somewhat to the left: that is, some people are performing at 0 and 1, although not too many; the bulk of the population lies in the 2's, 3's, 4's; and, by the time we get to 5, the actual performance has dropped off considerably.

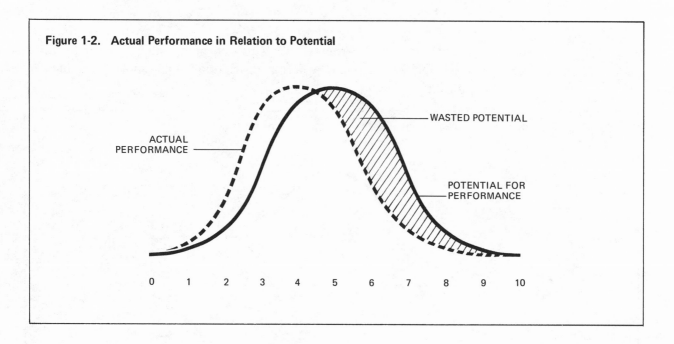

Figure 1-2. Actual Performance in Relation to Potential

By combining these two curves, we get an interesting proposition. As you can see in figure 1-2, the combination of these two curves results in a shaded area, which I refer to as wasted potential—that is, potential that is untapped by the organization. People in this area are performing below the level of their potential, and both the organization and the economy are losing power from one of their most valuable resources—human beings.

Many managers who've seen this diagram tell me that they would like everyone on their team to be outstanding; to be top performers; to be not just good, competent performers but to be at the tops of the appraisal and salary curves. I'd like that, too; it would make life a lot easier for everybody. In fact, I'd like to be able to tell you that, if you read this manual, I could make your team a winning one. But I can't. I don't know how to make a silk purse out of a sow's ear—consistently. Nor do I know anyone who can—consistently. Occasionally, yes. In one situation or another, yes. But everytime? No.

Instead, the tools and techniques in this manual will show you how to make a good sow's ear out of a poor one, how to make a good silk purse out of a bad silk purse. In other words, they'll show you how to take someone who is performing at 1 and move him to 3 or 4 or perhaps even to 6 or 7, how to take someone who is performing at 3 and move him to 7 or 8, how to take someone who is performing at 6 and move him up to 10. Instead of panaceas or "sure-fire solutions," I plan to offer some proven techniques that I've used with a variety of companies in establishing the type of achievement climate that triggers the Self-Starting Mechanism, which is inherent in virtually everybody. Once triggered, the SSM permits more individuals to contribute more positively to their organization's—and their own—goals.

**The Myth of the Disappearing Work Ethic**

Much of the blame for the productivity crisis has been attributed to the disappearing work ethic. Managers often lament that the work ethic has vanished, that "people don't want to work hard anymore." That's nonsense. People do want to work hard, and they do want to contribute to accomplishment. With a few exceptions, people have a sense of pride in accomplishment. The problem, then, lies not with "them" but with us, with our own management styles and the kind of climate we create in our places of work. We have failed to create the type of environment in which people take pride in their work, where everyone from the top of the organization to the bottom has a sense of accomplishment and contribution. We have not, in other words, systematically created the type of climate that fosters Self-Starters.

It's not that the work ethic has disappeared but, rather, that the work force has changed around us, and our organizations have not adapted to this changed environment. Too many managers are still locked into styles that date from the Depression. Unwittingly, they have forced the work ethic underground by failing to create the type of environment where people can grow. We are all guilty of misdirecting and misusing our human assets. And of misspending. We will spend $50,000 to buy a new machine and $7,200 a year to maintain it, but we won't spend 10% of that amount to make sure the operator is situated in a climate that encourages high performance.

I personally don't believe that the excuse that "people don't want to work hard anymore" explains away poor performance. Most (not all, but at least 90 to 95%) of the people in organizations today not only want to contribute to the organization's success but will do so willingly—*given the proper conditions*. I've seen plenty of high absenteeism, poor-quality work, discouraged and/or alienated first-line supervisors, poor sales, low margins, high error rates, and low productivity in a variety of organizations. The reason given: "People don't want to work hard anymore." Yet, within a few months, that same supervisor—with the same work force, the same equipment, the same sales force, the same product line—has been able to boast of decreased absenteeism, improved quality, radically reduced error rate, and improved productivity. Suddenly the people who didn't want to work hard anymore are working hard. Self-Starters are everywhere. They are contributing to the organization, and their contributions are paying off on the bottom line. Why the change? Because new management and supervisory practices altered—and greatly improved—the work climate.

A positive work climate is not only important, it's crucial. And the primary responsibility for creating the proper climate must lie with management. Charles J. Pitliod, board chairman for Goodyear Tire and Rubber Company, reports, "Management has an obligation to see that employees achieve a sense of personal satisfaction from what they do." The amount of personal satisfaction an employee derives from the job is, in large part, a function of the climate in which the work takes place. Just as a major league baseball player can derive personal satisfaction from his job climate, an employee should be able to derive personal satisfaction from the job. Employees who derive personal satisfaction from their jobs are going to be encouraged to contribute that extra little bit of effort that can be important in meeting the organization's overall goals.

I believe that there are a lot of 200 hitters in today's organizations who could be hitting 300 ball. Now the difference between that 200 hitter and a 300 hitter is only one hit every ten times at bat, but it's the difference between the minor leagues and the majors. The same thing is true in companies. The difference between the minor and major leagues may be only one hit in every ten times at bat. It's a small difference but a critical one and one that Self-Starters can make for you. Self-Starters can lead the way for your team, whether you're involved in manufacturing, sales, banking, insurance, retailing, health care, or real estate.

## Firstborns and the Self-Starting Mechanism

My own curiosity about the conditions that grow people into Self-Starters led me to uncover some interesting facts. I found that although firstborns account for only 33 to 38% of the population (depending upon the year of their birth), they seemed to account for more than their share of Self-Starters. For example:

- Most entrepreneurs (⅔ of them) are firstborn.
- A ten-year study of 1,503 superior ninth-grade students from Wisconsin showed that 49% of them were firstborn.

- Of the twenty-three astronauts, twenty-one were firstborn; the twenty-second had an older sister who died at an early age, and an age gap of thirteen years separated the twenty-third from his next eldest sibling.

- Fifty-five percent of high creative scientists (Ph.D. and a patent rate of more than one per year) at a major chemical firm were firstborn, but only 14% of those who were low creative (a Ph.D. and a patent rate of zero per year) were firstborn.

- Tests of nursery school, kindergarten, and day-care children showed that firstborns scored, on the average, 3.5% higher in creativity than did later-born children.

- A study in England in 1874 showed that firstborns were over-represented among fellows of the Royal Society.

- A study of 2,274 military personnel showed firstborns overrepresented in high-ranking positions.

- Eighty percent of a group of Air Force "military achiever" pilots are firstborns.

- A random sample of members of two-child families who entered Columbia University over a twenty-year period showed that, depending upon the year, 52% to 66% of them were firstborns.

- Sixty-four percent of the people from two-child families who were listed in *Who's Who* are firstborns.

Intrigued by all these facts, I started talking to firstborns to find out what separated them from the rest of the family. I talked with parents to find out how they treated firstborns differently from the rest of the family. I watched families in action to note differences. No matter where I turned, three *environmental* factors consistently emerged to distinguish firstborns from other children:

1. *There are higher expectations for the firstborns*. They are the ones who are going to be the all-star quarterback, the president of the senior class, or the captain of the cheerleading squad. In whatever direction expectations lie, they tend to be higher for the firstborn.

2. *Firstborns are given more responsibility at an earlier age*. If, for example, children are sent to the movies, the firstborn is given money to buy the tickets and popcorn.

3. *They receive more feedback and more attention is paid to what they're doing*. They get more attention from friends, neighbors, and relatives than the rest of the children. Parents even tend to take more pictures of the firstborn.

On the surface, this could suggest that unless you are firstborn, your chances of success and personal growth are low to nonexistent. On the surface, this could suggest that unless you were born with "it," you can't get "it." But that's simply not true. People who jump to that conclusion are overlooking the crucial element: the three factors are *environmental* factors. As you can see from diagram 1-3 the presence of the three factors in the environment is what counts; *it's whether or not the three factors have been, are or could be put to work that determine the presence of what I came to call the Self-Starting Mechanism.*

To test the importance of the three environmental factors, I went to one company and explained what I had found about the three environmental factors. I persuaded them to let me try an experiment by training their managers how to use the three factors. Productivity went up dramatically.

Encouraged by this confirmation that the environment is what counted, I trained managers in other firms how to use the three factors. Each time, the presence of the three factors in the work environment has increased productivity.

The factors have built high performance climates in manufacturing, sales, office, distribution, health care, research, financial and service organizations.

To study all sources of the three factors I researched other areas. This research further confirmed that it was indeed the environment that counted (and not being firstborn). Here are the conclusions of my second round of surveys:

- More members of the Million Dollar Round Table are later born than are firstborn. (MDRT members account for less than 4% of the insurance agents world-wide but each member sells over a million dollars of insurance a year.) But over 98% of them identified either themselves or a supervisor as the source for each of the three factors.

- A study I conducted of high performing and low performing sales representatives in wholesale/distribution showed that *more low performers* than high performers *were firstborn*. The same study showed, however, that the supervisors of high performers did a better job of creating the three factors of the Self-Starting Mechanism than did the supervisors of low performers.

- A study of company presidents who assumed that position before age 40 revealed that 67% of them could identify a supervisor from earlier in their career who created each of the three factors of the Self-Starting Mechanism in the job climate.

- My survey of high performing and low performing real estate agents showed that supervisors of high performers scored 22% higher on their ability to create the factors of the Self-Starting Mechanism than supervisors of low performers.

- Interviews with highly successful Self-Starters in a variety of fields showed that many of them *were not* firstborn. But each of those individuals could also identify the exact source of each factor of the Self-Starting Mechanism.

As figure 1-3 shows, there are other ways (besides being firstborn) that the three factors of the Self-Starting Mechanism can be or have been put to work:

- The three environmental factors (expectation, responsibility, and feedback) are more frequently at work where there is an age differential of three or more years between a child and the next eldest brother or sister.

- A manager or supervisor can create the type of environment—through expectations, responsibility, and feedback—that develops employees into Self-Starters.

- An individual doesn't have to be a firstborn or have a sibling at least three years younger. Nor does he or she need a supervisor to put the factors to work. Individuals can create their own three factor environment.

Of the five ways in figure 1-3 to activate the Self-Starting Mechanism, the third is most important to managers because it *gives us the opportunity to create the type of environment that will encourage high levels of performance and that will grow people into Self-Starters.*

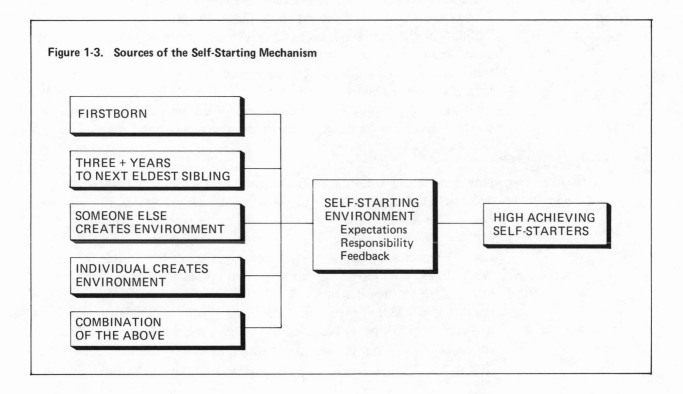

Figure 1-3. Sources of the Self-Starting Mechanism

**Elements of the Self-Starting Mechanism**

Figure 1-3 shows that there are four separate ways to trigger the elements of the Self-Starting Mechanism; the fifth one includes some combination of the first four.

It's significant that no matter which of the four primary sources of the Self-Starting Mechanism is responsible for the Self-Starter, *the environment is the same.* Moreover, it always includes expectations, responsibility, and feedback, the three factors that produce high-achieving Self-Starters. Any time the three factor environment is established, people will grow and flourish—and become Self-Starters. Self-Starters are *always* the result of the three factors but the three factors are only sometimes the result of being firstborn.

**A Closer Look At The SSM**

Let's, for example, take each of the factors of the Self-Starting environment and see how it pertains to people who are generally regarded as the ultimate Self-Starters—athletes. Even people who aren't Self-Starters on the job are generally Self-Starters in athletics. They may not put out as much effort as you think they should on the job, but watch them hit the tennis courts, the hockey rink, or the ball field. The same individual who puts in only 20% or 30% on the job will often put in 110% or 120% on the adult hockey team, the bowling league, or the weekend tennis match.

*Expectations*

Expectations influence results. If the organizational climate is negative, organizational results will be negative. Statements such as "We'll never sell that product" or "They don't have the problems we do" become self-fulfilling prophecies. While these statements may be false to begin with, they soon become entrenched in the value system of the organization. What was false becomes true. Athletes—especially professional athletes—wouldn't last long if the entire team kept saying, "We'll probably lose this game," "We sure are a sorry bunch of dummies," or "We'll only get one or two first downs." Even among us amateurs, high expectations tend to improve performance.

*Responsibilities and Goals*

How long would a halfback play football without knowing where the goal line was? How about a tennis player without a service line or a bowler with no pins? Probably not very long. Without the responsibility of a goal, none of these athletes would be very motivated to continue in his or her profession. The same thing happens when employees aren't responsible for a goal. When they're not motivated, they often don't do as good a job as they could in living up to their potential. That's not their fault, of course; it's our fault—for not letting them know specifically what that goal is. Just as a halfback wouldn't be a professional football player without a goal line, an employee can't do a professional job without knowing what the goal is. The first step in improving attitude and motivation then is to let employees know what goal we have in mind, whether it focuses on quality, attendance, sales, or prospecting.

*Feedback and Applause*  How long would the halfback play football without yardline markers to tell him how much progress he has made? How about the tennis player who couldn't see whether or not his shot went over the net? How long would a bowler continue to bowl if he couldn't see whether or not he knocked down the pins? Seeing how much yardage has been gained or where shots have rolled or landed represents feedback. One aspect of feedback is the *information* that tells us how we're doing. Because people think in terms of pictures, a chart or graph represents the best form of feedback for job performance. Obviously, the football player needs immediate feedback; it would be tough for a halfback to stay motivated about football if he didn't find out for a month whether or not he scored a touchdown. Employees need immediate feedback, too.

Football wouldn't be much fun without the yardline markers that show immediately how much progress has been made during any given play or series of downs. Likewise, a job becomes more motivating when someone can look back over the past few days or few weeks to see how much progress has been made as a result of his or her effort.

Of course, there is also *applause*, a special form of feedback. Try to picture Roger Staubach, O. J. Simpson, or Mohammad Ali performing without applause. These professional athletes all get paid extremely well; but without the applause, they wouldn't perform the way they do. Employees also benefit from applause, which, for them, doesn't take the form of clapping and cheering. One way or another, they like to know that their efforts are appreciated.

As managers and supervisors, we're usually quick to criticize when somebody does something wrong and slow to reinforce when somebody does something right. O. J. Simpson probably wouldn't be very motivated if the fans were quick to point out his every mistake and boo him—and then fell silent every time he did something right. Yet this is often what we do in our organizations. When employees make mistakes that affect quality, we're quick to point them out. But when they do something right or correct their mistakes, we rarely let them know that the effort or correction was appreciated. Small wonder, then, that people sometimes don't perform the way we think they should on the job.

In short, if we were to compare ways in which we could improve employee attitude, motivation, and performance with the same things that motivate people in terms of athletics, we would conclude that the following actions work well in both instances:

1. Communicate positive expectations about performance levels. Let employees know that you believe they can attain and sustain a high level of performance.

2. Establish a goal and responsibilities. Let everybody know what the goal is so they can see not only where they are headed but how much further they have to go to meet the goal.

3. Establish a feedback system that frequently lets people know specifically what progress is being made. And give a little applause. When either an individual or a work group progresses or does something right, express your appreciation. If the work group hits its goal, tell people that the effort they made was appreciated. Even if the target hasn't been hit but progress has been made, let them know it's appreciated.

By following these steps, managers have found that employees will become motivated Self-Starters.

Both in concept and in implementation, the Self-Starting Mechanism is relatively simple. Most things that work well aren't particularly complex *once we know how to use them properly*. And that's what you'll learn from this book — how you can use the Self-Starting Mechanism to accomplish such important tasks as improving teamwork, reducing costs, increasing sales, improving quality by growing the people that work for you into self starters.

Actually, you'll probably find that you already know something about many of the techniques described here. But by knowing exactly what to do in each situation, you'll be able to either begin doing some things that you already know you should be doing or to begin doing better, some things that you're already doing.

Probably more of the former than the latter. Most of us are in a position not unlike the county agent that is often used as an example of the point that most of us need to do more.

As you probably know, the function of county agents was to teach farmers about strip farming, crop rotation, and other farming methodologies that would help improve the productivity of their farms.

One new county agent decided to really get things going in his district. He gathered together sets of materials on all the modern methods that he could find and sent them out with a cover letter to each farmer in his district. He then sat back and waited for the fruits of his efforts to become apparent.

They weren't long in coming. About a week after mailing the packets of information out, he received one back in the mail. It was unopened and tucked in it was the following note: "Dear Mr. County Agent: Thank you very much for the materials on modern farming. I don't believe that I'll be needing them. I already know how to farm better than I do."

The same point is often true of us. We often know how to "grow people" better than we do. This book *will* help you know more, but most importantly, it will help you *do* more. It'll help you create more positive expectation, establish better goals, and provide better feedback.

# 2 What Is the Self-Starting Mechanism

Now that you have a feel for the rationale behind the Self-Starting Mechanism, let's look at some of the principles upon which this important collection of techniques is based.

**Not an Addition to the Job**

After looking through this manual and checking out the chapter titles and the number of pages, you might say to yourself, "I think this guy is trying to add an awful lot to our jobs." But the truth is, I'm really not *adding* anything to your job; I'm suggesting a new way of *doing* it.

The Self-Starting Mechanism is not a communication theory; it's a way of communicating with people. It's not a motivational approach; it's a way of doing some things you're probably already doing. When you use the techniques that comprise the Self-Starting Mechanism, you won't learn how to delegate, but you'll find that you're a better delegator. The Self-Starting Mechanism is not merely an approach to improved human relations, but you'll find that the human relations within your organization will start to improve. The Self-Starting Mechanism is not what is popularly called an "approach to team building," but you'll find that its application will help the members of your team work together better. What's more, you'll find improved team spirit throughout the organization as the ripple effects of the Self-Starting Mechanism begin to be felt.

**Organized Common Sense**

The Self-Starting Mechanism is not a theory; it's organized common sense. While it is based upon theories that have been tested time and time again, the Self-Starting Mechanism, in and of itself, is both practical and proven.

There are three ways to develop a theory. One approach is to sit in an ivory tower and think up reasons why people behave the way they do or why some people are more successful than others. The second approach is to sit in the ivory tower and look out at the real world and try to find out why something works and something else doesn't. The theorist using this approach tries to find things that seem to work and then builds a theory around them.

The third approach is the one I used in developing the techniques called the Self-Starting Mechanism. I went out and watched what happened. I interviewed people. I watched men and women build successful teams and successful companies. I spent considerable time running around the trenches to find out what worked. Finally, after I found out what kinds of things do—and don't—work, I went back and organized the techniques that people use into a set of practical techniques. Here's what you will find in the following pages.

First of all, you'll find a lot of common sense. And you'll probably find many things that you're already doing on the job: but perhaps you don't realize the full extent to which these common-sense approaches can be applied. The second thing you'll find is based on a computer technology term, GI-GO, which refers to "garbage in and garbage out." The same thing applies in terms of developing people who can be Self-Starters for you. Confusion in and confusion out, system in and system out. It is my hope that this book, as an organized approach to common sense, will provide a systematic approach to applying some common-sense techniques that work.

**The Self-Starting Mechanism Is Behaviorally Based**

This is perhaps the most important of all the principles used in developing the Self-Starting Mechanism. A behaviorally based approach is one that requires the manager to focus on specific behaviors of an individual rather than on general descriptions or general abstractions of those very specific behaviors. Frequently, people who are trying to develop Self-Starters say things like "Mike isn't aggressive enough. I wish Mike were more of a Self-Starter. I wish he were more aggressive." Because the individual trying to develop Mike into a more aggressive person has not articulated exactly what he wants in terms of behavior, he is often doomed to failure.

Perhaps his misguided efforts began when he sat Mike down and said, "Mike, if you're going to make it as a salesman in this company, you simply have to be a little bit more aggressive." Mike, not being sure exactly what his boss meant, no doubt nodded sagely and said, "Well, I'll put my shoulder to the wheel, Chief; I'll get out there and be a little more aggressive."

If we'd had the opportunity to sit down with Mike's boss before the heart-to-heart talk and ask him some questions, our dialogue might have gone like this:

"Who would you like to help be more of a Self-Starter?"

"Well, I'd like to help Mike."

"What could he do that would enable him to be more of a Self-Starter?"

"Mike should be more aggressive in dealing with the customers."

"Specifically, what do you mean by being more aggressive?"

"Well, he has to take the bull by the horns. He has to put his shoulder to the wheel."

"I'm still not sure exactly what you mean by being more aggressive. Could you give me some specific examples of things that Mike might do or not do that would lead you to conclude that he was being more aggressive?"

"Well, I think he ought to ask for the order more frequently during the sales call."

"Exactly how many times is he asking for the order now?"

"He's only asking for the order once or twice. And if a customer says no or doesn't show any particular interest, Mike gives up and doesn't ask for that order the second, third, fourth, or fifth time."

"I see. If I could summarize our conversation then, what you really mean when you ask Mike to be more aggressive is that you would like him to ask for the order—when it's appropriate—up to five or six times."

"Yes, I think that's an accurate summary of our conversation."

"Well, I'd like to suggest, Mr. Manager, that the next time you sit down with Mike, you point out that his success ratio might be a little bit higher if he were to ask for the order five or six times during the sales call."

With this specific piece of information in mind, the manager might conduct his next conversation with Mike this way:

"Mike, come on in and sit down. I've been traveling with you for three days now, and I've watched you very closely during the sales call. I think you do a good job of positioning the customer. I think you do a good job of relating to his needs. But I think you could do a better job in terms of asking for the order. I kept track of the number of times you asked for the order over the last three days, and it averaged out to 1.4 times during the sales call. This means that sometimes you ask for it once; sometimes you ask for it twice; once in a while, you ask for it three times. But the studies I've seen show that you can ask for an order five or six times, because frequently the customer doesn't even hear the first couple of times. And I'd like to see what you and I could do working together, Mike, to get the number of times you ask for the order up to a target of three. What do you think, Mike? How could we go about getting there?"

With this specific behavioral description in mind, Mike and his boss can now start to work on some very specific tasks that will develop the kind of behavior pattern the boss is looking for. Because the Self-Starting Mechanism is a behaviorally based approach, it requires the manager, who wants to develop Self-Starters among his team members, to identify some very specific behaviors a person might adopt if he or she is to become a Self-Starter.

The same thing applies to the relationship between motivation and behavior. Talk to a plant manager, a branch manager, a sales manager, or a hospital administrator about Self-Starters on the staff. Inevitably, you'll encounter someone who says, "What I really want are people who are motivated enough to become Self-Starters." Generally, this individual means that someone on the staff is not performing up to a desired level of performance. If he were performing up to the desired level the supervisor would say that he was "motivated." But when someone isn't performing up to a specific level, he or she would say that he's "not motivated."

Managers who are successful in developing Self-Starters, however, take a behaviorally based approach. In response to a question about sales, they might reply:

"Sales aren't as high as they should be. What behaviors should my sales people exhibit so that they'll get the kinds of sales results we're looking for? And, once we get that behavior pattern started, how can we maintain it so the individual becomes self-motivated, self-managed, and Self-Starting?"

The behaviorally oriented manager thus puts himself in a slightly different position than most other individuals when examining the behaviors or performances of people who are Self-Starters. Such managers look for specific examples of behavior that contribute to organizational results. Then they look for ways to develop that specific type of job behavior.

If we were to sort responses from managers into two types—those from individuals who probably could develop successful Self-Starters and those from people who probably could not—the result would look something like this:

**A. Responses from People Who Probably Would Not Be Successful In Developing Self-Starters**

1. That individual isn't very aggressive.

2. She has a bad attitude.

3. He's not very motivated.

4. She's really keeping her shoulder to the wheel.

5. That department isn't very cooperative.

**B. Responses from People Who Probably Would Be Successful In Developing Self-Starters**

1. That individual must ask for the order more frequently during the sales call.

2. She doesn't take the time to thank a customer for the order.

3. His sales-call reports come in on an average of two days late.

4. She does an extremely good job of identifying the customer's needs before she actually makes the sales call.

5. Whenever we ask for information from him, it takes a minimum of two weeks to get it.

As you can see, the Self-Starting Mechanism requires a manager to concentrate thoroughly on two areas: what kinds of job results are going to be required of this individual and what are some of the specific behaviors that lead to the accomplishment of those job results.

**It's Based on the 20-80 Rule**

The 20-80 rule is based upon studies originally done by Vilfredo Pareto, an Italian sociologist and economist who studied income distribution in various countries. He found that, despite different government policies in different countries, 20% of the people controlled 80% of the wealth. Today we know that the 20-80 principle applies to the following instances:

- 20% of the employees are responsible for 80% of the absences.
- 20% of the customers are responsible for 80% of the past-due accounts.
- 20% of the product line produces 80% of the profits.
- 20% of your in-laws cause 80% of your in-law problems.

Of course, it's not always 20-80. In reality, 27% of the employees account for 91% of the absences. Or maybe 35% of the accounts are responsible for 86% of the complaints. However, because of the 20-80 principle, it's also true that a very small change in behavior can lead to a big change in terms of job results. Frequently, the behavior we encourage an individual to develop can produce big changes in terms of job results. For instance, a small change in the type of account called on can make a big change in the number of new accounts. Or a small change in the way someone grinds a product can have a big impact on quality.

Figure 2-1. The Impact of Small Changes in Behavior Job Results

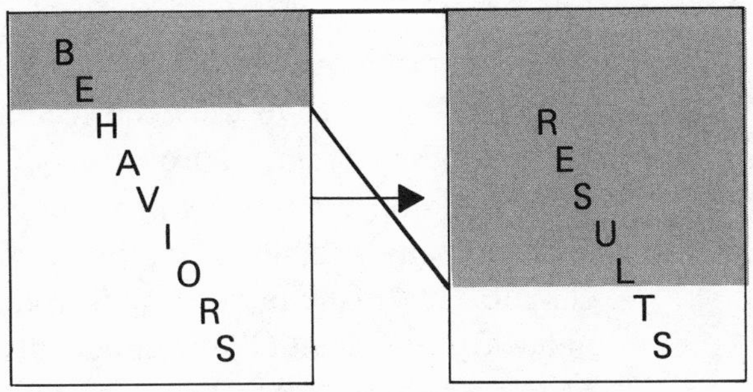

**The Self-Starting Mechanism Meets Dual Needs**

Both individuals and organizations have needs. And when individual needs and organizational needs don't jibe, it's bad for the people and it's bad for the organization. One of the individual needs the Self-Starting Mechanism helps to meet is the need to feel involved. Too frequently in today's job situation, people feel alienated from their work. Because they aren't involved, they feel no sense of ownership. As you read on, you'll find out why the Self-Starting Mechanism helps develop a feeling of involvement in people within the organizational setting. People also need to feel a sense of accomplishment. Individuals within the job situation generally are proud of accomplishment. While the refrain "People don't want to work hard" is frequently heard, this does not mean that, given the opportunity for individual accomplishment, people won't feel a sense of pride. Quite the contrary. Properly recognized job accomplishments give people a feeling of having done something worthwhile.

People also need a sense of individual worth. In many organizations today, the human assets are mistreated, demeaned, and mishandled. Put to work at meaningless tasks with little or no sense of responsibility, no feedback on how they are doing, and only an occasional bone thrown to them from someone up above, people often lose their sense of worth on the job. When this happens, they tend to look outside the job to find that sense of worth. They might turn to amateur athletics, local politics, or volunteerism—all of which are worthwhile. It is, however, a shame and a waste of an organization's human assets when people find they must look outside the job for all their sense of worth.

The Self-Starting Mechanism helps meet a company's need for motivated employees. Today the lack of motivation is a very real problem for an increasing number of organizations. In a variety of behavioral ways, employees indicate to management that they're not motivated. They don't come to work on time; they don't produce enough; they don't sell enough; the quality of the product they do produce isn't as high as it could be. In these and other ways, employees indicate to management that they are not what we would call motivated.

A company needs tools, techniques, and systems that have bottom-line payoffs. Fortunately, the Self-Starting Mechanism is able to give people the tools and techniques by which they can bolster morale and boost productivity. People who have used the techniques I propose have increased sales, reduced absenteeism, improved quality, cut error rate, slashed scrap and rejects, and upped company profits.

A company also needs employees who are committed to a success-oriented climate. Too many organizations today are filled with mental midgets, people who have essentially "retired" but are still collecting pay. Because these people's skills are not being properly tapped or utilized, the individuals themselves are not committed to the success of the organization. The climate is one of mediocrity or even failure rather than one of success. But the Self-Starting Mechanism, through the development of behavioral techniques, helps build a commitment to success-orientation in individuals. And when individuals are oriented to success, the organization naturally develops a climate that fosters success.

Fred T. Allen, chairman and president of Pitney Bowes, Inc., is keenly aware of the importance of this type of orientation and commitment. Says Mr. Allen, "When an individual or an institution invests in our stock, he or it deserves a regular and complete accounting. The employee who invests his working life in a company deserves no less and conceivably more. Consequently we have put a lot of time, money, and effort into making sure that our employees are informed about every facet of our company and that they feel they belong to, not work for, a company." It's this attitude of "belonging to" rather than "working for" that the Self-Starting Mechanism seeks to develop.

In short, the Self-Starting Mechanism helps overcome the "don't give a damnism" that is so costly to both individuals and organizations. It helps build a winning team by giving people an opportunity to be involved, a sense of accomplishment, and a sense of worth within the organization. It also helps the company improve its performance because it motivates employees and encourages their commitment to both individual and organizational success. Best of all, perhaps, the techniques of the Self-Starting Mechanism help produce tangible, bottom-line payoffs.

**Helps You Know Why You're Good**   The Self-Starting Mechanism is based upon what many successful managers do instinctively. As you read on, you'll find some things that you do already, some things that you perhaps could do more of, and some things that you're not doing at all that you ought to start doing. You'll probably also find some things that have worked for you from time to time. And, probably most importantly, you'll now find out *why* certain things work for you so that you can use those same sets of behaviors time and time again.

---

**Figure 2-2.   The Relationship between Conciousness and Competency**

|  | UNCONSCIOUS | CONSCIOUS |
|---|---|---|
| COMPETENT | UNCONSCIOUS COMPETENT | CONSCIOUS COMPETENT |
| INCOMPETENT | UNCONSCIOUS INCOMPETENT | CONSCIOUS INCOMPETENT |

---

If we were to look at an entire range of management skills, we would find that some individuals are pretty competent at what they're doing. We'd also find some people who aren't so competent at what they're doing. Let's represent the degrees of competence on a vertical scale. Another way of looking at people is to see how conscious they are of what they're doing; that is, the individual is either aware—conscious—of what he's doing or he's unaware of it. Let's represent the degree of consciousness on a horizontal scale. Combined, the two scales create a matrix, shown in figure 2–2, that represents the four types of approaches to developing Self-Starters: 1) conscious competent, 2) unconscious competent, 3) conscious incompetent, 4) unconscious incompetent.

Now let's see how each of these managers might go about developing—or not developing—Self-Starters.

The unconscious incompetent could not develop Self-Starters. If questioned about what a Self-Starter was, he would reply that he didn't know. Not only does the unconscious incompetent not know how to develop Self-Starters, he may not even *know* that he doesn't know.

The conscious incompetent deliberately sets out *not* to develop Self-Starters. Often, this is the individual who is threatened by having Self-Starters work for him, so he actively tries not to "grow people."

The unconscious competent is much like the natural athlete. The natural athlete is good: he knows that he's good, and others know he's good. He consistently helps win the game. However, when you ask the natural athlete how he succeeded, he is often unable to tell you. His skills come naturally, and, as a result, he can't describe what they are. Because of this inability to describe the skills and exactly how they work, most natural athletes make lousy coaches. They don't know *why* they succeeded as athletes, so they can't teach their skills to someone else.

Many top managers are like the natural athlete: they are natural Self-Starters. However, just because they themselves are naturally Self-Starters doesn't necessarily mean that they can develop others into Self-Starters. The fact that someone is a Self-Starter himself may be due to a particular talent or instinct that comes naturally. Unfortunately, this often prevents someone from teaching the same skills to someone else. Moreover, he can't develop other Self-Starters consistently. Therefore, his approach to building Self-Starters is only *somewhat* satisfactory because it's usually inconsistent in terms of results.

The purpose of this manual is to help you become *consciously competent* at developing Self-Starters. It's designed to help you find out why what you do works and why it sometimes doesn't and to help you build a systematic approach to developing Self-Starters.

## Not a "Shot in the Arm"

The ultimate goal of the Self-Starting Mechanism is something I call SSP—Sustained Superior Performance. Many management self-help programs have a shot-in-the-arm effect; but, with the passage of time, their potency diminishes. The Self-Starting Mechanism definitely isn't a shot in the arm. Nor is it an energy pill. It is rather, a collection of techniques that, once incorporated in your repertoire of leadership skills, can be applied continually in virtually every situation—profit or nonprofit, at home or on the job. Furthermore, the effects of applying the Self-Starting Mechanism can last for years. Some of the early applications made when I first began working with the techniques are still going strong. Granted, others have waned, not because the techniques weren't valid, but because I or someone else failed to apply them properly.

**Not a Cure-All**   The Self-Starting Mechanism isn't a panacea either. It doesn't cure corns, arthritis, or hay fever. It doesn't solve problems of cash flow, missing material, or broken machines. However, SSM probably will show you how to get people to sell more of the proper items so you'll have the cash you need. And it will probably show you how to reduce rejects to an acceptable rate so that the inventory is balanced. Building a climate in which the Self-Starting Mechanism begins to develop and help people grow takes time. While you'll start to see some results from using the techniques fairly quickly, the real payoffs come over time.

Because it's not a panacea, SSM neither promises nor delivers *immediate* solutions to problems you are facing right now. If sales are down, it will help you get sales back up to where they should be—but it won't do it overnight. For SSM to work for you, you'll have to study and absorb the techniques described in this book, and you'll have to practice them consistently and tenaciously. Once you've done your homework, helping people become Self-Starters will seem like second nature to you, and you'll eventually be the head of a team you're proud to lead.

**Employee Response**   People who have participated in the seminar upon which this book is based have asked, "What will my subordinates think when I start using these techniques?" The answer is simple: They'll probably appreciate your effort *if* you tell them what you're going to do beforehand. Ask them to read your copy of this manual. Tell them that you're going to use the techniques it describes, that you plan to practice them, and that you hope they'll use them, too, along with the people who report to them and to the other departments with whom they interrelate. Because there's no secret formula here, no nefarious manipulation, there's no reason you can't share with the people you'd like to help develop into Self-Starters the tools, techniques, and suggestions set forth in this book.

**A Process, not an Event**   The Self-Starting Mechanism is a process, not an event. It can't be seen, and you can't say, "There it is." You can say, "There's our machine" or "There's our computer." But you can't say that about the Self-Starting Mechanism. Nonetheless, it *is* there. The *results* of the Self-Starting Mechanism can be seen in increased sales, in reduced absenteeism, in improved quality, in less turnover and fewer grievances, but the Self-Starting Mechanism *itself* isn't a visible commodity.

For this reason, it takes energy to implement the Self-Starting Mechanism over time. When you install a machine, a lot of energy is expended initially, but once it's in, the machine keeps running. The same is somewhat true of the Self-Starting Mechanism. It takes some energy to get it going; but once it goes, it keeps on going. The difference between activating the Self-Starting Mechanism and installing the machine is this: the installation of the machine is a finite event, but the development of the Self-Starting Mechanism within key people who report to you takes place over time. The former is a single event at a specific point in time, while the latter is an ongoing process.

**Interdependence of Elements** The three elements of the Self-Starting Mechanism are mutually dependent upon one another, not separate and distinct from one another. A change in responsibility, for example, produces changes in both expectations and feedback; likewise, a change in either feedback or expectations could well produce a change in responsibility. Figure 2–3 illustrates this interdependence.

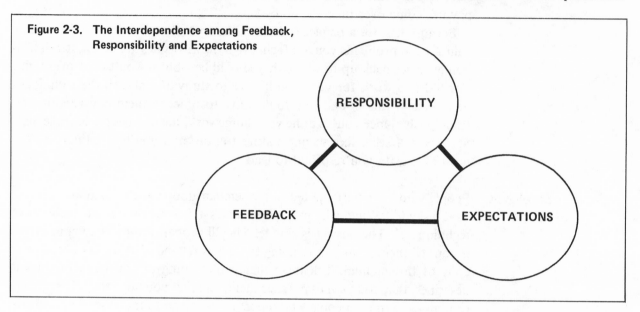

Figure 2-3. The Interdependence among Feedback, Responsibility and Expectations

RESPONSIBILITY

FEEDBACK

EXPECTATIONS

In a way, the three factors can be envisioned as a three-legged stool. If one leg is missing, the stool doesn't function too well. Developing Self-Starters is much like making sure that all three legs are on the stool. If you have responsibilities and expectations but no feedback, you don't have the Self-Starting Mechanism. Or, if you have responsibilities and feedback but very low expectations about performance, you still don't have the Self-Starting Mechanism. Unless all three elements are in place and working well, the Self-Starting Mechanism won't really pay off for you.

**Like Organizations, SSM Constantly Changes** The Self-Starting Mechanism is dynamic, not static. As figure 2–4 indicates, the Self-Starting Mechanism leads to high performance. This, in turn, leads to more Self-Starters in the organization, and more Self-Starters lead to higher performance. And so on and on and on. It's like a spiral that increases as it moves upward.

By the same token, if the Self-Starting Mechanism isn't working, the organization starts on a downward spiral. Without any Self-Starters in an organization, low performance results. And low performance leads to even fewer Self-Starters within the organization, which, in turn, means lower performance.

Organizations aren't static; they are constantly changing. The same is true for the Self-Starting Mechanism and the development of Self-Starters. The introduction of the Self-Starting Mechanism into an organization starts an

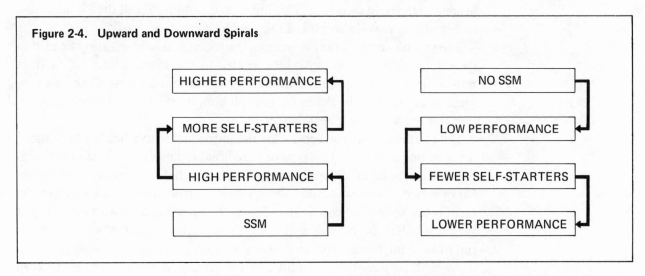

**Figure 2-4. Upward and Downward Spirals**

upward spiral. But the organization that doesn't use the techniques of the Self-Starting Mechanism cannot maintain its status quo; eventually, it starts to decline, and ultimately, it dies.

**Helps Develop "Professionals"** If you look at the people around you, you probably notice that some of them move a little more quickly than others. They get things done sooner. Let's represent that with a horizontal scale labeled "speed."

Another measure of how well people are doing might be the direction in which people are progressing. Some people are able to maintain progress in the right direction, while others frequently head off in the wrong direction. Let's represent direction with a vertical scale labeled "direction."

**Figure 2-5. Employee Speed and Direction**

| | LOW SPEED | HIGH SPEED |
|---|---|---|
| RIGHT DIRECTION | LOW SPEED RIGHT DIRECTION | HIGH SPEED RIGHT DIRECTION |
| WRONG DIRECTION | LOW SPEED WRONG DIRECTION | HIGH SPEED WRONG DIRECTION |

If we combine the two scales, we get figure 2–5, which gives us four different combinations.

Moving counterclockwise around the matrix the first combination we encounter represents the individual who's headed low speed in the right direction. While this person moves slowly and deliberately, he more or less is headed in the right direction. This individual, whom I'll call the Plodder, just inches along, making some headway each day.

The second combination represents the individual who is slowly headed in the wrong direction. Because he's headed in the wrong direction, he does pose a threat to the organization but not too serious a threat since he's progressing so slowly. The Schmoo, as I call him, is no real use to the organization but neither is he a real danger.

The third combination represents the individual who's headed high speed in the wrong direction. This type of individual *is* dangerous. These Holy Terrors can be found in all types of organizations, where they pose a real threat. Sample Holy Terrors include the quality control director who thinks the plant is run so the line can be shut down; the sales manager who wants to cut the price in half to increase unit sales; the librarian who thinks the library is run to keep the books from circulating; or the comptroller who suggests that if the business were run just a little bit differently, it would be easier to keep the books on it. Watch out for Holy Terrors!

Finally there is the person headed high speed in the right direction. Whatever his job title or job function, this individual is the Pro. Pros contribute. They develop. They create. They innovate. Nurture them for they shall help your organization succeed.

Self-Starters are the "Pros of the Pros." Not only do they do many different things but they are highly motivated to do them. Self-Starters head at an extremely high speed in the right direction, and this manual will help you grow that type of superior individual.

**What Is a Self-Starter?** By now, we all agree that Self-Starters are extremely important. But have we really determined what Self-Starters are? How would we define someone we consider a Self-Starter? After talking with people who call themselves Self-Starters or who have worked with others they called Self-Starters, I was struck by four elements that make certain individuals Self-Starters.

First of all, they are *consistently* high performers. Not just once in a while, or every other month, or on every fourth sales call, or toward the end of the year—but over an extended period of time. They consistently perform at peak levels, whatever their job responsibilities. The Self-Starter is the salesman who is out in the field making that extra call every day and spending a few minutes every night to mail cards to key accounts. It's the teller or the branch manager who puts a little extra effort into dealing with customers. It's the real estate agent who contacts one more prospect than do the other people in the office every day. It's the manufacturing supervisor who double-checks all the tools before the line starts up.

Second, Self-Starters are able to perform at this level with a *minimum amount of supervision*. They don't need someone standing over their shoulders directing their every move. They supervise themselves; they identify problems and potential problems and take corrective action on their own. When they encounter problems that they can solve on their own, they suggest alternative courses of actions and recommend possible solutions, rather than merely stating the problem. Because they are able to perform on their own with a minimum amount of supervision, geographic distance generally poses no barriers to having these people on the same team. Self-Starters can work the territory farthest from the regional office; they can run the plant that is seldom visited; they can function on their own on second or third shifts with no drop-off in performance.

Self-Starters also actively *seek out growth and new responsibilities*. Already strong individuals, they are looking for new ways to grow. They look forward to being on committees and task forces that have real jobs to do and that offer learning and growing opportunities. By the same token, Self-Starters shun responsibilities that aren't growth-oriented and that don't provide a challenge.

Finally, Self-Starters are an *inspiration to others*. They provide the models that others look up to. A Self-Starter is the top real estate agent whom everybody else in the office wishes to emulate. It's the go-get-em insurance agent who dazzles his or her colleagues. Or it's the manufacturing supervisor who's the envy of all the other supervisors.

# The Power of Expectations

About five years ago, I was helping Bob, the vice president of a medium-sized manufacturing company, think through some operational decisions for the coming year. "You know," Bob said at one point, "I've got something on my mind even more important than thinking ahead eight to ten months. I've just discovered that one of our major competitors is coming out with a brand new product. From what I hear about the product in their marketing plan, I'm convinced that we're going to get killed in the marketplace." He then proceeded to describe to me the new product and the competitors' marketing strategy. He told me that he had shared his concerns with his staff and asked me what I thought about the chances of his company taking a beating.

My response was a simple one and had nothing at all to do with the competitor's product or his marketing strategy. I answered, "Yes, you're going to get killed in the marketplace." And the reason I gave him was based simply upon the fact that he had created within his organization the *expectation* that they were going to get walloped.

We talked for a while about the power of expectations and how, frequently, something comes to pass just because we create the expectation that the event will occur. Upon realizing his error, Bob tried to rectify it. But it was too late. The expectation had been created, and the momentum was there. The company did, in fact, get killed in the marketplace by the competition. And, although it eventually came back, it took several years to regain its original momentum.

About three years after that incident, Bob left his job and assumed the presidency of a different firm. Shortly afterward, he invited me to speak at its annual management meeting. The usual events opened the meeting and one was a talk by Bob.

The situation he now faced was similar to the one he had encountered three years earlier. A major competitor had just come out with a new product, which was being heralded in the industry as a real breakthrough. What's more, it had a clever marketing plan. But the speech Bob gave about this situation showed he'd learned his lesson. He talked about the stupidity of his competitor coming out with a new product, when the fact was that *his* company had the best sales and marketing force in the industry. He acknowledged that the new product was probably a good one and, in fact, had several unique features. But he was quick to add that his company was going to knock the other one on its rear. He said it would be a tough battle but that eventually the competition would skulk home with its tail between its legs, licking its wounds.

And, as it came to pass, that's just what happened. When the new product came on the marketplace, the competition got killed. Why? Because Bob's sales force went out and outsold and outtalked the competitor's sales force. The power of the expectations fostered by Bob won the battle. His Self-Starters got the job done.

It's important to note here that Bob didn't deny the reality of a tough situation. The power of expectations has nothing to do with denying reality. Instead, it creates expectations that affect the situation positively. Had Bob chosen to ignore the advent of the new product in the second instance, he would have been denying reality—and he would have taken a second beating. During his talk, he told the sales force that the new product was a good one, that would be tough to sell against, but he was convinced that his sales personnel *could* sell against that product. He said—and quite accurately—that one of the most important things the sales force had in its favor was its ability to deliver against a very tight schedule. He said he knew that his manufacturing operations could outperform, outschedule, and outproduce the competitor. In other words, he planted in the salespeople's minds the expectation that they *could* outperform the competitor's sales force. By confronting reality with positive expectations about the outcome of a particular situation, Bob learned a valuable lesson.

**The Pygmalion Effect**

The Pygmalion Effect has it roots in ancient Greek mythology. Pygmalion, a Greek sculptor, carved a statue of an ideal woman and then fell in love with his own creation. Eventually, Venus, the goddess of love, transformed the artifact into a living woman. Thus, Pygmalion's *belief* in love helped him experience the real thing. Centuries later, George Bernard Shaw drew upon the Pygmalion myth to tell the story of Professor Henry Higgins and Eliza Doolittle, an illiterate Cockney flower girl. Higgins made a bet with one of his colleagues that he could pass Eliza off as a duchess. Thanks to his positive expectations (and a lot of hard work), he was able to do so. Shaw's play *Pygmalion* and the subsequent musical *My Fair Lady* dramatize Higgin's success in realizing his high expectations. In today's modern business world, the Pygmalion Effect refers to the impact of the positive expectations of one person upon another.

Perhaps no one has done more research on the impact of expectations upon human behavior than Robert Rosenthal, a professor of social psychology at Harvard University. Rosenthal has conducted a number of studies to test how the expectations of one person affect the behavior of another.

One of his more interesting studies was conducted with Lenore Jacobson, a staff member of a West Coast school system. Each child was given an intelligence test, which Rosenthal and Jacobsen said would accurately predict which students would become "intellectual bloomers." Each grade contained three classrooms—one for children of above-average ability, one for children of average ability, and one for children of below-average ability. At random, 20% of the children in each classroom were designated "bloomers." The teachers of these students were told that these children had scored high on the intellectual blooming test and would show remarkable gains in intellectual development during the school year. In reality, however, these students had been chosen at random; the only difference between these children and other children in the class was in the minds and expectations of their teachers. At the end of the school year, each child was again given the same IQ test. The children who had been randomly designated as "intellectual bloomers" showed an average increase in their IQ score that was four points higher than the other students in the class. Apparently, the children chosen at random as "bloomers" were influenced by their teacher's expectations. At the end of the school year, the teachers were asked to describe the behavior of their students. The children who had been randomly designated as "bloomers" were described as more interesting, more curious, happier, slightly more appealing, better adjusted, more affectionate, and less anxious for social approval.

Other children in the classes also gained in IQ during the course of the school year, but the teachers' reaction to the improvement in those children, who had not been designated as "bloomers," was negative. The more these undesignated children gained in IQ, the more they were viewed as less well-adjusted, less interesting, and less affectionate. In their cases, the improvement they displayed led to lower ratings on behavioral descriptions of their classroom activity.[1]

This last point has some interesting implications for managers. How do we view the performance of people who do better work than we expected them to? Think, for example, of the female manager. Since the managerial role has typically been perceived by males (and some females) as a "man's job," a woman who performs as well as, or even better than, expected might be perceived by superiors, peers, colleagues, and subordinates as being "hostile" or "aggressive" or "less well-adjusted" than other people. The same implications of negative perceptions of unpredicted or unexpected success could also apply to any group from which we might *expect* low performance but *receive* high performance.

Dr. Albert S. King[2] worked with a group of underprivileged workers who previously had been waitresses; housemaids; unemployed, unskilled laborers; and farm workers. Within the group were several trainees—seventeen pressers, twenty welders, and nineteen mechanics. King randomly selected fourteen trainees—four pressers, five welders, and five mechanics—and randomly designated them "high aptitude personnel." Supervisors for these individuals were told that the fourteen trainees could be expected to show unusual improvement and skill development during their training period. In reality, of course, the only difference between the fourteen randomly designated trainees and the other forty employees was in the minds of their supervisors.

At the end of the program, supervisors were asked to use eight criteria to indicate the degree of each trainee's adjustment. Ratings for those designated as "high-aptitude personnel" were much higher than for those not so designated. The high-aptitude trainees were considered more knowledgeable about jobs, more productive of neat and accurate work, better able to learn new duties, and more responsible, cooperative, and logical. In other words, these fourteen were, according to their supervisors, the best performers. Toward the end of the program, the trainees were asked to rank their colleagues according to whom they would 1) most like to work with, 2) most like to be with, and 3) judge the best overall performer. The "HAPs" scored higher in all three areas than did their colleagues.

Interestingly, when the welders and mechanics took practical and written tests during the course of their training, those labeled "high aptitude" scored significantly higher than did the other trainees.

King reports that supervisors probably revealed their high expectations of "high-aptitude personnel" in ways so subtle that the trainees could not even begin to detect or articulate them. For example, a pair of seemingly identical photographs was used to determine how visual cues might serve to convey the supervisor's message of high expectancy. Two pictures of the same supervisor were shown to trainees in the combination welder-mechanic training program. The pictures were identical except that one was modified to make the pupil size of the supervisor's eyes seem much larger than it did in the untouched photo. Both "high-aptitude personnel" and undesignated control members were asked the same two questions: "Do you see any differences in these pictures of your supervisor?" "Whether you see any difference or not, can you select the photo that shows how the supervisor usually looks at you?" In answer to the first question, none of the trainees noticed that the photos were different. But, surprisingly, all five trainees designated "high-aptitude" to the supervisor selected the photo with the enlarged pupils as representing the way the supervisor usually looked at them. Only two of the seven undesignated trainees chose the same photo.

Since all the trainees indicated that there was no difference between the two photos, why did those who were designated as "high-aptitude" and who subsequently performed best uniformly select the photo with the larger pupil size? According to psychological research, large pupil size can indicate more favorable attitudes and expectations. So eye contact in face-to-face relations is likely to serve as an unintentional, but certainly remarkable, indicator of the supervisor's interest in and expectations for his or her subordinates. Frequently, we communicate these expectations without being aware of what we are doing. Nonetheless, the impact upon subordinates is felt even though they themselves may not realize what is actually happening.

Such slight and imperceptible cues as pupil size might explain the high ratings given the "high-aptitude personnel" by their peers. In King's experiment, the supervisors' high expectations for the "high-aptitude personnel" probably were communicated to the entire group of trainees, alerting the rest of the trainees—subconsciously—that the supervisors expected more from the select fourteen.

J. Sterling Livingston described a similar response among managers in a *Harvard Business Review* article titled "Pygmalion in Management."[3] A district office manager of a large life insurance company had observed that outstanding insurance agencies grew faster than average or poor agencies. He also noted that new insurance agents performed better in these outstanding agencies. The district manager assigned his best agents to work with the best assistant manager. The six next-best agents were assigned to work with an average assistant manager, and the low producers were assigned to work with the individual regarded as the least able assistant manager.

The impact of these different combinations produced some interesting results:

1. The group selected as the top producers was frequently referred to as the "super staff." The esprit de corps of these salespeople was very high, and their production efforts exceeded even the most optimistic expectations. Thus, grouping the top assistant manager with the top producers in the office resulted in an overall increase in the sales among those producers.

2. Grouping the low producers with the assistant manager who was perceived as being the least able also had an interesting but predictable result. The productivity of these individuals, which was low before the regrouping, actually declined *after* the regrouping. Moreover, attrition among these individuals increased, as expected.

3. The average unit was expected to remain about the same. The district manager expected only average performance from this group, and, based upon what we now know about expectations, we might assume that its

production would remain constant, even though its members had been regrouped.

Surprisingly, though, the production of this group increased significantly. The assistant manager in charge of the middle group refused to believe that he was any less capable than the assistant manager of the "super staff" or that his agents had any less ability than those in the top group. In every discussion with his agents, he communicated his high expectations for his group and told its members that, through persistence and hard work, they could become just as good as the "super staff." As a result of his expectations, the average group increased its production by a higher percentage than did the "super staff."

## What Affects Expectations?

A number of different variables can affect the power of expectations.

*History*

History can be an important variable. An individual's beliefs and expectations are no more than the sum of his experiences to that point in time. As individuals, we are all conditioned by history, and our expectations become conditioned by that same history. If, for example, a salesperson has a history of trouble in landing big accounts, expectations could cause that historical pattern to be repeated time and again. Or, if a sales manager's historical perspective is that the people on his staff have trouble handling high volume accounts, he might unconsciously communicate that expectation to the sales team, which then has trouble handling such accounts.

*Status or Rank*

Status or rank also affects expectations. A company president telling a foreman that he's "the kind of individual who can improve quality" might well have a greater impact upon that foreman's own expectations and behavior than if the foreman heard the same thing from the training director. An airplane pilot who says to a small boy "If you eat your spinach and study hard in school, you can be an airplane pilot, too" would probably have more impact than would the child's mother or father saying the same thing. A physician advising her teen-age daughter that hard work, perseverance, and sacrifice are necessary if one is to become a top surgeon would have a greater impact than if a nurse's aide said the same thing to the same teen-ager.

It's important to remember, of course, that status and rank are often in the eyes of the beholder and in the social norms of a particular work group. To a reader of this book, a police chief would probably have more status and rank than a pimp or a drug kingpin. But a kid on the streets might not agree with you. To the street kid, the drug pusher has infinitely more status than the police chief, and, sadly, the kid might well respond to the drug pusher's expectations rather than to those of the police chief. It's important, then, that high expectations be communicated from a source that the receiver perceives to be high in terms of status or rank. What the status or rank actually *is* has virtually no impact at all; it is the sender's *perceived*, rather than *actual*, status that is critical in determining the impact of the expectations communicated.

*Biosocial Factors*   Biosocial factors also play an important role in affecting expectations. Sex, age, and race are probably the most visible and important of the biosocial factors. If, for example, a manager expects certain behavior from females, those expectations—whether positive or negative—are very often met.

*sex*   A branch manager, for example, recently revealed to me an interesting series of events that will illustrate this point. During the previous four years, he had employed three women to be members of the sales team—and subsequently let them all go because of poor performance. About three-quarters of the way through the fourth year, he participated in a seminar I conducted for sales managers from a variety of firms. As he sat through the seminar, I could see him taking copious notes in the margins of summary sheets in the notebook. At the conclusion of the seminar, he buttonholed me and poured out the following "confession."

"You know, I've been thinking about what you said about expectations and about the role plays we've been through. Over the past four years, I've hired three women and had to fire all of them from my sales team. Now I'm looking for a fourth to replace the one I recently let go. In each of these hiring situations, I was only responding to pressure from headquarters, which said I had to have a woman on the sales team. As I look back at my own behavior, I'll admit that my expectations in the first three instances weren't very high. In the situation I'd been forced into, I didn't see how a woman, no matter how bright or confident, could handle a 'man's job.' Now, I realize that I probably communicated these expectations to each of the women I hired—and fired. And, perhaps, in a variety of subtle and not-so-subtle ways, I also communicated them to other members of the team and other people in the branch.

"I think I'll go back and follow the suggestions you've outlined, in terms of communicating expectations, to the next person I hire and see what happens. Not only am I going to make it a point to communicate my expectations to that person, but I'm going to make sure that these expectations are communicated to other members of the branch. This time, I'm going to 'talk up' whomever I hire to the warehouse manager, to the people at the inside order desk, and to other key individuals."

I complimented the sales manager on the openness with which he had shared this information and suggested to him that his new approach would probably work well (combined with the other techniques we discussed during the seminar). I asked him to keep in touch with me and let me know what had happened.

About six weeks later, I received a letter from him. He wrote that he had hired a woman who, in terms of general background, skills, ability, and interest, didn't appear to be that much different from his three previous "mistakes." He did tell me, however, that he had communicated positive expectations about her performance not only to the individual herself but also to other key people within the branch. He reported that some people within the branch were mildly surprised about his positive expectations. But he had reassured them that this individual was going to be a good performer. What's more, he told them that, in a short period of time, she would be on a par with more experienced male members of the sales team.

About six months after that, I received another letter. If the most recent addition to the sales team could have read it, she would have known what it feels like to be a waffle with syrup poured over it! That's how lavish our sales manager was with his compliments. Not only had she caught on faster than anyone had expected, she was opening more accounts than almost anybody in the office, her average order size was already number three out of the ten members of the sales team, her gross profit dollars were in third place—and all this in only six months.

*age* Too often, people approaching fifty or fifty-five years of age are expected to "slow down." And, by the time they're sixty, they've lived up to our expectations and begun to retire—but they're still on the payroll. We managers then shrug our shoulders and say, "See, just what I told you. These old duffers aren't putting out the effort that they could." True, these individuals aren't performing at the levels of their potential, but that's probably because they're living up to our expectations, and, too frequently, their performance only *matches our expectations*. Thus, age is another biosocial factor that affects our expectations.

*race* The third biosocial factor that concerns us here is race. Each of us has certain biases, prejudices, and beliefs about other races. Whites expect blacks to behave in certain ways, and blacks frequently live up to those expectations—for better or for worse. Likewise, blacks expect whites to live up to certain expectations, and whites generally do—again, for better or for worse. That whites have expectations about blacks and blacks about Indians and Indians about whites and so on and on are facts of life and certainly not new ones. It's also a fact of life that "we" and "they" often live up to those expectations.

*Believability* The believability of an expectation is another important factor in determining the effect of that expectation. Telling a foreman, for example, that he can be plant manager might not be believable and, thus, would have no impact on performance behavior. Telling that same individual, however, that he might become a general foreman would seem much more believable and, thus, might well have a positive impact on the individual's behavior. Telling someone who cannot play the piano that he can perform in Carnegie Hall in six months would not seem believable; it would, therefore, be dismissed and have no real impact on that individual's behavior. Telling the same person, however, that, in one month, you could teach him to play "Twinkle, Twinkle Little Star," "Row, Row Your Boat," and "Mary Had a Little Lamb" does seem believable. It might, therefore, have a positive effect on the learning ability of the fledgling pianist who heard it. Telling a salesman that the new closing technique you've discovered will double his sales within six months would not seem believable and would be rejected out of hand. However, telling him that the new closing technique could improve his sales by 15% over the next six months might well seem believable and would, therefore, set him off on the right foot and in the right direction.

Here's how one individual I interviewed explained his reaction to expectations, believable and otherwise. He said, "If my manager has high expectations for me, I find myself responding to those expectations, as long as they're reasonable. If he thinks I can get the job done, I begin to have confidence in myself, and I, too, begin to think I can get the job done. I realize there might be some road blocks and things can't always go smoothly, but I begin to develop more confidence in my ability to do the job."

Correspondingly, this same individual admitted that if his manager had low expectations for him, he found himself responding accordingly. "It's not a deliberate thing," he continued. "It isn't conscious. But if my manager has low expectations and I have somewhat higher ones, I frequently find myself lowering my expectations to match my manager's. I guess it all depends on the type of climate the manager creates for me. If it's a climate of high expectations, I feel motivated, and I concentrate more on getting the job done. But if it's a climate of low expectations, my momentum slows down, and my performance drops off."

Jack Brickenden, an astute public relations consultant from Toronto, points out that the expectations of those within his client firms can either help or hinder his work. According to Brickenden, if there are negative views and expectations within the client firm, the public relations efforts must often first start by alleviating them.

A public relations effort to publicize a company's customer service policy is, after all, virtually worthless if there is no real customer service. On the other hand, Brickenden points out that if customer service people have positive expectations about themselves and their work, a good public relations effort augments and amplifies those expectations. "A well designed public relations effort," he says, "affects the expectations of both those inside and outside the company."

*The Placebo Effect* Placebos are well-known in the field of medicine. Often referred to as "sugar pills," placebos are pills that contain no actual medication. There was a time, when physicians were unable to identify a specific medical reason for a pain or illness, that placebos were routinely prescribed. The benefits of the "pill" were the results of what happened in the mind of the patient receiving the "medication." Perhaps they were also the effects of the physician's expectations.

In one experiment, researchers compared the effects of morphine with the effects of a placebo in controlling pain. Surprisingly, morphine was no more effective than the saline-solution placebo. And because neither the subjects nor the research investigators knew whether a placebo or morphine had been administered, there was no opportunity for the latter to communicate, either consciously or unconsciously, to the patients whether or not morphine was involved.

In another situation, a cancer patient was told of a "wonder drug" and then was administered that same drug. The patient's condition improved dramatically. But when the patient heard the drug was ineffective, he had a relapse. The patient then was reassured that the drug did, in fact, work, and he was given an injection of saline solution—and improved considerably. Finally, upon hearing that the drug was not at all helpful, he died.

A third example of the placebo effect occurred in Italy, where Professor Ranieri Gerbi of Pisa devised a cure that was guaranteed to prevent the recurrence of toothache for a whole year. It involved crushing a type of worm with the fingers and applying it to the aching tooth. A commission studied this methodology and found that 68.5% of the hundreds of toothaches investigated yielded immediately to the power of the worm, an unlikely but apparently most effective placebo.

The process of the placebo effect in medicine is a fairly straightforward, simple one. It goes something like this:

1. Physician examines patient.

2. Physician can't find anything specifically wrong that has a medical basis.

3. Physician decides that perhaps the reported illness is psychosomatic.

4. Physician decides, because of the psychosomatic nature of the illness, that a sugar pill (placebo) will probably cure whatever is wrong.

5. Physician *believes* that this sugar pill will cure the patient.

6. This belief is communicated to the patient, who takes the pill and *believes* it will cure the illness.

7. The illness is cured.

As managers, we also have the opportunity to create placebo effects for the people who report to us. Frequently, our *beliefs* and *expectations* of others are enough to bring forth the best (or the worst) in our colleagues.

Phil is an example of a sales manager who gave one of his salesmen a "placebo" that indirectly produced a dramatic increase in sales. Nick, one of

Phil's field salesmen, was suffering from a sales slump. Downcast and downhearted, Nick couldn't seem to break out of his slump, so he asked Phil to travel with him to see if perhaps he could find out what was wrong. As Phil later reported to me, Nick was doing virtually everything right—except for one thing: he didn't act as though he expected to make the sale.

After spending the day with him and talking with him at night, Phil concluded that the following sequence of events had probably taken place:

1. Nick had had a few rough days and a short slump in sales.

2. He didn't know what was causing the slump, so he began to watch what he said and did very carefully.

3. This careful examination of his sales behavior interfered with his natural selling abilities.

4. Because his natural selling abilities were being thwarted by this self-conscious introspection, sales continued to slump.

5. This confirmed his belief and expectation that he must be doing something wrong.

6. The more he brooded, the fewer sales he made.

7. In desperation, he came to Phil, convinced that something was seriously wrong.

About three-quarters of the way through their day together, Phil realized that nothing was wrong—other than Nick's belief and expectation that something was wrong. However, because of Nick's concern, Phil had to find something "really" wrong. He would then help Nick correct this "problem" and set him on the road again, full of confidence that he could sell as well as he used to.

With that plan in mind, Phil tried to decide what to give the salesman that would serve as a placebo. As they walked out of the final call that day, Phil reached into his trench coat pocket and found a stone from the beach that his daughter had given him after he came home from a trip. In the confusion of unpacking his bags and kissing his kids, he had thrust it in his pocket and forgotten about it. Now he surreptitiously took it out and placed it in his attache case.

When they got in the car, Nick asked, "Well, what am I doing wrong?" Confident that the placebo would work, Phil replied, "You're really not doing anything wrong. You just had a little slump and started worrying about it. All you need is some good old Irish luck to bring you out of it." "That sounds great," said Nick. "But where do I get Irish luck?"

"Fortunately," said Phil, "I have just the thing. Ten years ago, I was in a slump like this, and I was telling my uncle about it. He had just come back from Ireland, and he gave me this stone as a good luck piece. It broke *me* out of my slump, and I think it's just the thing to break *you* out of yours. You're a fine salesman. And I know you can do a much better job than you're doing. All you have to do is concentrate on the customer instead of on your sales techniques, which are fine. With the little bit of luck this stone will bring you, you'll be back in the ball game within two days.'' With that, Phil handed Nick the stone that had been worn smooth on the beach. The salesman took it and put it in his jacket pocket, saying that he felt better already. And he started to sell better, too: within two weeks, his sales were back up there to their previous level.

Phil isn't the only sales manager I've met who's reported giving his salesmen "placebos." Some of the other placebos I've head about are a variety of good luck charms, a certain way of tying shoes, a belt of a certain color, a special size of wallet or notepad, a worry stone, a colored business card, and certain types of pens. And the use of such placebos certainly isn't limited to sales managers. Financial institutions, manufacturing companies, retailers, and even government agencies have all, at one time or another, found different types of "placebos" effective in helping develop Self-Starters on their staffs.

## Impact of Low Expectations

Now let's look at the opposite of high expectations or of using a placebo to foster such expectations. Let's look at the impact of low expectations. People from whom little is expected tend to fulfill those expectations in several ways. A common reaction is to withdraw from the job—that is, retire but stay on the payroll. The individual who reacts to low expectations this way does just enough to get by. He or she justifies this attitude by saying, either consciously or unconsciously, "Well, that's all they expect me to do, so that's all I really have to do. They aren't paying me to do any more, so I'll do just what they tell me and no more."

People also react to low expectations by avoiding risk situations. Take, for example, the salesman who has an opportunity to develop new accounts. To do so, he feels a new method might be appropriate. But if a manager has low expectations of that individual, the individual will probably have low expectations for himself. He might, therefore, conclude: "If I try, I may fail—so I won't try." Or, "If I don't try, I can't fail; I may not succeed, but at least I won't fail—so I won't try."

Finally, the individual may literally withdraw from the job by resigning. Individuals who react this way probably have high expectations about themselves and are reacting to the low expectations communicated by their manager. Feeling that they have more to contribute than the minimum expected from them, they often leave and seek employment in more challenging environments. All too frequently, these individuals are our potential Self-Starters.

What I'm suggesting is that low expectations can be costly in both the short term and the long term. The short term cost is in low performance and the long term cost is in lost potential.

**Expectations and Leadership Styles**

Over the past several years, great debate has raged about whether Theory X or Theory Y is the appropriate style of leadership. According to Douglas McGregor, who coined the terms Theory X and Theory Y, some managers have a Theory X approach to management. They're the managers who believe that:

1. Work is inherently distasteful to most people.

2. Most people are not ambitious, have little desire for responsibility, and prefer to be directed.

3. Most people have little capacity for creativity in solving organizational problems.

4. Motivation occurs only at the physiological and security levels.

5. Most people can be closely controlled and often coerced to achieve organizational objectives.

Managers who practice Theory X structure the organizational environment very carefully and provide very close control and supervision for their employees. They tend to regard people as immature and often irresponsible.

And then there are the managers whom McGregor suggests practice Theory Y. They believe that:

1. Work is as natural as play, if the conditions are favorable.

2. Self-control is often dispensible in achieving organizational goals.

3. The capacity for creativity in solving organizational problems is widely distributed in the population.

4. Motivation occurs at the social-esteem and self-actualization levels, as well as at the physiological and security levels.

5. People can be self-directed and creative at work if they're properly motivated.

Most social scientists, consultants, professors, and training departments tend to favor Theory Y, which is a more humanistic approach to management. Clearly, it involves people more in the fulfillment of their job responsibilities. I, too, favor Theory Y; I like to be managed that way, and I like to manage that way. But I also know that that's not necessarily the case for all successful managers.

Several years ago, I was doing some consulting work with a company whose plant manager was hard as nails. He was more than Theory X: he was Theory XX. When I asked him if there were some particular reason why he used the leadership style he did, he gave me a list that sounded pretty much like the classic characteristics of Theory X managers—that is, work is inherently distasteful to most people, and so on. He told me that people (if they were to perform at a high level) had to be managed according to Theory X. And he was right—for himself anyway. Not because it was necessarily the right or the wrong way to manage but because his expectation was that, if he managed using a Theory X style, people would perform at a high level, and they did.

I talked with other managers who practiced a Theory X approach to leadership, and each of them firmly believed that this was the only way to succeed. In each case, their expectations were identical: a person who manages this way will have a well-run plant. And each of these individuals had just that.

Yet, in close geographical proximity to each of these Theory X plants, I found other plants, different divisions of the same company, with basically the same type of work force and producing similar products. The plant managers here generally espoused the Theory Y approach to management. And each of their plants was equally successful. When I questioned the managers about their leadership styles, they said that they had to practice Theory Y leadership to get the most out of people.

Interesting, isn't it? In each situation, the circumstances closely resembled each other. And, in each situation, people in the plants behaved exactly according to the expectations of their plant managers. Same people, same products, same union, but different leadership styles. In one critical way, however, both sets of managers and employees were alike: they both were helping match each other's expectations.

Using the Self-Starting Mechanism as a reference point on expectations, I would now like to suggest that both sets of managers were right in their respective situations because the *climate and expectations matched in both instances*. But what occurs when expectations don't match? Conflict and

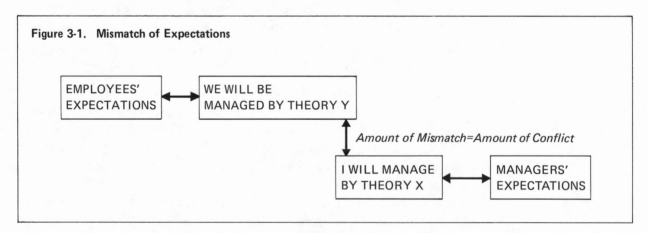

**Figure 3-1. Mismatch of Expectations**

EMPLOYEES' EXPECTATIONS ←→ WE WILL BE MANAGED BY THEORY Y

*Amount of Mismatch=Amount of Conflict*

I WILL MANAGE BY THEORY X ←→ MANAGERS' EXPECTATIONS

disharmony. As you can see in figure 3–1, when employees expect that they will be managed by Theory Y but the manager intends to manage by Theory X, conflict is almost inevitable.

In fact, numerous studies suggest that leadership style is really a function of three variables: the leader and his own personal leadership style, the followers and their expectations, and the situation at hand. The importance of these three variables is vividly illustrated when we compare the leadership styles practiced in a boot camp with those evident in a hospital. Basic training or boot camp depends upon a very directive style, one that wouldn't be at all appropriate with a medical staff. In each instance—the boot camp and the hospital—there is a different leader, a different set of followers, and a different situation. In a health care environment, a more laissez-faire approach to leadership would be appropriate. But look what happens when we change one of the variables, that of the *situation* in the hospital setting. Suppose an emergency occurs, and several steps have to be taken very quickly. In this situation, everybody involved expects that someone will take a strong stance and issue a stream of orders. Surely, hospital personnel wouldn't expect their leader to stand around saying, "Well, what do you think we ought to do now? Let's divide into little groups and make a decision about how we might handle this emergency." Thus, the expectations of subordinates about what they would regard as an appropriate leadership style often dictate what that style will be for a particular situation.

**Can People Respond to Expectations?**

No, say some. Yes, say others. Maybe, say still others. I say yes, people *can* change—for better and for worse. One company with which I was doing some work employed a particularly sour individual who was forever grumbling, "Things will never get better around here." When I asked him why, he said that things would never improve because people couldn't change. "Could they get worse?" I asked. "Hell, yes," he said. "People always can get worse."

Well, if people can get worse, they can get better. Often our expectations govern how people behave. If we *expect* that people can't or won't change, then frequently they can't or won't. If, however, we expect that, in spite of the situation, the individuals' ages or experience, or whatever, they can learn to change, then frequently they will respond to that expectation in a positive fashion. If we expect that people will never become Self-Starters, they won't. If we expect that people can and will become Self-Starters, then they will.

**Expectations and Team Performance**

The expectations we hold for other departments, other individuals, and other plants also affect the performances of these entities. Manufacturing supervisors, for example, might expect quality control to be a nuisance, and, sure enough, quality control ends up being a nuisance. If salespeople expect people in accounting to be nitpicking, they shouldn't be surprised when that happens. If the sales department expects the shipping department to miss schedules, schedules will be missed.

Unfortunately, such negative expectations can permeate—and hinder—whole organizations. Entire units can react to richocheting expectations. If sales expects shipping to screw them up and that's what happens, probably shipping will now expect sales to screw *them* up every chance it gets. And, sure enough, that's just what happens. Instead of trying to do its job, each department spends most of its time trying to "get" the other one and avoid being "got" itself. Each would rather be the "getter" rather than the "gettee," and so more energy goes into niggling little battles than into actual job performance.

By contrast, if sales expects shipping to be helpful, the latter department will usually begin to respond to that positive expectation. The two departments may never really like each other, but they at least begin to expect some teamwork and cooperation from each other.

Jack Martin, a staff associate of The Achievement Institute who specializes in helping companies build more effective teams, reports that differing expectations frequently account for much of what is frequently called "interdepartmental conflict." Reports Martin, "one of the most important steps in building a winning team is to identify some of the negative expectations and misconceptions that different departments have for each other." Once those are out on the table, we can then begin building a climate of positive expectations about success.

This same concept holds true in, for example, management-union relationships. In many respects, a first-line supervisor and a union committeeman have to work as a team. They have to resolve their differences within the confines of the labor contract and, at the same time, cooperate to make the company a better place to work for the employees. If the supervisor and the committeeman have negative expectations about each other's performance, they will function exactly like our quarrelsome sales and shipping departments. However, if the supervisor and committeeman have positive expectations about each other in their roles of helping employees, they'll be able to work more efficiently and get more done. I'm not naively suggesting that union-management relationships will always be harmonious; obviously, there is an adversary element built into the nature of the relationship. However, there are many instances when the two parties can operate together as a team, and it helps if each side has positive expectations about the other.

**How Expectations Affect Personnel Policies**

While expectations can directly affect the behavior of others, it's also possible that the effects may be more subtle. Personnel policies offer an area where the impact may be not quite so direct, but nonetheless quite severe.

*Testing*

Validity and reliability are two aspects of testing that must be considered here. A test that is valid has the characteristics of testing for those items or variables that it is actually testing for. For example, a test might be touted as being able to predict whether or not somebody would be able to sustain himself for a long period of time without actually making a sale; if the test actually can identify that variable, then it is a valid test. The reliability of a test, on the other hand, depends upon whether or not it is consistent over a period of time: a reliable test will continue to measure the same thing in the same way.

But just because a test is reliable, it isn't necessarily valid. Imagine a test, for example, that supposedly can measure whether or not somebody can sustain himself in a manufacturing environment with an assembly-line situation. If twenty people took the test and everybody received the same type of score on the same types of questions, the test might be considered reliable because it consistently measures the same thing. However, whether or not that's what is really being measured is another question entirely.

Enter the Pygmalion Effect and its impact upon expectations which further confuses the issues of testing validity and reliability. How? Because the administrator of personnel-policies tests may *expect* certain kinds of people to score in certain ways on the tests. And these expectations might well be communicated unconsciously to the test takers. One test administrator, for example, might expect that women would score low on a test; another might expect white males to score low; and someone else might expect blacks or Mexicans to do the same. The Pygmalion Effect suggests, I think, that people might respond only too well to those expectations, and their test results might show, for example, that females scored well on one section of the test and poorly on another. And those scores, whatever they are, might well have been affected by the expectations communicated, in one form or another, by the test administrator.

*Selection*  The area of selection also is vulnerable to the impact of the Pygmalion Effect. A manager, believing that an individual could succeed in whatever position he is selected to fill, might well choose that individual for that reason alone. If the criteria used for selection are good, of course, this selection method might aid the ability of the person filling the position. And the Pygmalion Effect even suggests that if the criteria used aren't good, the effect could still be positive.

An auto dealer once confided to me that he made it a point to hire only salesmen who wore loafers. When I questioned him about this rather unusual criterion for selection, he explained it this way: "I've got ten salesmen in my dealership, and at one point, I rank ordered them according to their sales and found that the three top salesmen were selling 75% of all of the units sold. I interviewed each of them separately to check into educational background, training, experience, other jobs, and hobbies, and I couldn't find anything that all three of them had in common—except that each one of them wore loafers. Then I looked at the other seven salesmen in my dealership and found that only one of them wore loafers, and he only wore them occasionally. So I decided that whatever it was that caused people to wear loafers must indicate some kind of skill that also enabled them to sell cars. From that day on, I've hired only loafer wearers, and, strange as it seems, it really works! When an applicant comes in, I immediately check the kind of shoes he's wearing. And if they're not loafers, I find some other reason not to hire him. But if the person *is* wearing loafers, I go through and check the other things to make sure he'll probably do all right in sales. Since I've implemented that policy, I've found that my sales have gone way up."

Although this fellow's criterion for selection was somewhat bizarre, the fact that he was successful can be readily explained in terms of expectations. He zeroed in on one peculiar variable (whether or not the salesman wore loafers) and used it as a basis for selection. When he found someone who wore loafers, he communicated, consciously or unconsciously, his high expectations to that individual, who then responded accordingly. And he probably communicated his negative expectations to the two or three people he hired who were not loafer wearers; he let them know, in one way or another, his expectations were low, and they, too, responded accordingly. Obviously, the key variable isn't whether or not somebody wore loafers but whether or not expectations of high performance were communicated to that individual.

*Performance Appraisal* Closely related to the selection process is the entire performance appraisal process, which is an important and valid tool in any management system. People have a need and a right to know how their performance is being judged against a predetermined set of standards. Because an organization *must* produce results, people whose performance is below par must be weeded out of the organization. Because our expectations can so greatly affect someone else's behavior, it's important that we don't let past appraisals influence present appraisals.

Consider, for example, an individual who has had three or four years of average or below-average performance appraisals from different department managers. During the fourth year, this individual is transferred to a new department; in an effort to find out what type of employee this is, the department head goes to the personnel file and pulls out the previous three performance appraisals. After reviewing them, department head Mary finds that Bill, the transferee, is only slightly above marginal. So when Bill walks into the department, Mary's expectations might be that Bill is only going to perform at a marginally acceptable level. In a variety of ways, these expectations are communicated to Bill, who, sure enough, lives up to Mary's expectations and performs only marginally.

But this need not occur. Just because a person has a history of poor performance doesn't mean that he can't perform well in a new situation. Quite the opposite. An individual with three or four years of only marginal performance can, when placed under the supervision of a manager with exceptionally high expectations, alter his performance radically.

A sales manager in a medium-sized manufacturing company related to me an incident that shows exactly how positive expectations can overcome a history of poor performance appraisals. A salesman, Ben, who had been in two other regions and had met with only marginal success, was transferred into my friend Mike's region. On Ben's first day at work, Mike called him into his office and said, "Ben, come on in and sit down. As we both know, you've been transferred into my territory. To find out what kind of a man I was getting, I went back and looked through the personnel files and dug out your two most recent performance appraisals, which I have here in front of me. I made a copy of each of them for you so you can refresh your memory." Ben, whose memory about his two previous performance appraisals didn't need much refreshing, picked them up and glanced at them nonetheless. Clearly, he expected to hear some lay-it-on-the-line, you'd-better-improve-or-else talk. But that's not what he heard.

Instead, the conversation went something like this: "Ben, when I looked at those performance appraisal files, I decided they didn't tell me very much about what kind of man was transferring into my territory. They did tell me a fair amount about previous performance levels, but that doesn't really tell me what kind of individual is going to work for me in the future. In fact, as I look at your performance appraisal reports and then at the other things in your personnel file, I see an individual who has an awful lot of unrealized potential.

"I'll tell you right now that nobody on my team is an average player. And, as a member of my team, I don't think you'll be an average player either. I think you have potential to perform at a much higher level than your records indicate. And I think the best way for both of us to make sure that that potential is realized is to forget the past history and start from scratch. That's why I'm going to tear up these copies of the performance appraisal reports and ask you to do the same. Now, as far as you and I are concerned, we're starting with a clean slate. First, I'd like to establish with you some short-term goals that can get us headed in the direction toward some long-term high performance."

The results of this conversation and those that followed were nothing less than spectacular. Ben's performance improved so dramatically that the previous two regional managers couldn't believe it when they saw his name consistently near the top of the list of sales achievers. Today, three and a half years after Ben joined Mike's sales team, he's still with the company and is still a top performer. Clearly, Ben is a Self-Starter in every sense of the word.

*High Potential Lists*  Maintaining a high-potential list is another practice that can have considerable impact in the area of personnel policies. When someone's name goes on a high-potential list, which many companies maintain, the individual knows it. Not only does he or she know it, but the bosses and the bosses' bosses know it, too. Frequently, other subordinates, peers, colleagues, and counterparts also know whose name is on, or is likely to be on, the high-potential list. Thus, people on the high-potential list are surrounded by high expectations. Small wonder, then, that their performance improves and that they measure up to that potential.

It's interesting to speculate what would happen if individuals were picked at random to be on the high-potential list. One wonders what would happen if the only difference between the individuals on the list and those not on the list existed in the minds of other managers. I suspect that we'd find that those individuals who had been placed on the high-potential list did indeed out-perform those whose names had been omitted.

The $64 question is: What would happen to overall departmental, plant, company, or divisional performance if *everybody* were placed on a high-potential list? That is, what would the overall results be if we had the same high expectations for everyone? My answer: We probably would have con-siderably higher performance than we would have had if those expectations hadn't been communicated. People tend to live up not only to their own ex-pectations of themselves but also to the expectations others have for them. The extent to which performance improves or declines depends upon whether those expectations are positive or negative.

## Positive Expectations Aren't Positive Thinking

It's important to note at this point that positive expectations aren't the same as positive thinking. Unless positive thinking is translated into specific be-havioral patterns, it has no impact. Moreover, the concept of positive expec-tations is a reality-based approach to performance improvement, while positive thinking often is not. Occasionally, people confuse the two, and the confusion unfortunately negates the effect of positive expectations. If sales are down, that's a fact. If quality is poor, that's also a fact. The existing situation represents reality. And once you accept reality, you can put positive expectations to work by expecting that the present situation can be changed.

One plant manager I know had the misfortune of confusing positive think-ing with positive expectations. His organization had been having some quali-ty problems, and he, determined to be positive, kept saying things like, "We have good quality, we're doing a good job on quality, and we're building quality products." The truth was that quality was awful, and everyone knew it. As a result of his cockeyed optimism, the plant manager lost considerable credibility. One can't just *wish* for improvement; one has to *behave* in ways that lead to improvement. And that's what positive expectations are all about.

## Others' Expectations Are Also Germane

So far, we've been concentrating upon *your* expectations and behaviors toward another individual. But it's equally important to remember that what *others* expect also plays a role. Consider, for example, the physician and the placebo. The physician gives the patient a prescription, saying, "This pill will work; it will make you feel better." The patient takes the prescription to a pharmacist, who shakes her head sadly and says, "I don't know why Dr. Bones gave you these." The patient goes home and his brother-in-law says, "I had some of those, but they didn't do me any good. In fact, they made me feel worse." His neighbor laughs when he hears the name of the medication. And the next day, a guy at work claims that his uncle was in the hospital for three weeks after taking the same medication. In this case, the physician had positive expectations and the patient did, too—until everyone else indicated negative expectations about the effect of the medicine. The probability of the medicine having any real effect is, therefore, greatly reduced because of the expectations of others.

Or consider the case of a manager who says to one of his staff, "I'd like you to attend this training course, which I'm sure will help you improve your job performance." But someone else in the department says, "That was just about the worst course I ever attended." Other coworkers also express doubts that anybody could be helped by that particular course. While the expectations of the manager were pretty high, they were effectively undercut by the negative expectations of people who had already been through the course or had heard about it.

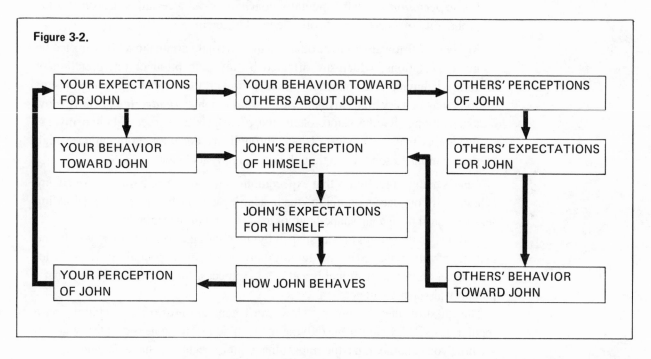

**Figure 3-2.**

Figure 3–2 shows that there are several places where the expectation system can affect human behavior and job performance. Let's imagine that we're concerned with your expectations for John. As you can see, there are a number of variables that can affect John's job behavior at different points in the system. Others' expectations for John certainly affect his job behavior; the way other people behave toward John affects his job behavior; your expectations and behavior toward John affect his behavior; and, most importantly, John's expectations for himself affect how he behaves. Clearly, a number of variables ultimately affect John's behavior. But don't forget that there are a number of places where *you* can influence that model and end up affecting, either directly or indirectly, John's behavior, his perceptions of himself, others' expectations for him, others' behavior toward him, and even the perceptions that other people have of him. I have indicated with an extra heavy line those areas where you can directly affect a part of the model. The lighter lines indicate those parts of the model not directly affected by you but through which your impact can be felt.

Note that each box is labeled in one of three ways: expectations, perception, or behavior. What, you may ask, are the differences among perception, behavior, and expectations? One critical difference is that perception and expectations are usually internal, while behavior is externally discernible and measurable. More specifically:

1. *Perception* is an interpretive reaction. I form a perception of John based upon my interpretation of his behavior.

2. My *expectation* is what I mentally conclude about a certain situation and the probability of a certain performance level occurring.

3. My *behavior* toward John or others is the external variable that is controlled by my expectations, which are affected by my perception or interpretation of John's behavior. It is important to note, however, that while my expectations for John may be very high, my behavior toward him may *inadvertently* convey low expectations. By the same token, the reverse is also true; although my expectations may be modest, I can, through my behavior, communicate high expectations to John, even though I don't really feel them.

What's being suggested is that expectations can play a strong role in influencing behavior. If you place a pumpkin vine in a large jar at the beginning of the growing season, you'll have a jar-shaped pumpkin at the end of the summer.

And just as the pumpkin was shaped by the configuration of the jar, you'll find that others will be shaped by the "configuration" of your expectations. Expect a lot from others and you'll probably get a lot. Expect a little from others and that's probably also what you get.

The question then becomes "How can I generate positive expectations on a regular basis?" By carefully studying the techniques in the next chapter, you will see how you can maximize the impact that your expectations have on others.

# Expectations
# and Self-Starters

Mary walked in and threw down her pen. "That son of a bitch," she muttered. "He has absolutely no confidence in me. He doesn't think I can do the job, and he puts me down every chance he gets." Having witnessed Mary's discussion with Bill, her boss, I wasn't surprised by her reaction. Nonetheless, I asked her what Bill had said.

"He said that he thought I was just the person for this type of project."

"So what's wrong with *that*?" I asked.

"It's not what he said," she replied. "It's more what he *didn't* say and the *way* he said what he did say that made me angry."

Mary's reaction was not an uncommon one. We often hear people say, "It's not what was said but the way it was said." Obviously, *how* something is stated can be every bit as telling as the statement itself. I've found that expectations can be communicated in a variety of ways, including both what we say and what we do. In Bill's case, the expectations he communicated were of a negative nature, even though the words he used were positive. Let's look and see why.

There are actually two elements involved in communicating positive expectations. First, as you can see in figure 4-1, there is the message itself, which consists of the words spoken, the vocal intonations used to communicate the words, and the body language that accompanies the words. Second, there is the environment in which the message (consisting of the words, the vocal intonations, and the body language) is delivered. The environment consists of things such as the setting (including furniture, barriers, desks, tables, and chairs), interruptions, and distance.

Each element plays an important role. This means that even though you may wish to communicate positive expectations, you stand a very small chance of being effective in developing Self-Starters if the words are the *only* part of the total communication process that is positive. What's more, the words constitute the smallest part of the message. According to Albert Mehramian, the *words* constitute only 7% of any message that is transmitted. The tone and vocal intonations constitute 30% of the message, and the body language constitutes 55% of the message.

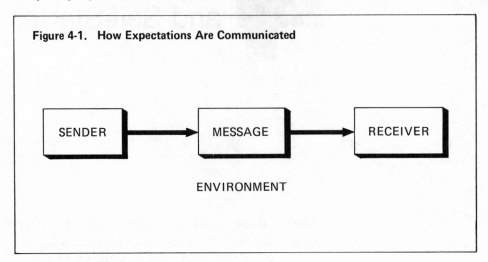

Figure 4-1. How Expectations Are Communicated

SENDER → MESSAGE → RECEIVER

ENVIRONMENT

Let's assume that the message itself accounts for 80% of the impact, and the environment in which the message is sent constitutes another 20% of the impact. Rounding the numbers off to the nearest 5% (a change of only 1%) gives us the following impact value:

| Message | Impact Value |
|---|---|
| Words | 5% |
| Vocal Intonations | 30% |
| Body Language | 45% |
| **Environment** | |
| Interruptions | 5% |
| Proxiemics | 5% |
| Setting | 10% |

This means it's possible to communicate only 5% positive expectations and 95% negative expectations, even though the words used are positive.

It's possible, but not necessary. Fortunately, there are techniques that will help you make sure your message communicates 100% the positive expectations that you intend it to. By making sure that not only the words, but the tone and vocal intonations, the body language, and the environment are all communicating positive expectations, you can encourage Self-Starters. After we've looked at how you do all those things to communicate positive expectations to people you want to be Self-Starters, we will come back and see where Bill and Mary went wrong. First, let's look at the message.

**The Words**  Generally, our concern about a message stops with the words themselves. Yet, while words are important, they constitute only 5% of the total impact, and anything that constitutes only 5% of the impact shouldn't be of primary importance. Nonetheless, certain words can communicate more positive expectations than can other words.

*Multilingual*  Developing Self-Starters requires you to be multilingual. Obviously, this doesn't mean that you have to speak English, French, Spanish, and German, but you do have to be able to use words that are appropriate to the individuals or groups of individuals to whom you are trying to communicate positive expectations.

"I anticipate success in this endeavor" might be a satisfactory way to communicate positive expectations to a group of research scientists. But if you use virtually those same words when speaking to a group of production foremen in a heavy-industry plant, you'll provoke head scratching and looks that say, "Why was this lightweight brought in to run the plant?" To the production foreman in the troubled plant, you'd be better off saying, "The Lyndon plant has been saying they can produce better than we can, but they're wrong. We're going to outproduce those sons of bitches with the highest quality that's ever gone out of this plant." To that, the production foreman might respond positively: "Well, damn! We've got somebody in here who knows about manufacturing, and we're really going to make this place hum." On the other hand, imagine addressing a group of research scientists this way: "Lab such and such is getting more patents than we are, but we're going to develop more patents than those sons of bitches can count." Considering your audience, this salty approach wouldn't be as effective at communicating expectations as would the more refined statement—"I anticipate success in this endeavor."

Also, you should try to use positive words. Words have value, and people respond to the words they hear. For example, as you read the word *lemon* and mentally picture yourself biting into a juicy slice of the sour fruit, your mouth probably begins to water. That's an involuntary reaction on your part. Your conscious mind reads the word *lemon*, and your subconscious mind reacts. The subconscious mind is unable to distinguish between positive and negative thoughts. It responds only to the image it holds. So if you say to somebody, "Don't forget to check and see that the order is on file," all the subconscious might hear is "forget to check and see if the order is on file."

The conscious mind hears the message and sends it to the subconscious, where it is accepted immediately and unconditionally. The subconscious mind then prepares the conscious mind to act in accordance with the received message. Since the subconscious mind is unable to distinguish between positive and negative statements, it acts only on what is said, not on the thought; in other words, it pays little attention to whether or not the words were preceded by the word *don't*.

This inability of the subconscious to distinguish between positive and negative means that even an offhand remark can have a debilitating effect upon your program to develop Self-Starters. You may not have intended to say or do something negative, but your intent is not important in terms of its impact. When you say or do something, it's the *impact* of what was said or done, rather than the *intent*, that counts. Even though your intent was positive, the impact might be negative in terms of how the individual received that part of the message. So, although words actually play a small part in a total message, they are nevertheless important and can affect the outcome of what you're trying to do.

To increase your impact on Self-Starters, state as many things as possible in positive terms.

| Instead of Saying | Say |
|---|---|
| "Don't send the report in without making sure all the parts are there." | "Make sure all the parts are there before you send the report in." |
| "Don't leave the scrap lying on the floor." | "Be sure to pick up scrap on the floor and take it over to a dumpster." |
| "Don't leave the customer on hold that long." | "The customer should always be taken care of within thirty seconds." |
| "Don't forget to thank the customer for the order." | "Remember to thank the customer for the order and tell him you appreciate his business." |
| "Don't yell across the office that way." | "If you need the help of somebody who's not near you in the office, walk over to where she is and speak to her in a normal tone of voice." |

**Verbal Intonations**

Verbal intonations have considerable impact on how expectations are expressed. Remember, they represent 30% of the impact. Consider, for example, the effect of emphasizing a different word in the same sentence. Let's take the sentence, "I think that Bill can do this." In the following paragraphs, we'll discover how different emphases can alter the meaning of the same seven words. As you read each sentence, emphasize the italicized word and say it out loud to yourself to see how changing the intonation and emphasis affects the meaning of the sentence.

*I* think Bill can do this. By emphasizing *I*, the speaker implies that he's quite sure Bill can do it. The implication might also be that other people *don't* think Bill can do it. Thus, if there was some question during a group meeting as to whether or not Bill would be the person to do something, your emphasis on *I* in the sentence would communicate to others that you thought he could, even though others didn't think so.

I *think* Bill can do this. While the communication still expresses a positive expectation that Bill can do it, there's also some unspoken doubt in your statement. If you emphasize the word *think*, it means that you don't *know* if Bill can do it, but you're reasonably confident in his ability to carry out the task. In fact, you might as well have said, "I'm not really sure he can do this, but I have some degree of confidence in his ability to carry out the task."

I think *Bill* can do this. By emphasizing the word *Bill*, you're implying that, although you think Bill can do it, you also think that other people cannot do it. This form might be appropriate if there was some discussion about who would be the appropriate person to carry out this task.

I think Bill *can* do this. This statement might be made in response to somebody else's statement that Bill couldn't do it. Maybe someone said, "I don't think Bill can do this; I'm not sure he has the ability." When you come back with "I think Bill *can* do this," you're communicating both to that person (and to Bill, if he's there) your positive expectations that Bill can indeed carry out this task, contrary to someone else's low expectation.

I think Bill can *do* this. This way of expressing the statement would be effective if there had been some discussion about, say, whether or not Bill was the appropriate person to carry out the task or whether or not the task was achievable. If you said, "I think Bill can *do* this" when the discussion was over, you'd be attempting to dispel any doubts about Bill's ability to carry out this task. It would probably supercede all doubts expressed earlier and would put them to rest. In effect, you'd be saying, "I listened to the discussion and heard all the reasons, arguments, strengths, and weaknesses, and I'm now convinced that Bill is the person who can do this particular task."

I think Bill can do *this*. By emphasizing the word *this,* you're indicating that you have confidence in Bill's ability to carry out a single task. For example, there are three tasks that Bill might possibly undertake. You've discussed tasks 1 and 2 and discarded Bill as a candidate for carrying out these assignments, but you decided Bill could carry out task 3. When you emphasize the word *this* you're saying, in effect, that Bill should be assigned to the third task, but not to the first two.

In each of these situations, you can see how changes in the intonation of and emphasis upon words in the same sentence can communicate entirely different types of positive expectations.

## Body Language

Body language represents 45% of the impact of a message. You can have the right words and intonations, but if the body language you use conflicts with those words or intonations, you're fighting an uphill battle. With positive words, positive intonations, negative body language, and negative environment, 35% of the impact communicates positive expectations and 65% communicates negative expectations. If you want to develop Self-Starters, you have to make sure that your body language is as positive as your words and vocal intonations. Here's how.

There are five primary body language categories: the position of the body itself, physical gestures, head position and head movement, facial expressions, and eyes. Each of these five categories must work in concert with one another to reinforce and support nonverbally the words and vocal intonations you're using. Because the nonverbal part of the message is even more powerful than the verbal part, you can say the right things with the right information but still inadvertently communicate low expectations.

One way, for example, of communicating low or negative expectations of somebody is to "close off" the body position. This means turning the front part of your body so it faces away from the individual, crossing your legs, and folding your arms. The term "giving somebody the cold shoulder" is not an idle one; it's just what we do when we assume the position shown in figure 4–2.

**Figure 4-2.**
**Communicating Low Expectations**

Over the past several years, I've conducted hundreds of videotaped interviews with people in which we've talked about their performance in a role-play situation. At the outset of each of these interviews, I've deliberately assumed the body position shown in figure 4–2. In only one instance has somebody failed to respond within thirty seconds to the body language I was "speaking." Everybody else quickly responded, nonverbally, in a variety of ways. Some people immediately crossed their legs and folded their arms. Others slid their chairs back and moved away from me. Still others refused to look directly at me.

After discussing performance-related issues with these people for several minutes, I then began to reverse myself. I relaxed my fists and opened my hands. I ceased "looking down my nose" at them and started engaging in a great deal of eye contact. I uncrossed my legs, unfolded my arms, sat erect in my chair, and leaned forward slightly with my arms resting on my desk in front of me. Depending upon how long I had been communicating negative expectations with my body language (as well as with my intonations, words, and barriers, such as the desk), people began to respond to the more positive body language I had switched to. Again, in only one instance did an individual fail to respond.

People began to respond positively in both verbal and nonverbal ways to my actions. Initially, they began by uncrossing their legs; then they would unfold their arms and drop them by their sides or place them on the table. Finally, they'd lean forward and begin to increase the amount of eye contact with me as we talked about job performance. Finally—and most significantly—they'd give their wholehearted commitment to an agreement to bring performance back to where it should be.

**TABLE 4-1**

## BODY LANGUAGE AND PERFORMANCE EXPECTATIONS

|  | THESE COMMUNICATE POSITIVE EXPECTATIONS | THESE COMMUNICATE NEGATIVE EXPECTATIONS |
|---|---|---|
| Body | Open<br>Erect<br>Leaning forward | Crossed arms<br>Legs crossed away<br>"Cold shoulder" |
| Hand Gesture | Open hands<br>Steepling<br>Hand to chest<br>Touching | Tapping fingers<br>Hiding mouth<br>Finger wagging<br>Closed/clenched hand |
| Head | Straight<br>Nodding up and down | Shaking back and forth<br>Tilted<br>Bowed |
| Facial | Smiling<br>Relaxed mouth<br>Alert<br>Ready to listen | Tight-lipped<br>Jaw muscles clenched<br>Grim smile<br>Raised eyebrows<br>Frown |
| Eyes | Pupils dilated<br>Wide open<br>Direct contact | "Looking down nose"<br>Lack of contact<br>Narrowed |

Table 4–1 shows some different ways of communicating both positive and negative expectations. To increase your effectiveness in growing Self-Starters, you should concentrate on those postures and gestures that communicate positive expectations and avoid those that communicate negative expectations.

*Body Position*    An open body position faces toward the person with whom you are trying to communicate and for whom you want to generate positive expectations. Body positions should be relatively erect, but if you lean forward slightly toward the person, it helps emphasize a positive attitude. When you turn away from the individual with whom you are communicating and cross your arms and legs away from him or her, you communicate negative expectations. You're giving the proverbial cold shoulder, and your listener will respond accordingly.

*Gestures*    Gestures are also part of body language. Touching your hands to your chest communicates a form of confidence, a belief in what you're talking about.

**Figure 4-3.  Belief in Expectations**

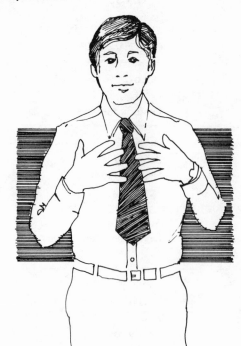

The person in figure 4–3, for example, might well be saying, "I believe you can do the job. I know you're able to do it." The words and gestures both say the same thing.

The individual in figure 4–4 is doing what we commonly refer to as steepling; the hands form a steeple that resembles a church roof. While it usually means that the person has self-confidence, it can also mean that he has confidence in his ability to help somebody grow. This person might be saying, "I know I can help you learn this new skill." Thus he expresses confidence in his ability to teach somebody that skill. If you are to develop Self-Starters, it is important that people believe you have confidence in your own abilities. This gesture might be followed by the hand-to-chest gesture and accompanied by these words: "Not only do I have confidence in my ability to teach you the skill, but I also have confidence in your ability to learn it."

**Figure 4-4.  Steepling as a Form of Confidence**

Open hands, as opposed to clenched hands or closed fists, also indicate an honesty and openness that people interpret as a show of confidence in them. On the other hand, gestures such as clenching your fists, tapping your fingers impatiently on a desk, hiding your mouth, wagging your finger, or pointing it at somebody often communicate negative expectations. Curiously enough, rubbing your nose with your finger (if you don't have a cold) can also communicate negative expectations.

*The Head*  Your head should face directly toward the person you're trying to communicate with, and any movement of the head should be up and down. If your head is tilted away or lowered, you're communicating negative expectations. If your head shakes back and forth (as in a negative response to a question), you also communicate negative expectations.

*Facial Expressions*  People are used to watching facial expressions, which are probably the most common and most readily identifiable of the elements of body language. Facial expressions that communicate positive expectations include a smile, a relaxed mouth, and a general alertness. Figure 4–5 shows somebody whose facial expression communicates positive expectations to someone else.

**Figure 4-5.  Facial Expressions and Positive Expectations**

Compare that expression to the individual in figure 4–6. This person is tight-lipped; the jaw muscles are slightly tensed; the smile is grim; and the eyebrows are raised. The combination communicates a disbelief or distrust in the other member of the dialogue.

Figure 4-6.  Communicating Low Expectations through Facial Expressions

*Eyes*  Finally, we come to eyes. Wide-open eyes communicate positive expectations. So do slightly dilated pupils; unfortunately, this is an involuntary action over which we have little or no control. Remember the experiment we
described in chapter 3 in which Dr. Albert King studied a group of hard-core
unemployed? In Dr. King's experiment, those individuals who had been
designated "high-aptitude personnel" were asked to choose, between two
photographs, the best likeness of their supervisor. Without hesitation, they
picked a photograph of the supervisor in which the pupils of the eyes had
been slightly enlarged. Those individuals not designated "high-aptitude personnel" picked the photograph where the pupils hadn't been enlarged.
Without realizing it, supervisors might well have communicated their
positive and high expectations for the "high-aptitude personnel" by involun-
tarily enlarging their pupils when they conversed with them. The old saying
"look them straight in the eye" is an apt one. It's also important that the
look be an open and friendly one that encourages confidence and optimism.

The individual who looks down his or her nose subtly implies a feeling of superiority toward the person to whom he or she is communicating. A lack of eye contact can likewise communicate low expectations; the subordinate subconsciously feels so unimportant that the supervisor would rather look out the window or at the wall—anywhere but into the eyes of the other half of the conversation. Narrowing the eyes or squinting also communicates negative expectations.

**The Environment**  Now let's examine the environment in which the message is transmitted. My observation has been that environmental impact is approximately 20%, with interruptions contributing 5%, distance 5%, and general setting 10%. We'll look at each of these in turn to see how they might affect the growth of Self-Starters.

*Interruptions*  If a manager sits down with one member of the team to talk about how that individual can perform better and attempts to communicate high expectations to that person, the frequency and duration of interruptions often can influence how the employee reacts to what's being said. If you're going to tell someone that you think he or she can do the job and that you have the highest degree of confidence in the individual's ability to achieve success, then *don't* take any phone calls, allow any visitors in, or shuffle any papers. Instead, concentrate fully on the situation at hand.

If you encourage, or even tolerate, interruptions, you're really communicating negatively to your listener; your're saying, "I consider this phone call more important than our discussion" or "I consider signing this letter more important than our discussion." If you allow someone to run into the office to "ask you a quick question about the ABC account," you're telling your listener that the ABC account is more important than the issue under discussion. While that may well be the case, it's probably also true that the ABC account can wait for a few minutes.

Instead, when you tell someone that you want to talk about something important, you should do just that, especially if the discussion involves communicating high expectations about that person's ability to succeed in a particular venture.

To ensure that no interruptions occur, do at least two things. First, ask that your phone calls be held and then stick to your resolve. Don't take that call from the important customer, the boss, the supplier, or the director of field operations. Devote your full attention to the conversation with the subordinate.

Second, close your office door. As a general rule, a closed office door should indicate no interruptions. If, however, someone does knock and then opens the door, ask the person to wait a few minutes. Or offer to call back when you're through with your conversation. Incidentally, if you repeatedly allow people to interrupt when your office door is closed, they'll assume that the closed door doesn't mean anything; they'll knock and automatically open the door, or they'll knock persistently until you open it yourself. If, however, they knock and you indicate to them that you can't talk right now, they'll soon learn that the closed door *means* no interruptions.

If you do shut off interruptions, be prepared to deal with some tensions and some preconceptions. When someone is talking alone to the boss, it generally means that he or she is getting chewed out. Thus, when you initially shut off interruptions, your subordinate might read that as meaning that a tongue-lashing is imminent. The best way to avoid this is to say at the outset what the conversation will be about. If you're going to discuss the quality control problem, say so. Field operations? Say so. If you want to prepare someone for a special task-force assignment, let the person know early on. This up-front tactic helps set the tone for the conversation and indicates the general direction of the discussion.

If you can't shut out the interruptions in the office, then hold the discussion out of the office. Go to the cafeteria, a restaurant, a conference room; go anywhere you can talk, uninterrupted and face to face, for an appropriate length of time.

The importance of curtailing interruptions recently was pointed out to me by the volunteer chairman of the education committee for a national association. Said he, "The full-time executive secretary who's running the association keeps telling me how crucial my position is. He tries to communicate to me the importance of the education committee in our future success. But, much as I'd like to believe him, I can't. Every time we sit down in his office to talk about the role of the education committee, he's busy signing letters, taking phone calls, or answering 'quick questions' from other members of his staff. Once he even forgot I was there and spent ten minutes talking to somebody in another part of the building before he realized I was waiting for him in his office. I really do think education is important or I wouldn't have volunteered to be chairman of this committee. However, I'm not so sure he shares my concern for the continuing education for our members."

Let this unfortunate example serve as an object lesson. Don't let interruptions communicate low expectations. Instead, let your full attention communicate positive expectations to those individuals whom you want to help grow into Self-Starters.

*Proximity*  Anthropologist Edward T. Hall has identified the four primary zones within which people have different degrees of comfort and which communicate different things to individuals. The four zones are:

1. The intimate zone. This zone ranges from zero to eighteen inches and is probably not one you would use for a business relationship. It's used for close relationships, such as making love, parent-child confrontations, or perhaps fighting.

2. Personal Zone. Eighteen inches to four feet. This zone is used for personal discussion, but the outer limits (three to four feet) can also be used to communicate positive expectations to whomever you are talking.

3. Four to twelve feet. This is the social zone, which is most often used for business. As a general rule, the nearer you position yourself to four feet, the more positive your communication can be.

4. Public zone. This is from twelve feet to infinity. It would be used for communicating to large numbers of people and is frequently used, for example, in political rallies.

Positive expectations toward potential Self-Starters could, of course, be communicated in any one of the four locations or zones, but we'll limit our discussion to zones 2, 3, and 4, for it is in these zones that most business relationships take place.

In the personal zone, you begin to establish with the other individual the fact that you're working together as a team. When you sit down *beside* someone to examine a sales report, document, production spec, or anything else as "partners" studying a mutual concern, your position communicates initial positive expectations.

In the third, or social, zone, such nonverbal movements as hand gestures or head movements would have to be a little more pronounced. One way, of course, to emphasize positive expectations when you're operating in that four-to-seven foot zone is to lean forward slightly to decrease the distance. Or if, say, you want to communicate to someone that you feel he can land a new account, you might turn your chair so you face him directly, lean forward with both your elbows resting on the desk and your hands clasped in front of you, look him straight in the eye, and say, "Nat, I *know* you can get this new account. Dealing with this type of individual is your forte, and with your experience and ability, I don't see why there'd be any reason you wouldn't get the account on the first call."

If you're operating in the public zone (twelve feet plus), you're probably addressing several people at once. Gestures that indicate confidence might include smashing your fist on a podium or lectern or throwing open your arms as you say, "People have indicated that they're not sure we can do this, but I know that each [pound of fist] of us has the ability [point finger forcefully], the skill [point finger], and the intestinal fortitude [point finger] to get out there and get the job done [karate chop]."

I'm not suggesting, of course, that these gestures always communicate positive expectations. I'm merely pointing out that a little dramatic body English can help drive home your points, be they positive expectations or something else. The most important thing to remember in using proximity to grow Self-Starters is to use the zone that is appropriate to the particular discussion. The second most important thing to remember is that, as a general rule, the closer people are to you, the better you can communicate with them and generate positive expectations. Even if the physical distance is great, there are things you can do to decrease the psychological distance and increase the impact of the communications.

*personal zone* Zone 2, the personal zone, is one in which a two-way conversation is generally conducted. Because you're relatively close to the individual with whom you're talking, the effects of facial expressions, small gestures, and eye contact are maximized. Trying to use zones beyond four feet for a one-on-one discussion would be inappropriate and probably would communicate negative expectations to the recipient of the message.

*social zone* The third, or social, zone is appropriate for a team meeting or conference. People might be seated around a conference table to discuss a particular issue; to maximize communications and to foster a team feeling, make sure that people are seated evenly around the table, as shown in figure 4–7.

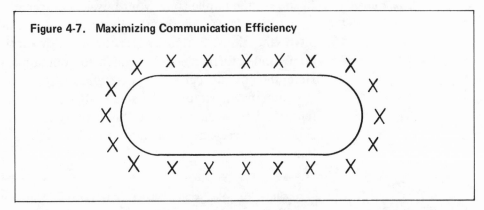

Figure 4-7. Maximizing Communication Efficiency

If however, you do not have enough people to make it all the way around, you have to be careful that you don't end up with an arrangement such as the one shown in figure 4–8. This is almost like two teams fighting with one another and it's difficult to draw everybody into the conversation. In this situation, it's important to psychologically draw everybody together. One

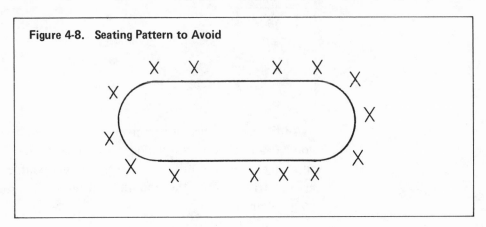

Figure 4-8. Seating Pattern to Avoid

way of doing this is put a chart across the table as shown in figure 4–9. This serves as a psychological block and in effect cuts off that other end of the table.

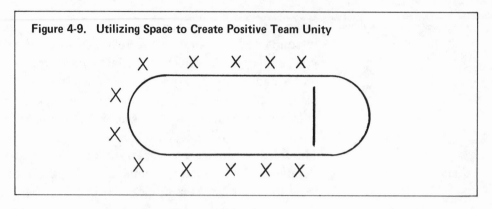

Figure 4-9.  Utilizing Space to Create Positive Team Unity

*public distances*

In zone 4, the public zone, your physical movements have to be exaggerated so that people can see them. Be careful that you don't use zone 4 for zone 3-type situations. In figure 4–10, the situation on the left would be inappropriate and a difficult one in which to communicate positive expectations. Here, the boss sits behind the desk and the four people with whom he wants to communicate sit around a small table at the other end of the office. The sensitive boss would correct this arrangement and have everyone sitting closer together, perhaps around a desk or table, as shown on the right in figure 4–10.

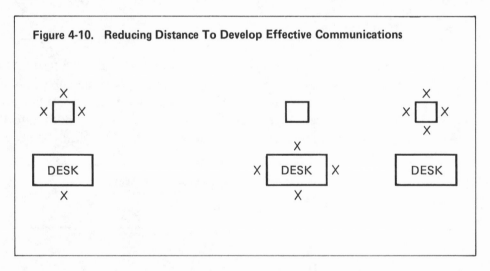

Figure 4-10.  Reducing Distance To Develop Effective Communications

Additionally, when you're using the public zone for communicating, it's a good idea to reduce the distance from time to time. This means that if you're speaking to a large audience, you should get yourself a neck mike so you can get out from behind the podium and reduce the distance between you and your listeners.

*Setting*  High expectations can best be communicated to another individual when the latter is comfortable with the physical surroundings. But this comfort level is difficult to achieve when two individuals are sitting across a desk from one another. To have a desk between yourself and someone is a good arrangement if you want to negotiate that person into a subservient position, but it's not a good way to communicate positive expectations. Sitting across the desk communicates a superior-subordinate relationship, and, although that may be the case in a discussion, it's not necessary here to emphasize your position in the office hierarchy.

Move your chair around so that the person you're talking with can sit next to you. And ask that person to bring his chair around to the side of the desk so you can both look at the same documents together. Or both of you sit at a round table that has no sides. Or sit on a couch where you can lay things out on a table in front of you. Whatever position you choose, communicate by the arrangement of your office furniture that this is a neutral situation, not a boss-subordinate situation.

This is not to suggest that you aren't, in fact, the manager or that the other person doesn't report to you. It suggests, rather, that although you're the manager, you're so comfortable with your position of power and authority that you can move around and nonverbally say, "In this situation, you're pretty much an equal. And because I'm comfortable with my position, I'm going to sit next to you so we can talk about this in a reasonable manner. One reason I'm doing this is because I have the highest degree of confidence in your ability to carry out this task."

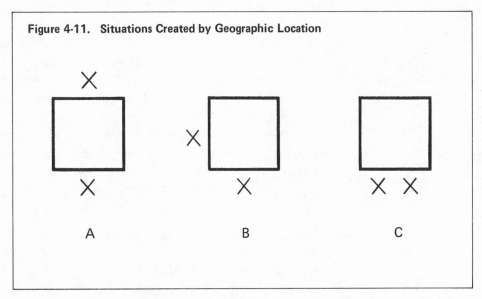

**Figure 4-11. Situations Created by Geographic Location**

Consider the physical locations of the people in figure 4–11. A shows two people sitting across the table from one another in what appears to be a competitive or negotiation-type situation. If you are, in fact, truly negotiating with somebody and want to gain the upper hand, you might use this arrangement, particularly if you could make your chair slightly higher than the other individual's and make his or hers slightly uncomfortable. Obviously, this isn't the arrangement you'd use when trying to communicate positive expectations to someone about success on a project or about work performance in general.

B, on the other hand, illustrates a more neutral type of position, one that you would probably use for an informal discussion. The two chairs might be positioned at the corner of a desk or table.

C illustrates a situation in which two people are sitting side by side and are, in effect, facing the project or the problem together. In this situation, you could, by the location of the chairs, indicate that both of you were tackling the problem or project together. If you then wanted to turn and face that person in an open position, you could turn your chair toward him, look him squarely in the eye, and say, "I know you can do this job."

**Bill and Mary Revisited**

With these thoughts in mind, let's analyze that unrewarding exchange between Bill and Mary. We already know how Mary feels about what transpired. Now that we've examined everything that can influence expectations, let's see why she feels the way she does.

*Words*

First of all, the words. The essence of what Bill said was, "I think you are just the person for this type of project." On the whole, these words are fairly positive. Bill, perhaps, could have been more specific about why he felt that way. As I questioned Mary, I learned that Bill hadn't referred to any of her past experiences, her special skills, or her background in market research. But the fact that he didn't mention these wasn't critical.

What was critical was his use of the word *person*. Mary told me, and it was confirmed by others, that Bill used *person* when he was assigning a project to a female member of the staff. As Mary explained it, he'd usually say, "You're just the one for the job" or "This is the ideal project for you." However, when he wanted to emphasize that he was dealing with a female staff member, he used the word *person*. Thus, on words, we'd give Bill a high score but not 100. Maybe around 80.

*Vocal Intonations*

Bill emphasized the word *this* in his statement: "I think you are just the person for *this* type of project." This suggests that Bill didn't think Mary was the right person for *other* types of projects. Therefore, his confidence that this was her type of project was actually demotivating. Score on intonations: 10.

**Body Language**   I had an opportunity to observe both the body language and the environment in which the message was communicated. Here's what I "heard" as I watched them talk.

*body position*   Bill stood with his arms crossed and his body turned slightly away from Mary. In other words, he was giving her the classic cold shoulder. Body position score: 5.

*gestures*   Although his hands were not closed or clenched in fists, they did remain clamped firmly on his arms. Bill did, however, pat Mary on the back several times, but then he'd quickly recross his arms. The pats on the back that I observed were the kind you'd give a small child. This said to me that Bill was looking down at Mary and treating her condescendingly. Not very good on gestures: 5.

*head*   Bill's head was tilted up and turned slightly away. He was, in effect, looking down his nose at Mary. Rating on head position: 5.

*facial expressions*   The only facial expression I saw was a grim smile, which had the unfortunate effect of tightening Bill's jaw muscles. Score on facial expressions: 5.

*eye contact*   From where I was seated, I noticed that Bill spent a lot of time looking away from Mary rather than looking her straight in the eye. What little direct eye contact he did establish would last for only a few seconds. Score on eye contact: 20.

**Proximity**   Bill and Mary were approximately three to four feet away from each other, at the outer reaches of the zone that's appropriate for the situation. The psychological distance, however, was increased slightly because Bill rested one foot on a box and leaned back slightly. The additional three or four inches of distance between Bill and Mary negatively affected the expectations being communicated. Proximity score: 40.

**Interruptions**   Bill and Mary were standing in the hallway, and every time somebody walked by, Bill stopped talking to Mary and smiled at the passer-by. He'd greet everyone, and once he even stopped to sign a work order. Six interruptions in two minutes certainly affected—negatively—Mary's receipt of Bill's message. Score on interruptions: 0.

**Physical Setting**   As I mentioned, Bill had found a box in the hallway upon which he could prop his foot. Bill managed to keep this and a couple of other boxes between Mary and himself. He also managed to meet in a busy hallway. Not particularly devastating, but combined with the other things certainly didn't do anything to help the situation. Score on physical setting: 60.

Below is a summary of how Bill scored.

| Message (80%) | Bill's Score | Impact Value | Net Result |
|---|---|---|---|
| Words | 80 | 5% | 4.0 |
| Intonations | 10 | 30% | 3.0 |
| Body Language | 20 | 45% | 9.0 |
| | | | 16.0 |

| Environment (20%) | Bill's Score | Impact Value | Net Result |
|---|---|---|---|
| Interruptions | 0 | 5% | 0.0 |
| Proximity | 40 | 5% | 2.0 |
| Setting | 60 | 10% | 6.0 |
| | | | 8.0 |
| | | Total Score | 24.0 |

As you can see, Bill didn't score too well. And no wonder. He scored high on only one item (words), and they only count for 5% of the total picture.

Fortunately, Bill soon learned—and you will, too—that Self-Starters thrive on the carefully conceived and thoughtfully delivered communique. In the office and out, both medium and message can make or break a people-growing project.

# 5 Responsibilities and Goals

Without responsibilities and accountabilities, there can be no goals. Individuals, departments, plants, divisions, and even entire companies wander off in a multitude of directions. When everybody marches to the beat of his own individual drummer, there is no real sense of purpose and very little organizational accomplishment.

Frequently, you hear the refrain, "That's everybody's responsibility." But when profits, sales, quality, or customer relations are at stake, that's nonsense. While everybody may play a role in fulfilling a particular responsibility, someone has to be solely accountable for the ultimate fulfillment. What was "everyone's responsibility" quickly becomes no one's responsibility, and when no one is accountable for something, it doesn't get done.

In a misguided effort to motivate people and to develop Self-Starters, too many organizations try to make everyone responsible for "profits," "quality," or "customer service." Rather than helping people grow, however, this merely confuses people and diffuses responsibility so widely throughout the organization that no one can perform at his maximum. But, you may argue, making people accountable or specifically responsible for something may place too much stress on them. True, making them accountable for too much, particularly over too short a period of time, could place an undue amount of stress on someone, but we'll see later in this chapter how to prevent that from occurring. What's more important is that, without some degree of accountability, people cannot grow. And without a specific set of responsibilities, it's virtually impossible for people to assume more and more responsibility for managing themselves instead of having others look after them. If a person, both as an organizational member and as an individual, is to grow and become more of a Self-Starter, he or she must learn to accept and fulfill increasing degrees of responsibility.

A good way to look at accountabilities is to consider first an organization as a system. As figure 5–1 shows, there are a number of elements in a system. One such element, of course, is *inputs*, which usually take the form of money, time, and people. Most of the things we have to work with within the

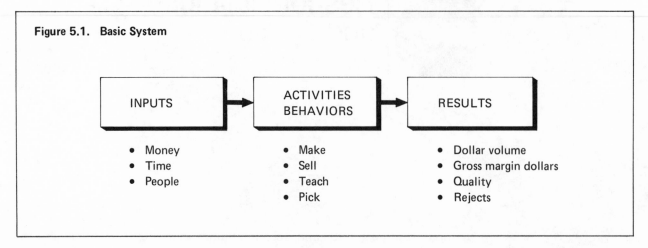

Figure 5.1. Basic System

| INPUTS | ACTIVITIES BEHAVIORS | RESULTS |
|---|---|---|
| • Money | • Make | • Dollar volume |
| • Time | • Sell | • Gross margin dollars |
| • People | • Teach | • Quality |
| | • Pick | • Rejects |

organizational setting belong in one of these three primary categories. A second element in a system consists of *activities*, behaviors, and organizational processes. Making, selling, teaching, picking, packing, stocking, designing, and testing are all activities that people engage in within the organizational setting.

George S. Odiorne, professor of management at the University of Massachusetts and a pioneer in the use of goals in management, points out that too many managers and staffs get caught up in the activity process. Odiorne calls this involvement "the Activity Trap." He suggests, and accurately so, that people can become so immersed in "getting there" that they forget where "there" is. People caught in this trap include the salesman who acts so busy making calls, he forgets why he makes them and the instructor who insists that the job would be much nicer if it weren't for all the damn students.

Finally, these activities yield certain results or *outputs*, which would include dollar volume sold, gross margin dollars, quality, rejects, reworks, absenteeism, tardiness, projects completed, students graduated, average length of stay in a hospital, and so on. Different types of organizations, of course, will have different kinds of organizational results.

Building a set of accountabilities for someone is rather like charting a route for an automobile trip. Rarely do we run out, hop in the car, and ask, "Where shall we go today?" Instead, we start out by saying, "Well, we'd like to go to Cleveland or Chicago or Sacramento or Lake Placid." In other words, we determine our destination, our *goal*. The same principle applies to the management process: we have to slow down, back up a step, and then establish the goals we want to accomplish. Figure 5–2 illustrates a system based on goals.

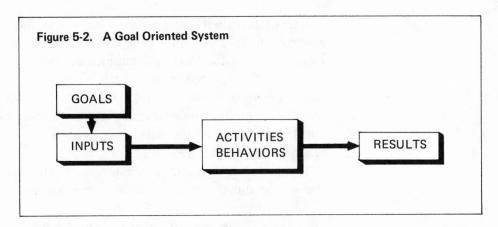

Figure 5-2.  A Goal Oriented System

GOALS

INPUTS → ACTIVITIES BEHAVIORS → RESULTS

It's important to note that the goals are simply the results we expect to accomplish. Ideally, we should sit down at the beginnng of some period of time and outline those results that we want to accomplish at the end of that period of time. Goals equal the results we want to accomplish or, in other words, the destination we want to reach.

**Start with a Results-Oriented System**

To identify individual accountabilities and responsibilities, we will consider the dynamics of the first four elements—goals, inputs, activities, outputs—that constitute an organizational system. (Later, we'll see how to fit feedback into the system.) Using a results-oriented system as a basis for identifying accountabilities and responsibilities has a number of benefits. First of all, it's based upon both corporate and individual performance. By specifying, in terms of goals, what is expected of the company as an organization, as well as of individual plants, departments, and individuals within those departments, both individual and corporate goals can be successfully integrated.

Moreover, it's based upon common sense. It stands to reason that individuals can perform better if they have a goal toward which they can direct their efforts. Once common goals are identified, cooperation from all members of the management team can be expected, and the individual manager or employee is better able to direct the work of people in the department toward the common goal.

Finally, a results-oriented system provides a way of allocating scarce resources. By identifying results to be expected from departments, projects, people, and plants, entire organizations determine those areas most in need of resources. An input-output analysis can be conducted to identify those program areas with high resource needs but low output or results. These could then be examined carefully for possible budget trimming. By the same token, program areas needing relatively few resources but showing a high level of expected results may be identified as being worthy of more resource allocation.

Results orientation begins by identifying what can be accomplished. Over the years, we've found that well-qualified members of organizations often fail to perform with maximum effectiveness merely because they aren't aware of the specific results expected of them on their jobs. Too frequently, managers think they have communicated specifically what a person is expected to accomplish; but, if you ask the subordinate what he's accountable for, his answer might be quite different from what the manager would describe. Such misinformed employees are unaware of both organizational and individual goals, the purpose of their work, and how their own goals relate to those of the system as a whole.

Try the following awareness test in *your* company to see how closely you and a subordinate concur on his or her job responsibilities.

1. Take a single sheet of paper and on it list the answers to the following questions about one of your key subordinates:

   a. What are the key areas of this individual's job for the coming year?

   b. In each of those key areas, what are the critical performance indicators that you will use to measure results during that time?

   c. For each indicator, identify the level of performance that you expect to see achieved and identify the date by which you think that level of performance should be obtained.

2. Ask that same subordinate, who will remain unaware of your response, to answer questions a, b, and c.

3. Compare the two responses.

Countless bosses and subordinates have taken this "test" in all types of organizations and among all levels of management. Over the years, the difference between answers averages about 25%. Obviously, the implications of this average "score" are pretty serious. If a subordinate and a superior can't agree on what specifically constitutes the subordinate's job, appraisal reports lose much of their validity.

The fact that someone is not a Self-Starter may not be due to inferior performance; it may be because the individual doesn't know what his or her job is. In fact, an individual might be very much a Self-Starter—but a Self-Starter heading off in the wrong direction. Exhorting or encouraging someone to be more of a Self-Starter when the individual isn't sure what specifically constitutes the entire job doesn't do much good. Instead, it urges that individual to work harder toward irrelevant or incorrect goals and, ultimately, toward becoming a Holy Terror.

One significant point emerged after we probed for the reasons for the mismatch on the superior-subordinate questionnaires: seldom was there an agreement or an articulation of specific goals at the beginning of the time period. Neither the manager nor the subordinate had agreed upon specific responsibilities and accountabilities, identified the performance indicators that would help measure performance in each of those areas, or identified the specific level of accomplishment to be reached and when it was to be reached.

**Activities: Means to an End**

I'm a firm believer that accountabilities should be considered in terms of goals. Too frequently, accountabilities have been described in a number of ways that aren't goal-oriented. For example, we often try to describe accountabilities in terms of activities rather than in terms of results to be accomplished. But there's a critical difference: activities are what go on during the course of the day, while results are the completed work that is left behind when the employee goes home. Activity is a *process* by which the work is completed; results are the *completed work* itself. Installing engines, for example, is a work activity, but the work output or result is the installed engine. While there is only a slight semantic difference between the two terms, there is a very important practical difference. To say that an employee engages in "processor activities" tells us only what *occurs* on the job, while the results tell us what is *accomplished* on the job and are more useful in determining the level of performance required within that job situation. Washing linen in a hospital is an activity, but the result of doing an effective job is that we have a low linen cost per patient day. Running a stamping machine is an activity, but results focus around things like units produced per day, rework, scrap, and rejects.

Certainly, activities are important processes; they are the steps that must be taken to reach the goal. But the primary focus in developing accountabilities must be upon goal accomplishment itself. We wouldn't want somebody to run a machine if he weren't producing enough or if he produced low-quality products. Nor would we want a salesman to make calls all year if those calls didn't lead to new accounts, more dollar volume, or higher gross margin dollars. Thus, we're suggesting that activities are the *how* of accomplishing the *what*; they're the *means* leading to the *end* result. And while they're very important, they're not the starting point for developing job accountabilities.

**Specificity Is All**

The second problem in helping people develop responsibilities or accountabilities concerns specificity. Dr. Albert W. Schrader, director of the Division of Management Education at the University of Michigan's Graduate School of Business Administration and an authority on management practices, notes that managers too often describe responsibilities to their employees in vague, generalized terms. A manager might, for example, call Mary in and say something like, "Mary, if you're going to succeed as part of our sales team, you'll need a lot more perseverance, so I want to encourage you to get out there and hit the ball." To Mary, "perseverance" might mean a variety of different things, including making more sales calls, following through on more leads, making more telephone calls, reducing entertainment expense, spending more time with the distributor's sales staff, spending less time with the distributor's sales staff, or any number of other behaviors. Actually, the boss probably meant that Mary would have to develop some type of tool that would allow her to determine what kind of progress she was making with a particular customer before she decided it wasn't worth the time to make additional calls on that account. Here again, what's needed is the identification of specific results and agreement on those results, not general advice couched in abstract terms.

## Three Steps to Better Goals

Donn Coffee, an organizational consultant from Long Island and an expert in the field of goal setting, has outlined an effective three-step method for developing goals. Coffee suggests that the following steps will lead to the development of firm goals:

1. Specifying key areas

2. Developing performance indicators

3. Establishing goals

To give you an idea of how this process might work, let's apply these three steps to the job of a baseball player. Then let's look at your own job responsibilities and the job responsibilities of others.

### Specifying Key Areas

For a baseball player, some typical key areas might be offense, defense, self-development, public relations, and intrateam relations. Also called major responsibilities or result areas, these are the parts of the job where the ball player is expected to obtain results.

### Developing Performance Indicators

Now, let's consider indicators for just one key area—offense. Some typical indicators for offense might be batting average, runs scored, runs batted in, slugging average, and stolen bases.

### Establishing Goals

Next, we'll select just one indicator—batting average—and see how we might establish a goal for that. A good goal has several elements. It should:

- Have a specific end result to be accomplished (which means it's measurable).

- Be realistic (which means it's achievable and isn't a "mission impossible").

- Be observable (which means we can see, count, hear, measure, or describe it).

- Have a completion date.

- Be under the control and/or influence of the individual who is accountable for it.

- Identify any trade-offs or costs that we're willing to live with in obtaining that goal.

Thus, a goal for the baseball player might be "to increase my batting average from 270 to 310 in time for the All-Star Game and without reducing the number of extra base hits from last season." As you can see, the ball player's goal—to increase his batting average from 270 to 310—is a measurable, specific end result to be accomplished. It's realistic; a 310 batting average makes sense for this player, but a 410 average would probably be out of the question. It's observable; it's something we can see, count, hear, measure, or describe. It has a date for completion. It's certainly under the control or influence of the individual who is accountable for the goal. And it clearly identifies the trade-offs the ball player and others are willing to live with (in this case, with no reduction in the extra base hits from last season) in obtaining that goal.

**From Ball Park to Business**

This same three-step process can be applied to the job situation. On the job, the term "key area" is frequently used interchangeably with the terms "key responsibilities," "major result areas," or "key job responsibilities." All these descriptions refer to the particular area where someone contributes results. Representative key areas for professional managers might include the following: financial results, new service development, scheduling, selection/placement, staff development, staff utilization, personnel relations, budget management, service delivery, program planning, interdepartmental relations, customer relations, self-development, profitability, product quality, product integrity, user department satisfaction, and customer satisfaction.

Notice that all these terms describe *areas* in which results are needed; they are neither indicators (measurements of performance) nor actual end results. To repeat, key areas identify the types of results needed in the area in which someone will be working; but they don't attempt to specify a completion date, a level of accomplishment, or any costs or trade-offs the employee is willing to live with. Key areas do not have to have the same elements as a goal. They simply ensure that the goals we're working on are directly related to our present job responsibilities.

**Key Areas and Authority**

It's not enough to give people responsibilities in order for them to grow and become Self-Starters. They also must have the authority necessary to carry out those responsibilities. Without the proper authority, employees become so stressed that they may decide it's not worth it and lose their drive and enthusiasm for the job. Yet managers frequently complain that their staff doesn't accept authority. Fortunately, there are some valid answers to the questions people sometimes pose about whether or not they have the authority necessary to carry out the appropriate tasks.

There are four classes of authority that might be delegated to an individual.

- Class I authority is full authority to take the necessary action and carry out a responsibility without consulting or reporting to an immediate supervisor.

- Class II authority is full authority to take necessary actions in carrying out the responsiblity, but the immediate supervisor is to be informed about the action taken.

- Class III is limited authority. An individual with Class III authority is expected to present recommendations to his immediate supervisor and not take action until a decision is reached.

- With Class IV authority, no authority is given under normal circumstances. However, an individual should be familiar enough with the responsibility to carry it out in an immediate supervisor's absence.

I've already suggested that you should reach agreement with each of your subordinates on his or her respective key areas. Now, I'd like to suggest that you go one step further. Jot down on a sheet of paper that list of five or six key areas. Show your subordinate the four classes of authority just described and ask him or her to assign to each of the key areas you've agreed upon the appropriate class of authority. Without looking at the responses, you do the same. Then compare the two lists. The studies I've conducted show that these two lists rarely will match.

In comparing the responses of managers and subordinates, we usually find that a manager will give his or her subordinate a fair number of Class I authorities in various key areas, a lot of Class II authorities, some Class III authorities, and very few Class IV authorities. The subordinate, on the other hand, will assign himself or herself no, or very few, Class I authorities, a couple of Class II authorities, a lot of Class III authorities, and perhaps one or two responsibilities in which he or she has Class IV authority. This dissimilarity occurs not because the subordinate isn't a potential Self-Starter, but because we, as managers, haven't done our part to articulate specifically what authority that individual has in each area. More importantly, we've failed to behave in a manner consistent with the level of authority we have delegated.

In most cases, you'll probably think that you've given your subordinates more authority than they think they have. That's because we think we give people lots of authority when we say something like, "Bill, you've got complete authority to make all the decisions necessary to carry out this responsibility." Now, that *sounds* like Class I authority. But having given that initial authority, we managers then start to take it back, bit by bit. Not overtly, not deliberately, perhaps not even consciously, but through little things we say, small decisions we make, and subtle behaviors in which we engage, we indicate that that person really doesn't have the authority necessary to carry out completely a particular responsibility. We might, for instance, question some of the subordinate's decisions, or we might even reverse some of those decisions that we question. Have you ever told someone he could spend $400 without checking with you? Then, when a bill came through for $375, you blew your stack and called your subordinate every name in the book? While you verbally said that he or she had the authority to carry out a responsibility, your actions told something quite different—and actions always speak louder than words.

In the space of five minutes, I once had the opportunity to ask a vice president, a regional manager, and a unit manager what amount of money the unit manager could spend without checking with the regional manager. I asked them each separately because they were each in different rooms at headquarters, and then I got them all together to discuss their different responses. The unit manager said she thought she could spend up to $50 without getting any kind of approval. I asked the regional manager how much she could spend without first checking with him; after thinking about it for a minute, he allowed that $100 would be an appropriate amount of money to check with him on, but she could spend anything less than $100 without checking. I then asked the vice president the same question: how much could the unit manager spend without first checking with the regional manager? He replied that he really hadn't given the matter much thought, but $200 to $250 would seem like an appropriate amount. When I asked all three of them together how each had arrived at his or her conclusion about the appropriate amount of money, some intriguing facts came to light.

Apparently, the vice president and the regional manager had each done several subtle things that caused the unit manager to believe that she could spend less and less money without first checking with her superior. There was the time, for example, when she decided to buy some advertising space. After she submitted the invoice to the regional manger, he went through the ceiling. "Don't ever spend this much money for this type of thing again without first checking with me!" he thundered. Of course, all the unit manager heard was "don't ever spend this kind of money again without checking with me." As it happened, the advertising budget was something over which she had relatively little control and even less authority; however, because there was no specific agreement on different levels of authority for different responsibilities or key areas, the unit manager generalized the regional manager's outburst to include *all* of her responsibilities. On another occasion, the vice president made an inspection tour of our manager's unit. When he noticed a particular brand of industrial soap in the supply room, he asked her why she bought that product and from what source she purchased it. He ended the conversation by suggesting that she look elsewhere to purchase another type of detergent. After several instances such as these, the put-upon unit manager quite naturally concluded that the less she spent without checking with somebody, the better off she was.

Both the regional manager and the vice president had complained to me that this particular unit manager was not a Self-Starter, that she wasn't grabbing the ball and running with it, that she didn't seem to take charge the way they thought she would when they first hired her. Actually, though, her two superiors were effectively, if unconsciously, sabotaging their own desires to develop a Self-Starter. All the unit manager needed was some discussion about and agreement on the areas where she could take initiative and those where she had to check before she could carry out the action.

**Developing Indicators**

Developing indicators is the next step in the process of achieving accountability through goals. Indicators function as the performance measures that tell us how well an individual is doing within a particular key area. Within the key area of quality, for example, we might be concerned with such indicators as rejects, rework, scrap, or customer-returned material. Within the key area of cost control, a hospital might be concerned about linen cost per-patient-day, dietary cost per-patient-day, average receivables, and maintenance cost per square foot of floor space. And, within the key area of employee relations, we might be concerned about such indicators as absenteeism, tardiness, and turnover or about even more specific indicators, such as turnover within six months of the hire date.

Some jobs, of course, do not readily lend themselves to the development of indicators. At one company with which I worked, the general counsel sat in on one of the training sessions I conducted. While the notion of establishing goals appealed to him, he didn't see how it could be done for the general counsel's job. When I asked him if he wrote reports, briefs, and recommendations for other key members of management seated around the room, he replied that he did. I then wrote on the chalkboard: "Key area: management information/reports."

"I understand that," he said, "but I can't come up with an indicator. How do you measure how good a job I'm doing at providing these individuals with recommendations? You really can't say that I've got to provide two a day. Sometimes it's one a day and sometimes one a week; other times, it will be four or five in one day."

I then asked both the general counsel and the group to brainstorm things they thought people receiving the reports might look for in those reports. "Let's regard the receiver of the report as a 'customer' of the general counsel," I suggested, "Not an external customer, of course, but an internal customer or a user department."

Then we brainstormed a list of things that user departments might look for in a report and boiled it down to five variables—report accuracy, report timeliness, coherence, applicability to the situation, and speed of response. Next, we drew a scale, similar to the one in figure 5–3, that went from one to

**Figure 5-3. Developing Indicators for Goal Setting**

| | LOW-POOR | 1 | 2 | 3 | 4 | 5 | HIGH-GOOD |
|---|---|---|---|---|---|---|---|
| How do you find the accuracy of this report? Comments | | ☐ | ☐ | ☐ | ☐ | ☐ | |
| How was the timelines of this report? Comments | | ☐ | ☐ | ☐ | ☐ | ☐ | |
| How coherent was this report? Comments | | ☐ | ☐ | ☐ | ☐ | ☐ | |
| How applicable was this report to your situation? Comments | | ☐ | ☐ | ☐ | ☐ | ☐ | |
| How was the speed of response to your request for information? Comments | | ☐ | ☐ | ☐ | ☐ | ☐ | |

five, with one being "poor" or "low" and five being "high" or "good." And we added a section for comments after each of the variables.

I then asked the general counsel if his secretary would make copies of our scale, distribute one with each recommendation or report, and ask that it be returned to his office. He said that would be a simple thing to do and might even provide some useful information. I then asked the other key members of the management team if they would take a few minutes to fill out one of these as a means of providing the general counsel with some information on how his recommendations and reports could be made more useful; they agreed to try.

Within three months, there was general agreement that the reports had become much more useful. The area that showed the greatest need for improvement and, of course, that finally showed the greatest improvement was "coherence." It seems that the general counsel had been unintentionally writing the reports in "legalese." But once he received feedback on how the reports were being perceived, he changed his writing style so that the reports became more lucid for the user departments. The key area then became "management information," the indicator became the average rating on reports, and the goal in this case became "to improve the average rating on reports from 3.2 to 4.1 by December 1 without spending any more time on the reports and without adversely affecting the quality of the reports."

In this instance, the performance indicator didn't really have to be developed. It was there all the time, but it was hidden away in the system. To develop a good performance indicator often requires taking information that is already somewhere in the system and bringing it out to use as a performance measure.

Of course, the more lead time the indicators give you, the more useful they are. Indicators that highlight problems while there is still time to take corrective action are much more useful than those that report problems when it's too late to solve them. The quality of incoming raw materials clearly gives us more lead time than does scrap, and scrap gives us more lead time than does customer-returned material. Thus, it's probably more practical to focus on quality of incoming raw materials rather than on either scrap or customer-returned material.

Among other things, the indicator step helps us achieve balance in the job. Indicators can measure one of four things—quality (how good), quantity (how many), timeliness (how long), and cost (how much). To focus on any one of these classes of indicators to the exclusion of other classes can lead to problems. Focusing solely on quantity, for example, can cause problems with quality, timeliness, and cost. By considering potential indicators in each class, we can help people develop balance between the quantity, quality, timeliness, and cost of their job outputs.

## Writing the Goals

The third and most important step in the goal-setting process, of course, is writing the goal. And a good goal should exhibit six characteristics.

*Specify End Results*

First of all, it must state the specific end result to be accomplished. This means the goal must be measurable; therefore, if you've developed a good indicator, it will be used as part of the goal. An example of a goal that lacks a specific end result to be accomplished would be to say to somebody, "I'm going to rough you up a bit." If, however, you said, "I'm going to break your arm," you'd be *quite* specific. In fact, your end result is even measurable, and there would be no ambiguity about the goal you have in mind.

*Be Realistic*

The second element of a good goal is that it's realistic. It should involve some stretch, which would force people to grow, but it should still remain within reach. It shouldn't be a mission impossible. To say "I'm going to double our sales this year" is probably to express an unrealistic goal. And for a smallish company to announce that it's "going to be number one in terms of sales" in its industry within a year is equally unrealistic. It's important that goals require people to stretch, to grow on the job, but it's also important that the goals be neither so high as to be unobtainable nor so low as to be undemanding.

The probability of obtaining a goal and the motivation or involvement in trying to obtain it follows a curve that looks something like the one in figure 5-4.

This curve suggests that, if there is zero probability of success in goal obtainment, there's not very much motivation or involvement. It also suggests that if there's 100% probability of success, there's probably not much involvement or commitment either. Most importantly, the curve suggests that,

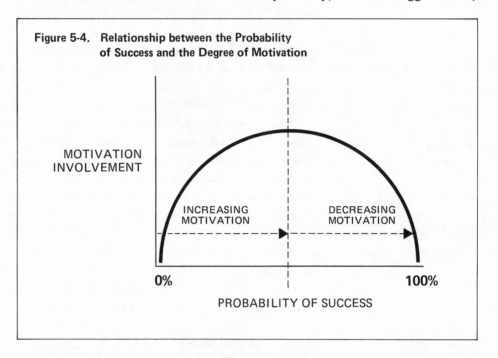

Figure 5-4. Relationship between the Probability of Success and the Degree of Motivation

MOTIVATION INVOLVEMENT

INCREASING MOTIVATION

DECREASING MOTIVATION

0%

100%

PROBABILITY OF SUCCESS

at that point where there is some risk of failure, there's also a relatively high motivation level. The key variable must be that the individual controls many or most of the variables that determine whether or not that goal becomes obtainable. Knowing this, we can help people grow to their maximum on the job. If people don't have control over the variables that affect that goal attainment, then the probability of success is very low. And, equally disheartening, the probabilities of both motivation and goal attainment are low, too.

*Be Observable*  A good goal should be observable so we'll know when we get there. To tell someone that he's looking at a very fast boat isn't the same as making that fact observable. But to be able to point to the records that show that this boat won twelve out of its last fifteen starts makes the situation vividly observable. The same principle is important to remember in establishing performance goals. A good goal is one whose attainment is observable.

It's helpful to think of this aspect of goal development in terms of "how would you know when you saw one." When managers present preliminary goal statements that say things like "My goal is to improve communications," I always ask them, "How will you know when you get there? How will you *know* that communications have improved?" Generally, the response is something like, "Well, if we had some good communications around here, the number of stock-outs due to misordering would drop." And my retort is, "Then you should *say* your goal is to reduce the number of stock-outs due to misordering from fifty a week to five a week by November 1st without adding to inventory."

*Include a Completion Date*

A good goal should have a date for completion. Too frequently, a goal either doesn't have a date, or, if it does, the date is inappropriate. Completion dates shouldn't necessarily correspond with the end of a fiscal year or a calendar year. The organization that gives all its goals year-end completion dates finds that the work load is unevenly distributed throughout the year. For the first seven months of the year, everybody coasts along at a relatively casual pace. Suddenly they realize that they have a whole list of goals to accomplish, and the work pace during the last five months becomes hectic, even frantic, as people rush around trying to meet all their goals. And, of course, they never do meet them all because trying to cram all that extra work into five months is simply impossible. That's why I recommend setting a specific completion date, be it April 1, June 10, or November 2. Whatever the appropriate completion date is, make it as specific as possible. Even a completion date of "by the end of the second quarter" is better than a completion date that corresponds with the end of the fiscal year.

*Be Controlled/ Influenced by Accountable Employee*

Finally, the goal should be under the control or influence of the individual who is accountable for its accomplishment. It's not very effective to assign a general foreman control of a goal that is affected by depreciation, schedules, amortization tables, taxes, wage rates, or the general economy. But that same foreman might logically oversee goals that concern units of production, volume, scrap, reject, rework, absenteeism, and turnover. That's not to suggest that everyone needs control over all the variables that affect goal attainment. A production foreman, for example, certainly doesn't influence *all* the variables that affect his attendance rate. However, he controls enough of these variables and influences enough of the others that it would make a reasonable goal for somebody in that type of position.

*Identify Any Trade-Offs or Costs in Reaching the Goal*

Anything pursued to its ultimate eventually conflicts with something else. Beauty that is pursued endlessly might well conflict with personal health. Physical fitness pursued to its ultimate might conflict with having enough time to earn a living.

Just as balance is necessary in our personal lives, it is necessary in our business lives. Any single measure of accomplishment pursued to the exclusion of all other measures leads to an out-of-balance organization. A manufacturing firm who focused its efforts exclusively on the volume output of its plant might well encounter cost or quality problems. (When you hear someone shout, "I want production at all costs," that's usually what they get. Production—but at all costs.)

Another company might focus its attention solely on sales volume but neglect to watch margins. Or the credit department might eliminate all credit losses but also cut out the development of any new accounts.

To insure that the people establishing goals keep the appropriate perspective, it's helpful to include as part of the goal any necessary trade-offs or costs required to reach the goal.

**Evaluating Written Goals**

Some of the following sample goals are well-written and some are poorly written. I've evaluated each one to give you an idea of what constitutes a good—and an inferior—goal.

**Goal Critique**

| | Yes | No | Comments |
|---|---|---|---|
| 1. *To improve communications* | | | |
| Specific end result? | ☐ | ☑ | It's an activity. |
| Realistic? | ☑ | ☐ | |
| Observable? | ☐ | ☑ | How would you know when you got there? |
| Completion date | ☐ | ☑ | |
| Under control/influence | ☑ | ☐ | Probably—depends upon what's meant by communications. |
| Trade-off identified | ☐ | ☑ | |
| 2. *To reduce error rate by October 10* | | | |
| Specific end result? | ☐ | ☑ | From what error rate to what error rate? |
| Realistic? | ☐ | ☑ | No commitment to end result |
| Observable? | ☐ | ☑ | Only if you put in a number or percent |
| Completion date | ☑ | ☐ | |
| Under control/influence | ☑ | ☐ | Probably—if the goal belongs to the appropriate individual |
| Trade-off identified | ☐ | ☑ | |
| 3. *To improve quality from 94% to 96% yield by changing the scrap disposal sequence without affecting units of production* | | | |
| Specific end result | ☑ | ☐ | Has specific end result but also includes *how* (changing scrap disposal sequence) |
| Realistic | ☑ | ☐ | |
| Observable | ☑ | ☐ | |
| Completion date | ☐ | ☑ | |
| Under control/influence | ☑ | ☐ | Probably—if the goal belongs to the appropriate individual |
| Trade-off identified | ☑ | ☐ | |

4. *To reduce overtime from 5% of payroll to 3.5% of payroll by November 15*

| | | |
|---|---|---|
| Specific end result | ☑ ☐ | |
| Realistic | ☑ ☐ | |
| Observable | ☑ ☐ | |
| Completion date | ☑ ☐ | |
| Under control/influence | ☑ ☐ | Probably—if the goal belongs to the appropriate individual |
| Trade-off identified | ☐ ☑ | |

5. *To increase sales from $100,000/month to $350,000/month in the next 90 days without decreasing gross margin*

| | | |
|---|---|---|
| Specific end result | ☑ ☐ | |
| Realistic | ☐ ☑ | Unless you know something that I don't |
| Observable | ☑ ☐ | |
| Completion date | ☑ ☐ | |
| Under control/influence | ☑ ☐ | Again—if the goal belongs to the appropriate individual |
| Trade-off identified | ☑ ☐ | |

## Goals versus Standards

I often hear the question: How high do I set the goals? Remembering the motivation/probability-of-success curve (figure 5–4), my answer is: You want to set goals that have some stretch in them but that aren't missions impossible.

One way to maximize the probability of being somewhere at the top of that motivation curve is to use the min-max or standard-goal approach, which I'll explain shortly. Here's why.

With just one single goal, there's a tendency to use that target as an evaluation and punishment tool rather than as a growth and developmental tool. If, for example, an employee sets a goal of 12 but only reaches 11 at the end of the year, he'll frequently be reprimanded, his performance evaluation will be low, and he won't receive a generous merit increase—all because he didn't meet his goal. No wonder this employee starts to look at goal-setting as a punishment process, rather than a growth process.

But, just as we don't want to be unduly harsh or unrealistic, we don't want people wallowing in mediocrity or complacency either. That hardly develops Self-Starters. Therefore, we have to have some basic standards or "passing grades" that we can use as a basis for evaluation. Many organizations have found it useful to have a different set of goals for *evaluation* than they do for *growth and development*. Initially, this might sound confusing, so let's see how it works.

An organization might, for example, set 10 as a standard and make that standard widely known. From now on, 10 is the minimum passing grade; that's the least anybody can do. If you get 10, that entitles you to the same job at the same pay (with cost-of-living allowances) for another year. However, the organization's powers that be might announce, "We'd like you to stretch and grow here. And, to do that, we'd like you to set a breakthrough goal somewhere above that minimum-performance standard." Let's say that somebody sets a goal of 15, and, at the end of the year, she hits 13. At that time, you, as manager, have two choices: you can tell this employee that she missed her goal by 2, or you can tell her that she exceeded the standard by 3.

You'd be best off telling the employee that she's exceeded the standard by 3; although she didn't hit the goal of 15, she's still 3 above standard. Organizations that have used this approach have found that it fosters perceptible growth and motivation. This tack then encourages employees to set a higher target the next year. As manager, you might explain this procedure to your subordinates this way: "The standard for this particular part of the job is 10; you set a goal of 15, and you hit 13. For performance appraisal purposes, you're 3 above standard. You've exceeded it by 3, and you've made good progress toward the goal. What do you think the goal should be for next quarter?" (Or the next year, or whatever time period you're looking at?)

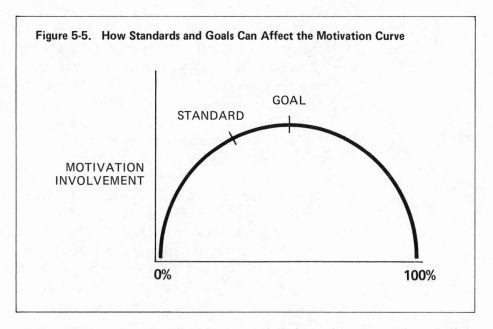

Figure 5-5.   How Standards and Goals Can Affect the Motivation Curve

The technique just described has several distinct advantages. First of all, it maximizes the probability that the employee will operate at the top of the motivation curve. And, rather than being committed to a single target, we're able to consider a range of expectations, from low to high, as illustrated in figure 5-5. We've also encouraged people to establish stretch goals, because they know that their performance is going to be measured against an ongoing standard.

One problem of continuously measuring people against the breakthrough goal is that they learn they will be punished if they miss that goal. Therefore, employees too often try to protect themselves by setting low goals, which they can accomplish and which will look good at performance appraisal time. As they set lower and lower goals, their expectations, as well as ours, tend to be lowered. When this happens, performance falls even more. And, as performance falls, employees are punished still more for not achieving their breakthrough goals. This downward spiral, fueled by lower goals, expectations, and performance, becomes increasingly difficult to stop and eventually reverse.

The question then becomes: How fast do we move up that standard when performance consistently exceeds the standard? I feel strongly that the standard has to be moved up—but not automatically as soon as somebody hits a particular level of performance. Let's return to our example where we had a standard of 10, a goal of 15, and a year-end achievement of 13. Now, if we automatically move the standard up to that most recent performance of 13, we create a figurative rubber band that snaps behind that achiever as soon as she takes a big step forward. If we tell her that 13 is now the new minimum standard and then ask what her new goal will be, she'll remember the rubber-band effect and say, "Well, maybe this time I'll only try for an improvement of 3, which would bring me up to 16." Then, when she hits 16 at the end of the year, 16 automatically becomes the new minimum standard. Thus, people learn to take shorter and shorter steps—and, subsequently, their goals become lower and lower, too. Their expectations about performance are lowered, so performance follows in a downward pattern. This downward spiral also fuels itself because, as performance goes down, the next goal-setting cycle is lowered even more.

That's why I suggest replacing the rubber-band effect with the sliding scale effect. Let's say the standard is 10; somebody sets a target of 15 and then hits 13. Leave the standard at 10 and ask the employee what goals she'd like to set for next time. And what if she hits 16 the next time? Then it's probably fair to move the standard up to 12 or 13. This way, we're always able to say two very important things to people about their job performance. First, "You've exceeded the standard and are succeeding within the job situation." And, second, "There's still room for improvement, so let's set a breakthrough target you can shoot for in the coming months."

**Employee Participation in Goal-Setting**

Dr. Kenneth H. Blanchard, a San Diego-based consultant and one of the nation's top authorities on leadership style, suggests that this style is a function of several variables. The first variable he suggests we consider is task behavior, which he defines as the extent to which a leader directs subordinates in the completion of their tasks. Specifically, it involves the degree to which they are told what to do and when, where, and how to do it. Relationship behavior, on the other hand, is the extent to which a leader engages in two-way communication by stressing the development of personal relationships.[2]

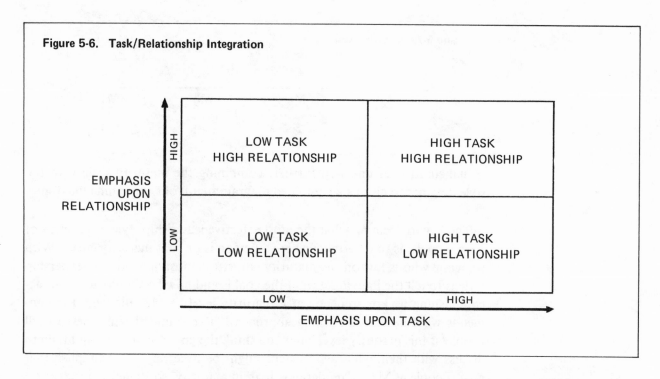

**Figure 5-6. Task/Relationship Integration**

Figure 5-6 illustrates the four quadrants of leadership behavior:

- High-task and low-relationship behavior is characterized by one-way communication: the leader closely defines the roles of the followers and tells them when, how, and where to do various tasks.

- High-task, high-relationship behavior is characterized by attempts to get the followers to buy, psychologically, into decisions that must be made.

- High-relationship, low-task behavior is characterized by shared decision-making by both leaders and followers. Two-way communication is utilized.

- Low-relationship, low-task behavior is characterized by letting the followers run their own show, with only general supervision.

Some leadership-style "experts" claim that one style is better than another. But Blanchard is too practical and realistic to do that. Instead, he says that different styles are appropriate at different times and with different types of people. One key variable that Blanchard stresses is the *maturity* of the followers with whom you're going to be establishing the goals. Suppose we draw a scale that looks something like figure 5-7, with "maturity" ranging from very high to very low.

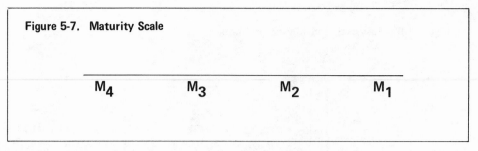

Figure 5-7. Maturity Scale

M₄ M₃ M₂ M₁

Blanchard goes one step further, combining the maturity scale with the style diagram to give us a combined diagram that looks something like figure 5-8.

The key to deciding what the most effective leadership style is, in terms of setting goals, is to determine where a person is on that maturity curve. With someone who is low on the maturity curve, the most appropriate leadership style is to tell the individual what the goal is and how he should go about accomplishing it. For someone at a maturity level of M2, Blanchard recommends what he calls a "selling approach." I've found that it's best to tell people at this maturity level what you think the goal ought to be and then to discuss with them what action steps might be necessary to accomplish that goal. People at M3 are moderately high in maturity, so Blanchard suggests a participative approach here. Frequently, this involves joint discussion about what the goal ought to be and perhaps assistance from the subordinate in developing the action plan necessary to accomplish that goal. For highly mature individuals, Blanchard recommends a delegating approach. At this stage, the employee is probably a true Self-Starter, proposing goals to you and, with almost no guidance whatsoever, developing the appropriate action steps.

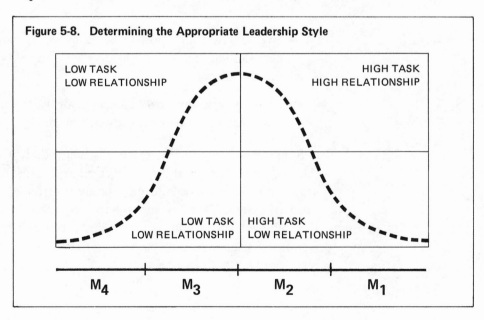

Figure 5-8. Determining the Appropriate Leadership Style

Obviously, it is crucial that you select the appropriate leadership style that corresponds with the appropriate maturity level. The effectiveness of a particular style depends largely upon the maturity of the individuals involved in the goal-setting process. Using the delegating approach with someone who is extremely mature is quite appropriate. But trying that same approach with someone who is at M1 on the maturity curve would be entirely inappropriate and probably would lose the ball game for you.

**Integration of Goals Encourages Accountability**

Rensis Likert, director emeritus of the Institute for Social Research at the University of Michigan, has suggested that organizations consist of a series of *linking pins*. His widely known theory is particularly relevant to a discussion of goals and responsibilities. Not only do goals require the appropriate leadership style, but they must also be used to forge organizational strength. Likert notes that if the diverse elements of an organization are to work well together, each individual operating within the organization must function as a linking pin. In the three organizational levels indicated in figure 5-9, we can see how three different linking pins might work. Each level integrates the level above it with the level below it. If an organization is to work well, individual, departmental, and divisional goals must be set so that each unit works together to accomplish some overall target. The diagram shows how different organizational units must function well together to meet an overall target.

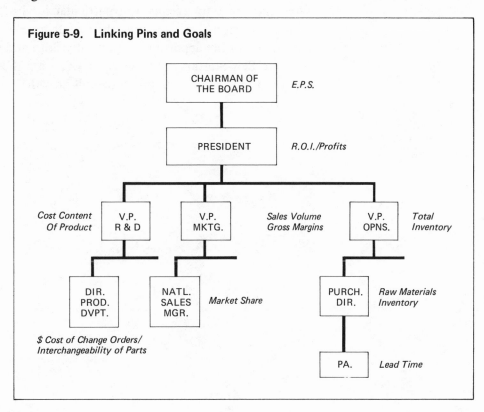

Figure 5-9. Linking Pins and Goals

Imagine a situation in which the company president has an objective to improve return investment from X% to Y% by the end of the fiscal year without missing the organization's standard sales forecast. The director of research and development might have a related objective that reads: "To reduce the cost content of the product by an average of 14%." The director of marketing might have an objective that reads: "To increase unit volume from 300,000 to 320,000 units while staying within the existing advertising budget." And the director of operations might have an objective that reads: "To reduce inventory levels from $1,000,000 to $100,000 by June 1 without affecting scheduling."

Each of these objectives ties into the president's objective, which ties into the chairman of the board's objective of earnings per share. If we trace a path through that organization, we can see how other objectives must be integrated to help meet the overall objective. Down a couple of levels from the vice president of operations is the director of purchasing, whose objective reads: "To reduce raw material inventories from $750,000 to $450,000 without affecting out-of-stock conditions." And tying into that is the purchasing agent's objective, which reads: "To land raw materials on our docks four weeks before we need them rather than three weeks before we need them." Thus, high priority objectives can be traced up and down in the organization. This integration not only helps encourage team work but assures accountability at each and every level of the organization.

Accountability for results at a particular level of the organization is imperative. As individuals see how they contribute to the overall growth and profitability of the department, plant, division, and company, they begin to grow into Self-Starters. The better they can see the big picture, the harder they'll look for ways to improve overall growth.

# 6 | Action Planning for Goal Accomplishments

Using goals encourages primary accountability. Unfortunately, most organizations stop there. Self-Starters should not only be accountable for accomplishing certain goals or targets, they should also be accountable for and committed to the basic steps necessary to reach that final goal. Goals are *what* we want people to accomplish. Goal planning or action planning is *how* they are going to get there. Too frequently, we establish goals by one method or another and set out the targets people are to shoot for, but we overlook the second level of accountability. When people have the targets but lack the action-planning steps to accomplish those targets, they frequently miss the targets. Managers then hold subordinates' feet to the fire because goals weren't accomplished. But the real culprit here was the manager, who didn't insist that the subordinate lay out the action-planning steps necessary to reach the goal.

Goals without action planning give us, first of all, no milestones against which to check goal progress. Part of the action-planning process involves setting certain interim or milestone target dates by which to accomplish certain steps. Without these interim milestones, it's difficult to tell if any progress has been made toward accomplishing the original goal. Second, without action planning, there's no insurance that the goal will be reached. Action planning functions like an insurance policy: the fact that we *plan* our goals helps assure the accomplishment of them. Without the insurance of a plan, a manager can't be assured that the goal will be reached.

And, finally, a lack of action planning means no individual steps have been assigned to reach the goal. Not all the action-planning steps are necessarily taken by the individual who is accountable for the original goal; frequently, another department or even someone outside the organization has to help accomplish the goal. But without the planning stage, the outside help and interdepartmental cooperation necessary to reach the goal are missing. And when they're missing, there's no goal accomplishment.

To see how the absence of action planning can cause problems, let's consider a company whose director of personnel had a definite objective. He intended to increase the percent of racial minorities in the work force from 14% to 24% (which would equal the percent of minorities in the local community) by November 1 at an additional cost of $14,000 and not more than 200 staff hours. He turned accomplishment of the goal over to his recruiting and selection manager, and he asked for a quarterly progress report on the percent of goal accomplishment.

In this particular instance, the company had to hire 116 additional minorities to raise the percentages to the right level. At the end of the first quarter, the personnel director asked for a report on progress toward the target and was told that the company was 25% of its way toward the target. Our administrator dutifully reported to the president that twenty-nine more people had been hired to bring them to a total of 16.5%. The same thing happened at the end of the second quarter; the progress report from the recruiting manager was approximately 50%, and the personnel director reported that they had hired another twenty-nine people, thus bringing them up to a total of 19%. At the end of the third quarter, the recruiting manager reported that they were 75% of their way toward the goal; and, again, the personnel director reported that they had hired an additional twenty-nine people, thus bringing the total percentage to 21.5%.

These same percentages were reported to a government inspector who was checking compliance with certain government laws. At the end of the third quarter, the government checked to see how this particular company was doing. The records indicated that, although the company was making some progress, it actually had nowhere near the number of people or percentages it had reported. The problem? An unfortunate case of miscommunication about the action plan.

Here's what went wrong. The person responsible for implementing the objective had developed a plan to accomplish that goal, which was realistic but difficult to reach. However, because of the hiring patterns and seasonality of the company's business, most of the actual hiring would have taken place in the fourth quarter. During the first three quarters, the personnel department was setting up the procedures for seeking out, interviewing, and selecting those people to be hired during the fourth quarter. To the person in charge of recruiting, therefore, 25% of goal accomplishment meant that they had completed that portion of the action plan that was to be accomplished during the first quarter. Fifty percent of the goal accomplishment meant that they had completed the second quarter of the action plan, and 75% of the goal accomplishment meant they had completed the third 25% of the action plan. During those three quarters of a year, the company actually had hired fewer than seven minorities, but it had established the systems and had, in fact, identified the people to be hired during the fourth quarter. Needless to say, this breakdown in communications created some awkward problems with the government.

In another company, a department head established a goal "to implement a new scrap-disposal system by November 1 without affecting the production schedule." He made a commitment to the plant manager to accomplish this and gave each of his general supervisors a pep talk on the importance of reaching the goal. Every couple of weeks or so, he would ask them how they were coming in terms of accomplishing the goal, and the responses would range from "pretty good this week" to "we're really working on it" to "looks like we're getting it under control." As the time drew near to implement the new scrap-disposal system, however, the department head found

---

**Figure 6-1. Sample Action Plan**

KEY AREA:  Sales Expansion

INDICATOR:  Increased Unit Sales

OBJECTIVE:  To increase unit sales from 150,000 to 300,000 on an annual basis to existing accounts by 1/15. Cost not to exceed working hours within present budget.

| ACTION STEPS | BY WHEN | INVESTMENT $ | HOURS | BY WHOM US | OTHERS |
|---|---|---|---|---|---|
| Consult with management about plans and results desired. | 8/15 | 0 | 2 | TKC | |
| Determine which accounts did not purchase 50% of their units from us last year (by analyzing figures obtained from accounting). | 7/14 | 0 | 2 | CBG | |
| Analyze competitive program now being sold to accounts (using competitive file). | 7/21 | 0 | 2 | CBG | |
| Develop sales plan to include brand, prices, terms, delivery, and warranty. | 8/15 | 0 | 5 | TKC | DMW |
| Present plan to one preselected account (key district). | 8/18 | 0 | 2 | TKC | DMW |
| Revise, if necessary. | 8/25 | 0 | | TKC | DMW |
| Present to all districts involved. | 9/1–10/1 | 0 | 10 | | DMW |
| Review results with one major district. | 12/1 | 0 | 1 | | BBC |
| Review results from sales printout. | 12/15 | 0 | 1 | TKC | |
| Review on a monthly basis. | | | | TKC | |

that virtually no progress had been made toward introducing the new system. Why? Because he had failed to develop with each general supervisor an appropriate action plan that would ensure that the target date would be met with the available funding resources. Had he developed an action plan, such as that shown in figure 6–1, he would have had appropriate check points to monitor and, thus, could have seen that progress was being made toward that goal. The truth of the matter is that, while the department head complained about "not having Self-Starters," he hadn't done his fair share to grow them.

One health care organization also discovered the importance of action planning the difficult way. Its objective was "to reduce the average length of stay from 7.2 days to 6.9 days, commensurate with the level of care, from one fiscal year to the next and with no loss in the quality of patient care as measured by the physician survey form and the patient-satisfaction form." While the organization did a good job of establishing the objective and obtaining commitments from everyone involved, it failed to develop the steps necessary to reach that particular goal.

Because little progress was made during the first quarter of the year, key administrators decided to turn up the heat during the second quarter. Despite this, virtually no progress toward the goal was evident after six months. Finally, pressure from the administration became so intense that everybody ran around working to accomplish the goal. By now, though, it was too late in the year to implement all the steps necessary to reach that goal. Had the decision makers sat down at the beginning of the year and thought through all the steps necessary to reach their goal and then implemented those steps, they would have had an insurance plan to virtually guarantee the accomplishment of the goal.

In another instance, a department head identified a goal, reached agreement with each subordinate manager and supervisor on the importance of the goal, and jointly developed the steps necessary to accomplish that goal. Unfortunately, he and his colleagues forgot to relate the accomplishment of the individual steps to the appropriate parties. One step in particular dealt with the review of certain credit actions and the establishment of new policies; three different people each might reasonably have been the person to execute that step. And each, of course, thought the other two were doing it. When it came time to implement the new credit procedure, it was discovered that nobody had been working on it. Introduction of the new procedure then had to be delayed for two months while someone reviewed certain credit actions. Hindsight showed that this unfortunate incident resulted because there was no individual accountability built into an otherwise adequate action plan.

Make sure that your foresight is better than your hindsight. Put accountability for the accomplishment of each action step into the plan. Use initials, specific departments or whatever is appropriate. But put the accountability into the plan.

**15 Steps to Better Action Plans**

Fortunately, there are several things we can do to help people grow with action planning. In the remainder of this chapter, I'll describe fifteen steps to develop effective goal plans. By taking them yourself and with your subordinates, you'll help individuals grow and become the Self-Starters your organization needs.

*1. Establish Checkpoints.*

People need checkpoints so they can take corrective action when things get behind target. A goal plan should outline certain steps that will let everyone involved in all the steps know what kind of progress is being made. It's not enough just to develop the goal and then the plan. Checkpoints are imperative because they permit speeding up or slowing down certain steps and revising, modifying, deleting, or adding others. Thus, the original target can be met even if the original conditions change.

*2. State Each Step Specifically.*

Each goal-planning step should be stated specifically enough so that people involved in the goal-planning process can tell when that step is completed. This means that steps such as "improve communications," "develop more morale," and "get more commitment" don't work very well as action steps. Specific steps, such as "reduce the number of interdepartmental meetings due to miscommunications" or "reduce the frequency of absenteeism" or "implement project," are far more useful.

*3. Specify Who Is Responsible.*

The person or persons accountable for the accomplishment of the objective and those directly responsible for specific segments of the process should be named and clearly identified. As our sample action plan shows, it's important to note specifically who is accountable for each step that must be taken to reach the goal. Someone within our organization or our department or even someone outside the organization might be the accountable individual.

Incidentally, it's not necessary to write out the entire name of an individual or company. Usually, it's more convenient and practical to use abbreviations or initials or some other shorthand form of communication. Just make sure that your shortened forms of communication clearly identify the person responsible for the accomplishment of each specific step.

*4. Identify Communication and Collaboration Needs.*

Frequently it's as important for individuals and departments to share information about the action steps necessary to accomplish goals as it is for them to share information about the goals themselves. Often, another department must help the originating department reach a goal; in those instances, the assisting department must know about the additional demands that will be placed upon it to help the other department meet its goal.

Action steps sometimes conflict with one another and produce a push-pull situation. That's what happened to one company whose director of manufacturing proposed this objective: "To improve return on investment from A to B by November 1, without affecting the production schedule."

The goal of the director of marketing was "to improve customer service levels from 85% to 92% by October 15 without increasing the marketing department budget." When these goals were presented at an executive staff meeting, everybody nodded wisely, proclaimed the two goals "very important," and wished one another good luck in accomplishing them.

As you might guess, one important step in the manufacturing manager's action plan was "to reduce the inventory levels of finished goods, work in process, and raw material inventory from X to XX." This he did with great dispatch. As you might also guess, the marketing director was determined "to increase inventory levels from A to AA." So he worked like mad to raise the inventory level.

Now, the manufacturing manager's action step dealing with inventory levels was number 3 in his action plan, and the marketing manager's action step dealing with inventory levels was number 6. This meant that the manufacturing manager went to work on his third step before the marketing manager got to *his* sixth step. And this accident of timing adversely affected service levels. Thus, by the time the director of marketing reached his step number 6, he had completed the first five steps of his action plan. And, although those steps had a positive impact on customer service levels, they were offset slightly by the reduction in service levels through the reduced inventory. The net result, then, was a slight reduction in service levels.

Alarmed by his failure to approach his goal, the marketing manager vigorously tackled his sixth action step. By exerting a lot of sales effort and doing plenty of pushing, controlling, and coaxing, he was able to push inventory levels up to the point where service levels were starting to reach an acceptable level. The manufacturing manager, meanwhile, had completed his third action step and was working on other steps in the action plan. Suddenly he noticed that inventory had popped up to a level that threatened the accomplishment of his goal. He immediately set to work pushing it back down—and he succeeded.

Thus, for approximately four and a half months, the directors of manufacturing and marketing were both busy fighting fires with the finished goods inventory. The director of manufacturing would push it down, and the director of marketing would push it back up. Manufacturing down, marketing up—until finally someone said to them, "Hey, you two guys better figure out what you want, and then we'll do it." But it wasn't until this outspoken subordinate blew the whistle and told the two directors to shape up that they realized what they had been doing, not only to themselves but, more importantly, to the people who were trying to manage the inventory levels properly.

So how did they resolve this conflict? They agreed upon a band or range of inventory levels within which they could both live comfortably. Not one that either would really consider a maximum contribution toward the accomplishment of his goal but something within which they could both function. And as long as inventory stayed within that band, both of them were satisfied.

**5. Allow for Sufficient Involvement and Initiative.** When the individuals who will be affected by the action plan are sufficiently involved in and familiar with that plan, you can be sure of two things. First, there is a high probability that the plan will be technically excellent. And, second, the individuals involved in executing it will be totally committed.

Many action plans are technically well-conceived, carefully designed, and fully integrated within the overall operation. But the best plans won't succeed if the designers forget to seek and obtain the involvement of those individuals who will be affected by them.

One publishing company, for example, moved its offices from an old, cramped location to a new, more spacious and modern one. The old offices had been in a converted house. Storage areas were the basement, clothes closets, and a small corner of one room where the roof slanted sharply. The offices themselves were in redone bedrooms, with a portion of the former kitchen also serving as office space. The basement was small and crowded but did provide some room for people working on projects that required a lot of bench space. Heating and cooling were erratic, the carpeting on the stairs was worn through in places, and all the rooms had creaky, loose floor boards. The women's restroom was on the second floor and contained a broken bathtub; the men's room was on the first floor, and its bathtub leaked if the water was turned on. Bats occasionally visited from the attic. Not surprisingly, there was plenty of good-natured grumbling about that "damn old house."

The new quarters, by contrast, were more attractive and spacious. There was much more space, and shelves had been erected in a large room that was specifically for storage. Each editor had his or her own office (something that wasn't possible in the old building), and each administrative assistant and secretary had room in the work area immediately outside his or her boss's office. Parking was easier, the location was more readily accessible to virtually every member of the staff, heating and air conditioning worked regularly, and there were no bats to contend with.

The central staff planned the move to the new quarters carefully to minimize disruption and to reduce the amount of work that individuals would have to do in either planning or actually making the move. Nonetheless, the first two weeks in the new setting were disastrous. Nothing seemed to work quite right in the new location. It was either too hot or too cold. The new quarters lacked "charm"; they were too "sterile." The storage shelves weren't the right height. The colors were all wrong. The environment wasn't conducive to creative work. And, while the old place wasn't great, it was sure a lot better than the new one.

All true? Yes—but only in the minds of the disgruntled staff. Within five or six weeks, things settled down to normal, and everybody was busily engaged in his or her projects. But during that interim period, a lot of individual and organizational energy went into ironing out problems that hatched simply because people hadn't been involved in developing the various steps necessary to accomplish the move. Technically, the moving plan was excellent. But because the individuals it affected weren't consulted or involved in developing and refining the steps, the plan had less than their full commitment. When the move actually took place, individual team members reacted, either consciously or unconsciously, to their lack of involvement and made life difficult for themselves and others.

The moral of this little cautionary tale is simple: Make sure that people who are going to be affected by an action plan can take part in developing it. That way, there's ownership not only of the goals but of the specific steps necessary to reach the goal.

*6. Give the Plan Stretch.*

Just as goals should stretch people, action plans must stretch them, too, because action plans consist of the steps necessary to accomplish the goals. These steps should be difficult but not impossible. They should force people to learn new skills, to try out new behaviors, to grow in some way on the job. If a plan simply lists activities that would have been carried out even if there were no breakthrough goals, there's not much sense in developing that particular plan. It would be better to shelve it until it can be created to help people develop, apply, or seek out new skills to use on the job.

One organization made the mistake of asking people to list, as part of an action plan, a whole series of steps that, taken together, constituted their jobs. Obviously, people perform quite a number of things in the course of doing their normal duties. So by the time these employees listed all these routine tasks, they each had twelve to fifteen pages of activities they were to carry out, 90% of which were normal, routine, and taken for granted. Ironically, they'd spent so much time developing their lists of activities and almost an equal amount of time reporting on how they were carrying them out that they had little time left to actually *do* each task well. Thus, they fell further and further behind schedule until, finally, they said they didn't want anymore to do with either goal setting or action planning. In this case, management learned a bitter lesson: employees should be encouraged to identify breakthrough goals involving stretch and let the normal activities take place as a matter of course.

*7. Help Your Team Tackle Future Problems.*

A good action plan is designed to **help the organizational team learn how to be more effective in tackling future problems.** An expression frequently heard around organizations is, "Throw them in over their heads and see if they can swim." While this tactic is perhaps better than not putting someone in the water at all, there is an even better way to do it: throw them out a little bit farther than they were before and make them swim that extra distance.

The problem with throwing someone in too deep is that he may not have learned to swim well enough to make it back to shore at all.

When people are thrown in too far over their heads, they don't learn how to tackle future problems effectively. Instead, they learn not to "go swimming." Throwing people in *too far* over their heads can actually discourage rather than encourage risk-taking. Moreover, when people are unsuccessful at tackling problems that are simply too difficult for them, they often become discouraged about their own problem-solving abilities and hesitate to confront some problems they probably could solve.

*8. Encourage Both Group and Independent Action.* Design action steps in such a way that *some will require cooperation* among individuals and departments and some will be performed independently. And make sure that everyone gets a chance to perform in both situations. Many people endowed with the Self-Starting Mechanism, for example, perform poorly when asked to work with a team. Yet the same individuals, when properly directed, can encourage the whole team to be more Self-Starting than it was previously. The Self-Starter team member who is well directed can teach other people how to be Self-Starters and also can learn how to work more effectively in a group.

As our society becomes more complex, people who are used to working alone are going to have to learn how to work through, with, around, or near teams, and these team experiences will help them grow. In fact, it even helps strengthen their Self-Starting abilities because, after working in a team, they see even more clearly how they can work faster and better on their own in particular situations.

On the other hand, some individuals work well only within the security of a group. They prefer the team decision because it means less individual accountability. But these individuals really ought to take some of the necessary action *beyond* the confines of a group. As they succeed in these solo situations, they'll learn what it's like to accomplish things on their own, and, thus, they'll improve their Self-Starting abilities.

*9. Let the Activists Help Plan the Action.* In other words, *involve those who will carry out the steps in the action planning phase.* Kenneth H. Blanchard has noted that there is an important distinction between goal-*directed* activity and goal activity. If, for example, the goal is to consume food, the goal activity would be to actually eat the food, and the goal-directed activity would be to prepare the food. The more individuals are involved in establishing a goal, the higher their level of involvement. The same holds true for goal-directed activity: the higher the level of involvement in developing the activity that will reach the goal, the higher the level of motivation.

Some people may not be organizationally mature enough or experienced enough to set a goal. They might, however, be entirely capable of developing the action steps necessary to reach that goal. This point becomes particularly important when we are setting stretch goals and when our back-up action plans to reach those goals are also stretched. The more the individuals are involved in establishing the goal and the action steps, the longer they will engage in goal-directed activity before they become frustrated and give up. As a general rule, then, the more stretch that is involved in the steps of the action plan, the better it is to involve subordinates in establishing those steps and deciding which steps must be taken to reach the goal.

*10. Foster Self-Starters' Creativity.* Most new things, both great and small, have flown in the face of conventional wisdom. In other words, someone has to stick his neck out and take a chance. And usually that someone relies upon his Self-Starting Mechanism to force either individuals or organizations to try the new and different—and, frequently, the successful. Of course, trying something new also can lead to failure. Self-Starters know more failures than do people who aren't Self-Starters. On the other hand, they also have many more successes because they simply try more things.

Trying the new is not always easy, of course. Society at large, organizations in general, and everyone (except you and me) tend to reject out of hand anything new that might disturb the status quo. Consider, for a moment, the irony of such an attitude as illustrated by the following examples:

- The first successful cast iron plow invented in the United States in 1797 was rejected by New Jersey farmers under the theory that cast iron poisoned the land and stimulated the growth of weeds.

- An eloquent divine in the United States declared that the introduction of the railroad would require the building of many insane asylums, as people would be driven mad at the sight of locomotives rushing across the country.

- In Germany it was proved by experts that if trains went at the frightening speed of fifteen miles an hour, blood would spurt from the travelers' noses, and the passengers would suffocate going through tunnels.

- Commodore Vanderbilt dismissed Westinghouse and his new air brakes for trains by saying that he had no time to waste on fools.

- Those who loaned Robert Fulton money for his steamboat project stipulated that their names be withheld for fear of ridicule were it known they supported anything so "foolhardy."

- In 1881 when the New York Y.W.C.A. announced typing lessons for women, vigorous protests were made on the grounds that the female constitution would break down under the strain.

- Men insisted that iron ships would not float, that they would damage more easily than wooden ships when grounding, that it would be difficult to preserve the iron bottoms from rust, and that iron would deflect the compass.

- Joshua Coppersmith was arrested in Boston for trying to sell stock in the telephone. "All well-informed people know it is impossible to transmit the human voice over a wire," said the skeptics.

- Chauncey M. Depew confessed that he warned his nephew not to invest $5,000 in Ford stocks because "nothing has come along to beat the horse."

- Scientist Simon Newcomb said in 1906 just as success for the airplane was in the offing, "The demonstration that no combination of known substances, known forms of machinery and known forms of forces can be united in a practicable machine by which men shall fly seems to the writer as complete as it is possible for the demonstration for any physical fact to be."

- When Buffington took out patents for the steel-frame skyscraper in 1888, the *Architectural News* predicted that the expansion and contraction of iron would crack all the plaster, eventually leaving only the shell.

- According to the theory of aerodynamics, the bumble bee cannot fly. The bumblebee is unable to fly because the size, weight and shape of its body, in relation to the total wing spread, make flying impossible. (But the bumblebee, ignorant of these scientific truths, goes ahead and flies anyway.)

*11. Don't Take "Can't" for an Answer.*

When people come to you to report that a goal can't be accomplished, simply ask, "*What would have permitted us to accomplish the goal?*"

Charles F. Kettering, the creative genius in the early days of General Motors, told the story about the development of ethyl gas in which he used this technique. A brilliant chemist, Midgely, worked for Kettering and his staff on the gasoline problem. Kettering was particularly interested in the project for it tied in closely with engine knock in cars—for which Kettering was originally blamed. When manufacturers put the self-starter in automobiles around 1912, they took off the magneto and put on the better ignition. Some say that's when Kettering put the knock in motors.

According to Kettering, what actually happened, however, was that just after they put the self-starter on automobiles, women began to drive and more people began to buy cars. This required more gas, and, in the rush to fill the demand, a poorer gas, which actually knocked more, was unknowingly produced. Kettering's group was searching for an additive to put in the gas that would stop the knock.

After much work, Midgely and his staff were ready to give up. They walked into Kettering's office with a stack of books and reports that detailed everything they had done. Placing it on his desk, they announced, "We give up."

"Do you want me to read all that?"

"Yes. These are all the reasons why we can't do it and it won't work."

"I don't want to read all that, and I don't have the time. Can you tell me on one page what, in your opinion, would have made the idea work?"

"Well, we'll try."

The only thing the staff could come up with was that if they could create a red flame front in the wave of flame inside a cylinder, they could accomplish their objective. They didn't know why red did it, but they did know red would work. Kettering said, "That's the answer. We'll go after some chemical that we can put in the gas that will give us the red front." After much work and experimentation, they finally came up with ethyl gas. And they solved the problem.

The point is that Kettering asked "What would work?," and the question produced creative results.

Alex F. Osborne, author of *Applied Imagination*, has developed a list of 75 questions designed to spur creative thought. Here's part of his checklist for new ideas:

Adapt?      What else is like this? What other idea does this suggest? Does past offer parallel? What could I copy? Whom could I emulate?

Modify?     New twist? Change meaning, color, motion, sound, odor, form, shape? Other changes?

Magnify?    What to add? More time? Greater frequency? Stronger? Higher? Longer? Thicker? Extra value? Plus ingredient? Duplicate? Multiply? Exaggerate?

Minify?     What to subtract? Smaller? Condensed? Miniature? Lower? Shorter? Lighter? Omit? Streamline? Split up? Understate?

Substitute? Who else instead? What else instead? Other ingredient? Other material? Other process? Other power? Other place? Other approach? Other tone of voice?

Rearrange?  Interchange components? Other pattern? Other layout? Other sequence? Transpose cause and effect? Change pace? Change schedule?

Reverse?    Transpose positive and negative? How about opposites? Turn it backward? Turn it upside down? Reverse roles? Change shoes? Turn tables? Turn other cheek?

Each of these could be used as a variation on the question: "What would have permitted us to accomplish the goal?"

*12. Write Down All Your Action Steps.* Remember, the *faintest word is better than the fondest memory*. Too often, someone says, "Sure, I've got an action plan all figured out to reach that goal." And, in his own mind, he does. However, when you ask him to commit the steps to paper, along with the estimated completion time and cost for accomplishing each step, he finds that he's already two months behind schedule in reaching the goal. Both Self-Starters and employees who still have a long way to go should commit the steps to paper because this procedure forces them to think through carefully what must be done and by whom to attain the goal.

Frequently, Self-Starters set overly ambitious goals and don't think through the action steps necessary to reach those goals. Because these individuals *are* Self-Starters, they're raring to accomplish goals even though they have neither mapped out necessary action steps nor discussed them with their subordinates. The sorry results? Missed goals and frustrated Self-Starters.

But when these same individuals commit to paper some of their thoughts, it increases the probability that other people will become involved in the action plan, as well as the probability that the goal will be reached. And when fledgling Self-Starters share this success, they themselves will begin to demonstrate more Self-Starting characteristics. Self-Starters often fail to help others develop Self-Starting attributes. But, by committing to paper the steps necessary to reach goals, they can become more effective mentors and models.

*13. Develop a Contingency Action Plan* Nothing ever goes exactly the way it was planned. And when things do go awry, people often are at a loss to cope with the new situation. Once the action steps are laid out, ask the individual in control of the project what might go wrong that would hinder the completion of the action plan. Ask how he or she would *know* that something had gone wrong. And, if those events do come to pass, what can be done about it? Fostering this type of thinking should lead to the formulation of contingency action steps that could be taken if major conditions changed. This contingency action plan would serve to back-up the one shown in figure 6–1. In the event that one of the contingent events identified did come to pass, they would be prepared to put a modified action plan into effect.

Even better than these general questions are specific ones, such as "What if a major supplier went on strike?," "What would we do if a major customer went bankrupt?," "What would be the impact of a 50% increase in the inflation rate?" These queries force people to start thinking creatively about what steps they might take. And creative thinking about these steps encourages people to think about all the things that *might* happen and how they would deal with them. When people get used to rolling with the punches, they become adept at formulating contingency action steps, which will ensure the accomplishment of the original goal, no matter what.

*14. Avoid Killer Phrases.* "Killer phrases" are expressions that tend to stifle creativity and diminish enthusiasm. Their impact upon the creator of a new idea or approach is deflating and defeating. Every time we use one of these phrases, we stem the flow of fresh new ideas, projects, solutions, theories, and so on.

Needless to say, the following forty-five killer phrases should be excised out of our organizational lexicon and avoided like the plague.

## Killer Phrases

1. Won't work.
2. Done this way for forty years.
3. Tried it before.
4. Stupid.
5. Can't do much.
6. No time.
7. No money.
8. Our problem is different.
9. People won't cooperate.
10. Top brass will say no.
11. The union won't buy it.
12. Unrealistic.
13. Never been tried before.
14. We've tried that.
15. Too new.
16. Costs too much.
17. Who the hell thought of that?
18. What's wrong with the tried and true way?
19. You're scraping the bottom of the barrel.
20. Ridiculous.
21. Accounting will never agree.
22. Production is tied up in other details.
23. The union will object.
24. Let sleeping dogs lie.
25. We've tried it before and it didn't work.
26. That's not the way they do it at the main plant.
27. The boss won't like it.
28. No!
29. That's too simple.
30. Don't like it.
31. It can't be done.
32. We have always made money this way.
33. Get back to work!
34. That's not our problem.
35. Come back later.
36. Where'd you get an idea like that?
37. Let someone else do it.
38. It'll take longer that way.
39. No good.
40. Too expensive.
41. This is the best way.
42. I don't approve.
43. You are wrong.
44. They will never accept it.
45. I am doubtful.

*15. Use Booster Phrases Instead.* The following booster phrases are calculated to up the level of creativity in organizations, offer support, and challenge people embarking on creative endeavors.

---

**Booster Phrases**

1. Let's find out more about this.
2. You've hit on a brilliant idea.
3. Money's no object.
4. Let's try it.
5. Go ahead—I'll listen.
6. Yes.
7. We'll talk about it.
8. It's worth a try.
9. Sure, we'll try.
10. You have a good idea.
11. It's worth talking about.
12. Everything is worthwhile.
13. I like your thoughts.
14. Who says it can't be done?
15. Let's be different.
16. A real possibility.
17. It should work.
18. Look into it.
19. I'll get Joe to give you a hand.
20. Buy one and try it.
21. Give it a go.
22. Let's look into this.
23. Management will buy that.
24. What a saving.
25. Sit down—let's talk it over.
26. Let the competition try to top this one!
27. Friendly laugh.
28. Tell me again what you believe.
29. There's real possibility here.
30. Let's see if we can draw this.
31. At last!
32. When do we start?
33. Why hasn't someone tried that before?
34. Just what we need.
35. The boss'll like this.
36. Price sounds good.
37. That idea will apply to the whole plant.
38. That really took some thinking!
39. Excellent.
40. Very good.
41. Wonderful!
42. Let's consider the facts.
43. Very progressive.
44. We will make it work.
45. We can do it.

---

Action planning, then, is the *how* of achieving the **what**. It is a means leading to an end. In action planning, the creative part of the management process is most apparent; once we've decided what we want to accomplish, we'll usually discover a variety of different ways to get there. Most importantly, action planning helps us develop Self-Starters because it serves as insurance that goals will be accomplished.

**The ABC's of Performance**

Just as there are ABC's in formal learning, there are ABC's in why people do what they do (or don't do). The ABC's of behavior can be explained in psychological terms as Antecedent—Behavior—Consequence. The A (antecedent) comes before the behavior, the B (behavior) is what the individual does, and the C (consequence) is what occurs after the behavior. Each of the ABC's play an important, but distinctly different, role in helping us to understand human behavior.

Examining the antecedent tells us whether or not a behavior will occur the first time. Antecedents on the job include statements of positive expectations (I know you can do it); goals (I need 20 an hour, but I'd like 23); action plans (If we rearrange the material flow, we'll get to at least 22); and other varieties of these such as statements of confidence from peers, job tickets, directives, bulletin board notices, talks at company meetings, and other cues, signals, or trigger mechanisms that start behavior. Without the proper use of antecedents, behavior does not start.

| ANTECEDENT | BEHAVIOR | CONSEQUENCE |
|---|---|---|
| *What happens before the behavior.* (Chapters 1–6) | *What you want the person to do.* | *What happens after the behavior.* (Chapters 7–11) |

Too often, however, we stop our efforts at this point and go no further. Usually for a simple reason—the behavior we want has started. However, unless the consequences for the behavior are positive, the behavior soon drops off and we are faced with the roller coaster performance described on pages 116 through 120.

The relationship between the ABC's is a simple one. Antecedents *start* behavior. They get it going. Behavior begins to take place as a result of the proper antecedent(s). The first six chapters of this book have focused on different ways of starting behavior. However, antecedents do nothing to continue behavior, so they alone are not enough.

Behavior continues only as a result of the proper consequences—postive in the form of reinforcement or information. The proper consequences, then, are necessary to *maintain* behavior. So far, we have concentrated on antecedents which start the behaviors that will make an individual a Self-Starter. In Chapter 7, we are going to begin examining ways of *maintaining* some of those behavior patterns, and that, after all, is where the rubber meets the road. Starting a behavior does no good (except in the short term) if the behavior pattern cannot be maintained at an appropriate level.

# 7 | How to Sustain Performance

In this chapter, we'll begin our discussion of the last of the three elements that compose the Self-Starting Mechanism—feedback. Actually, there are two aspects to the feedback element: the *information* aspect and the *applause* aspect. If we compare feedback to our sports model in chapter 1, we might say that the yardline markers on the football field represent the informational aspect and what the fans do represents the applause aspect. Actually the fans might do one of three things: they might applaud; they might boo; or they might do nothing. And, as we'll see later on, there is an even more important source of applause—the individual himself. A real Self-Starter is someone who is able to give himself his own applause and pats on the back and who can say, "Hey, I did a really fine job today." But most potential Self-Starters need some help from us, and that's what this chapter is all about—how to applaud the players on your team or, in psychological terms, how best to reinforce them.

While the difference between the informational and applause aspects of feedback might seem small, it's a very important one. Just how important was made clear to me some time ago by a regional sales director for a major pharmaceutical firm. During a seminar, I explained to his group the difference between the informational and the reinforcing aspects of feedback.

"You know," he said, "you just made me realize something I hadn't been able to figure out. About six months ago, I called a meeting of my district sales managers. As part of the meeting, I asked them to lock themselves into a room for three hours and to figure out what they wanted me to do, do differently, or stop doing to help them in their jobs. One of the things they said they wanted was more feedback from me. I couldn't believe it! And I didn't understand what they meant. Sometimes I thought I'd been providing too much feedback. I'd have meetings with them; I'd talk to them on the phone; I'd go over reports with them in person and by phone; I'd travel with them.

If anything, I thought I was overloading them with feedback.

"But your explanation of the two aspects of feedback made me realize what they were saying. They didn't want more feedback in the form of *information*; they wanted more feedback in the form of *reinforcement*. They wanted me to let them know when they were doing a good job. It's clear as a bell now. All I was doing was *sharing information* with them. And while that's certainly an important part of the job, it's also important to use that information as a basis for *reinforcement* or *applause* when my subordinates do a good job."

He was right. Both forms of feedback are important, and one without the other doesn't really do much good. So now let's look at reinforcement as a form of feedback. And then, in chapter 9, we'll look at the informational aspect of feedback.

## Reinforcement As Feedback

Reinforcement actually is nothing more than a consequence that the individual perceives as being positive. It might be a kind word, a smile, a favorite meal, a trip to a conference, a night out on the town, a reserved parking place, a trophy award, or any one of a thousand things that people perceive as being positive.

But feedback doesn't always take such a positive form as reinforcement. There's also *punishment*; that's when something negative happens as the result or consequence of a behavior. And, finally, there's something called *extinction*, which is neither positive nor negative.

To distinguish among these three types of feedback, let's look at a real-life situation. If I were to tell a joke at a cocktail party and everybody laughed, that would be positive reinforcement. If, on the other hand, I told a joke at a cocktail party and everybody groaned and somebody said I shouldn't have told the joke at all, that response would be negative and punishing. Extinction would occur if my joke at the cocktail party was greeted with stony silence. Curiously enough, extinction is usually more punishing than punishment.

|  | Usually | Should |
|---|---|---|
| Reinforcement = positive = good attention |  | When someone does something right |
| Punishment = negative = bad attention | When someone does something wrong | When someone does something really wrong |
| Extinction = 0 = no attention | When someone does something right | When someone does something a little wrong |

Another way of looking at these three forms is to see reinforcement as equaling good attention, punishment equaling bad attention and extinction equaling no attention at all. What we should be doing, then, is reinforcing individuals' good behavior and minimizing the amount of attention they receive for poor behavior. Unfortunately, the opposite usually occurs. Usually, when people do something wrong or poorly, they get attention: it might be negative attention, but they *do* receive attention for it. And, either consciously or unconsciously, just about everybody likes attention in one form or another.

But what happens when a person makes an effort to correct himself and starts to perform well? Unfortunately, we generally say to ourselves, "Well, Harvey finally started doing something right." Rarely do we go to Harvey and tell him he's making progress in the right direction. And because we thus extinguish or ignore the improvement, we decrease the probability that it will continue. Ignoring improvement in somebody's job behavior is just like not laughing at a joke at a cocktail party. As we'll see in the next chapter, extinction can work two ways: if used appropriately and at the right time, it can effectively discourage undesirable behavior, but it can also put the kibosh on behavior that is improving.

## Why Reinforcement Works—and How

There are a number of reasons why reinforcement works so well. First of all, it takes only a small amount of reinforcement to maintain a behavior pattern once that pattern is established. It's like building a habit. Once the habit is started, momentum builds up, and it becomes extremely difficult to stop the momentum of that habit. Or think of pushing a stuck car: it takes a lot of energy to get the car moving, but once it's rolling down the highway, it doesn't take much energy to maintain the momentum. The same basic analogy applies to human behavior. It might take a lot of energy to get someone to do something, but once the behavior starts, we can maintain it with a little reinforcement.

Behaviors often can be started by using the tools and techniques I suggested in the earlier chapters. For example, expressing positive expectations ("I know you're capable of doing this job") will start a desired behavior. Goals and action plans ("Here's where we're going and how we're going to get there") will start behaviors, too. But it takes reinforcement to maintain that behavior. Remember, though, that *reinforcement comes after the behavior, not before.* Only after someone has done something can we actually reinforce that particular behavior. Just as reinforcing a desk strengthens that desk, reinforcement strengthens behavior. And it increases the probability that the individual will engage in that same behavior pattern again.

## Reinforcement Is Situational

What is reinforcing to one person in one situation may not be reinforcing to another individual in the same situation, nor may it be reinforcing to the first individual under different circumstances. Picture this scene. Just before a strike vote, you walk up to a union employee, who is standing next to the zone committeeman, the chairman of the local committee, and the president of the local, and tell the employee that you appreciate the extra help and effort he put in today to get out those shipments. Probably not too reinforcing due to union-management relations. Now compare the effectiveness of this reinforcement in a different situation. You catch up with the employee as he walks out the door after work and say, "Mike, I really appreciate the extra effort you put in to get out the Acme shipment." I think you'll agree that the probability of reinforcement actually occurring is higher in the second situation due to the one on one contact without the possibility of union-management relations interfering with the reinforcement process.

Use of positive reinforcement for strengthening behavior is a specific technique that you can adapt to your particular leadership style. In fact, you *must* adapt it to your personal style. If you don't, your subordinates will be suspicious of your motives.

In one seminar I conducted, a foreman in the manufacturing operations unfortunately misconstrued what I said about reinforcement. John was a tough, hard-driving supervisor who had a no-nonsense way of dealing with his work group. He was fair and he was firm, but he was tough. And he was a good supervisor; productivity in his work group was among the highest in the plant. After the seminar, John started practicing what he thought was "reinforcement." Very politely and with lots of emotion in his voice, he began to thank people for doing a good job. He told them how much he "appreciated" what they had done and said he thought it was "really nice" that they were putting in the extra effort. So what happened? Productivity in John's work group plummeted. About a week and a half after the seminar, he cornered me in the aisle and said that he didn't think this "positive reinforcement stuff was working too well." He'd tried using it, and productivity in his work group had dropped. However, he also said he was willing to give it one more shot before he gave it up for good.

I asked John if I could hang around his department for an hour or so. He said I could, and what I observed gave me a clue to the problem. John was reinforcing people in a style that was clearly not his own. Even the words he used sounded strange coming from this naturally tough-talking he-man. I could see the puzzled reactions from people in the work group as John tried to "reinforce" them. His timing was good; the behaviors he selected to reinforce were good. But his style was all wrong, because it wasn't consistent with his overall management approach.

I took him aside and told him to continue to do exactly what he was doing. But, instead of his saying, "I really appreciate the excellent job you did on that part," I suggested he say something like, "Mark, you may be a mean son-of-a-bitch, but you're the best damn mechanic in the shop" or "Bill, the grinding on that job is slicker than bat shit." He smiled, said he understood what I meant, and returned to his work group. Within another week, productivity had not only returned to where it was before but it had increased 12%. The last I saw of John, he was rounding the corner with his arm around a member of his work group, telling the individual that, in spite of his ugly mug, he was one of the most productive employees in the plant. Both of them were smiling, and both glanced at a chart posted in the work area that showed productivity was up another 6%.

**Immediacy Is Important**

To be most effective, reinforcement should be as immediate as possible. The more immediate the reinforcement, the more powerful it is. Reinforcement that takes place a week, a month, six months, or a year after the behavior occurs doesn't have much effect on that particular behavior. It might sound nice, but it doesn't do much in the way of encouraging an individual to continue a desired behavior. Nonetheless, organizations still insist upon using delayed reinforcement or feedback as a basis for trying to change behavior. Because the principle of immediacy is so important, delayed performance appraisals seldom make any *permanent* impact on people's behavior. They are simply too far removed in time from the behavior under discussion. Sure, they might generate a temporary sense of pride or, if they're negative, of chagrin. But their effect is short-lived.

The immediacy of the reinforcement is much more important than the intensity of it. (The same, of course, is true with punishment.) If Mary puts together a good report on Tuesday, it doesn't do much good to wait four weeks to tell Mary that that was a particularly good report. The best time to tell Mary is on Tuesday, while the accomplishment is still fresh in her mind and in yours. Both consciously and subconsciously, the effect on Mary is greater.

Of course, such immediacy is not always an option; sometimes Mary is geographically removed from the supervisor to whom she reports. The key thing to remember here is that immediacy is also related to the next opportunity for the reinforcement to occur. If Mary submits the report on Tuesday and we won't see Mary until Friday, as soon as we do see her, we should comment favorably on the report. This reinforces the behavior and locks it in.

In developing Self-Starters, we are trying to encourage certain patterns of self-sustaining behaviors that we won't always have to reinforce. And the quickest way to make a behavior self-sustaining is to give it immediate reinforcement. Immediate reinforcement operates on both conscious and subconscious levels, and a behavior that is immediately reinforced is strengthened more positively than one that is reinforced long after it occurs.

The relationship of immediacy to the next opportunity for the reinforcement to occur can be particularly important when dealing with individuals who are geographically remote from the manager, such as branch managers or salespeople. A sales manager, for example, may see a member of the sales team only once every five or six weeks. But this doesn't mean that immediate reinforcement is impossible.

Let's say, for example, that you want salesman Joe to make more frequent calls on high-potential accounts. For several months now, you've worked with Joe, encouraging him to devote more time to nailing big accounts. But unless Joe is prodded to do so, he generally doesn't go out on his own to find potentially lucrative customers. But now, as you review his call reports from last week, you notice that Joe, on his own and without any prodding, called on three high-potential accounts.

You receive this information in the Tuesday afternoon mail, and you'll be having breakfast with Joe on Friday morning. Let's further suppose that two of Joe's sales calls took place last Tuesday and one of them took place last Wednesday. If you phone Joe as soon as you receive the reports, that's approximately a week after he made the calls. In terms of absolute time, that's not very immediate, but it is an opportunity for positive reinforcement. So you try to contact Joe by phone right away in order to strengthen his promising behavior.

Let's suppose, however, that you can't reach Joe by phone; he's out on the road, you're not sure which hotel he's staying at, and you won't see him again until Friday morning. In that case, there's nothing you can do but make a point of reinforcing those three sales calls *as soon as you can* when you see Joe on Friday. Waiting until you've traveled with him for half a day and then mentioning them at lunch would be better than not mentioning them at all. But it certainly doesn't have the psychological impact that mentioning them first thing in the morning would have.

## Reinforce Improvement As Well As Excellence

All well and good, you say, but what if somebody isn't really doing a good job. How can you reinforce someone like that? Simple. You merely use a technique known as *shaping*.

It's a fact that most of us don't have too much trouble reinforcing the top performers, the natural Self-Starters, the people who get out there on their own and get the job one. They're a pleasure to have on the team; they're easy to work with; and we're delighted to have the opportunity to reinforce that type of individual. Unfortunately, however, reinforcing the person who isn't yet a Self-Starter but *who is making progress* doesn't come quite so naturally to most of us.

Let's say that people who are Self-Starters generally perform at 9 and 10 (on a scale of 1 to 10). Below that ninth level is the majority of employees, the ones we want to build into Self-Starters. Suppose Ann goes from 4 to 5. That might be quite a step for her, but, unless we reinforce it, Ann probably won't continue to make that sort of effort. In fact, she'll probably retreat to 4 because her progress, which required a great deal of effort on her part, wasn't reinforced. She received no applause for making an effort, and if there's little or no applause, Ann—and countless employees like her—will stop making the effort.

Actually, the situation is somewhat analogous to lifting weights. We could hardly expect somebody to walk in off the street and press 210 pounds. But if someone did, we'd think that was pretty great, and we'd probably say so in no uncertain terms. However, if somebody came in off the street and lifted twenty pounds, we wouldn't say very much. In fact, we might nudge each other in the ribs and say, "Big deal."

Now let's suppose that that second person came in and said, "Last week I was lifting twenty pounds; today I'm lifting thirty-five pounds." Our inclination might be to say, both to ourselves and to that individual, "Well, that's not very much. Lots of people can do much better." However, let's look at what that person has done: he's improved 75% in just a week's time. He's added fifteen pounds to the amount of weight he was lifting, and, while that may not be spectacular, at least it's an improvement. A minimum performance standard for that individual in that particular situation might be forty-five pounds. And, although he's not even up to the minimum standard yet, it's still possible to reinforce him for his improvement. That's how you get people to grow—by encouraging improvement rather than focusing on absolute levels.

Of course, there's no way you can tell an individual who has gone from poor to marginal that he's doing a good job. That would be lying. And because it would be insincere, it would be perceived that way and would have no effect. It might also cause problems at performance appraisal and salary administration time. It is, however, possible to be entirely sincere and tell that person that you appreciate the effort that resulted in the improvement.

Remember, reinforcement is strengthening, and whatever is reinforced, you get more of. If we reinforce a particular *level* of performance, we will get more of that *level* of performance. If, however, in helping people to develop and grow, we reinforce *movement* in the right direction, we will get more *movement*. And, as we build up movement, we get more momentum. And momentum is what helps people grow. So don't just reinforce good performance. Make a point of reinforcing people who are *trying* or who are *making progress*, however slight that progress might seem to us.

**Timing Is All**    Does it sound as though it might take an awful lot of reinforcement to attain momentum? Maybe so, but that isn't really the case. Actually, we can follow two primary types of reinforcement schedules: *continuous* and *intermittent*. As figure 7-1 shows, with *continuous reinforcement*, the individual gets reinforced for everything he does that's either right or is a step in the right direction *Intermittent reinforcement* is administered on a random basis. Intermittent reinforcement is like a payoff schedule on a slot machine: you're sure it's going to pay off, but you're never sure exactly which quarter will trigger the jackpot.

Continuous reinforcement is the best way to develop new behaviors, so it's used most frequently and appropriately with new employees, whom we wish to acquire certain types of skills. Once they have acquired those skills, however, and have reached a desired performance level, we can reduce that schedule of reinforcement to an intermittent schedule. From now on, you can reinforce them on a random basis. Although it might seem that the more reinforcement, the better, that's really not the case. Once somebody has reached the desired level, you can maintain that level with a very small amount of reinforcement, which is sure to come but which doesn't occur on a predictable schedule.

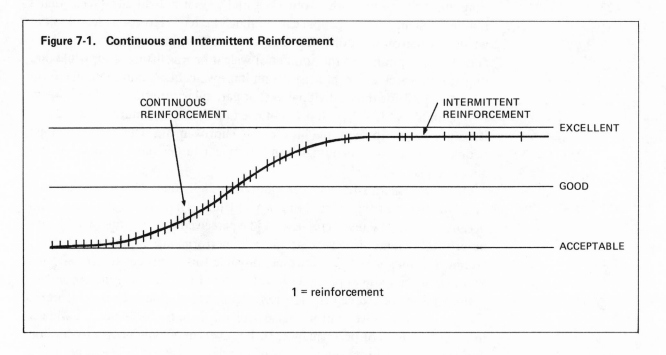

Figure 7-1. Continuous and Intermittent Reinforcement

One advantage of intermittent reinforcement is that it reduces the problem of overload or satiation. You, for example, might like chocolate milk shakes, but if I gave you one every time you did the least little thing right, you'd get pretty tired of chocolate milk shakes in a hurry. In fact, drinking the chocolate milk shakes might even become punishing after a while. If, however, you receive the chocolate milk shakes on an intermittent basis, maybe one this week, two next week, one the week after that, and three the week after that, you know that the milk shake is going to be there for the desired behavior, but you're never quite sure when the payoff is going to occur. This pattern, which can become almost compulsive, is known in psychological jargon as "slot machine behavior." And you can see why. Think of the individual who stands in front of a slot machine, pouring in quarters and waiting for his payoff.

The relationship between continuous and intermittent reinforcement means that, if we wish to develop Self-Starters, we may have to provide more support and reinforcement initially than we would really like to. It may mean providing more support and reinforcement initially than we would consider appropriate for somebody who is going to be a Self-Starter. However, it doesn't mean that the recipient of all our support and reinforcement won't eventually become a Self-Starter. In developing new behaviors, an individual must leave an old behavior pattern, which is probably comfortable and familiar, and try something new. A change of that magnitude requires some extra support and reinforcement. However, once the individual reaches the desired level, we can reduce the amount of reinforcement and support we've been providing. Of course, we'd never want to take it away entirely, but we can offer our support less frequently. Then, as the amount and frequency of support decrease, the person becomes more of a Self-Starter. He provides more and more of his own reinforcement, and we provide less and less.

## Naturally Occurring Reinforcers

Once an individual starts to provide much of his own reinforcement, he's well on the way to becoming a Self-Starter. And once he is able to provide *most* of his own reinforcement naturally, he is indeed a Self-Starter. Naturally occurring reinforcers flow from the job or task itself. A sense of accomplishment, pride in one's work, and a feeling of a job well done are examples of the naturally occurring reinforcers that all Self-Starters draw upon.

Unfortunately, such reinforcers are sometimes difficult to come by, especially when a person is just learning a new skill or is new to the job. As managers, we have to supply extra reinforcement until the person gets up to speed. For salespeople, naturally occurring reinforcers frequently diminish during slumps in the economy. That's when we managers have to provide a little extra reinforcement to help keep people motivated, despite a difficult economic situation.

We can also bolster the reinforcing powers of naturally occurring reinforcers. In the following three examples, I'll show you how to strengthen the impact of naturally occurring reinforcers and, thus, how to expedite the development of Self-Starters.

| | |
|---|---|
| *Situation*: | Employee asks you to look at a completed piece of work. |
| *You say*: | Looks real good, Bill. I can tell you feel a real sense of pride in turning out a quality job like that. |
| *If employee responds*: | Yup. I guess I do. |
| *You can say*: | Well you should. It's a good job. Keep up the good work. |

| | |
|---|---|
| *Situation*: | Regional Sales Manager points out someone who has really improved in the last few months. |
| *You say*: | Alma, the developmental work you've been doing with him is really paying off. It must be gratifying to see someone come on so strong as a result of your efforts. |
| *If Alma responds*: | Well, yes, I guess it does feel kind of good. |
| *You can say*: | It should, because that kind of development is the mark of a real pro. |

| | |
|---|---|
| *Situation*: | Someone does a particularly good job but doesn't mention it. |
| *You say*: | Carol, I just found out that you organized that Maple job so that we met our original completion date in spite of our earlier setbacks. I also know you kept your extraordinary efforts quiet. That's the kind of attitude we need around here. |
| *If Carol responds*: | Well, I just try to do my job the best I can. |
| *You can say*: | You sure do. And you do most of it on your own. That type of independent action is good. |

**Rippling Ponds and Roller Coasters**

Another real advantage of reinforcement is its rippling-pond effect. When you reinforce one behavior in a behavioral class, it increases the frequency of other behaviors in that same class of behavior. If, for example, you reinforce somebody for submitting report A on time, you increase the probability that other reports will come in on time.

This principle is particularly important in developing Self-Starters because it means that we can identify a particular desired behavior that occurs in a variety of areas and increase the frequency of that behavior in all those areas with relatively little reinforcement.

Joan, for example, was in charge of a department that was responsible for submitting five different types of monthly reports. The reports were frequently late and incomplete. One day, Joan received a report from Dave that was exactly what she was looking for. It was concise, well-written, and to-the-point; it had a beginning, a middle, and a conclusion; it had a summary paragraph at the end of each section; and it was on time. Pleasantly surprised, Joan immediately told Dave, "I just wanted to take a minute to thank you for the really outstanding job you did on the monthly report. It was concise, well-written, and to-the-point; you included a summary paragraph at the end of each section; and you submitted it on time. That's the kind of report that really makes our lives easier around here, and I appreciate the effort I know you must have put into it."

Now what Joan reinforced was just one behavior in a whole class of behaviors. She reinforced the submission of one report and, specifically, she reinforced those things about the report that were good and that should have been common to all reports. The effect was just like dropping a stone in the middle of a pond: a ripple moves out and affects the entire pond. Joan continued to reinforce Dave, who continued to submit superior reports right on schedule. The reinforcement of the first good report spurred Dave on to do a good job on a particular part of another report, which was likewise reinforced. The following month, three out of the five reports were on time, and they were all of a much higher quality.

"So what?" you say. "Why didn't Joan just tell Dave to turn in the report?" As a matter of fact, she had—several times. What would happen, however, is that, after she spoke to Dave, the reports would improve for a while, but their quality would then decline. Then she would speak to him again, and the reports would improve, but only temporarily. Bill had developed what I call a roller-coaster performance pattern, certainly not something you would expect from a Self-Starter. Actually, this not uncommon roller-coaster pattern is easy to identify and correct.

Let's say that we have three possible levels of performance—acceptable, good, and excellent—as illustrated in figure 7-2. Now, let's imagine that

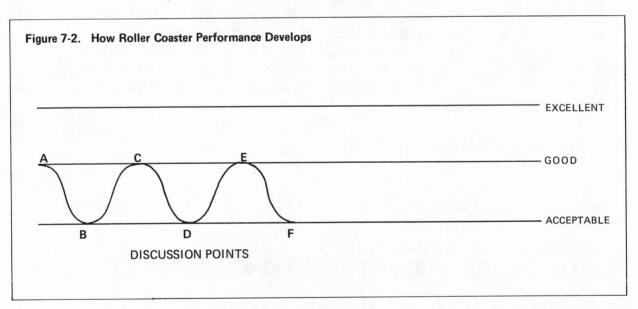

Figure 7-2. How Roller Coaster Performance Develops

somebody is coasting along at "good" (point A), when he suddenly drops to "acceptable" (point B). When he reaches point B, the manager calls him in for a heart-to-heart discussion about his performance. The first discussion is usually a mild one and seeks to determine the cause of the performance drop and the things that might be done to get performance back on track. As a result of this discussion, performance usually improves, back up to point C.

When performance reaches point C, it's acceptable once more, and the manager says to himself, "Well, old Charley is back to where he should be or at least back to where he was." However, *he doesn't say anything to old Charley* (extinction) and, after a little while, old Charley's performance drops off again, down to point D. The second heart-to-heart talk is a little sterner than the first one. As a result of it, Charley's performance climbs back up to "acceptable." The manager says to himself, "I guess Charley had it in him all along, but he just wasn't doing it." Still, however, *he says nothing to Charley* (extinction) and, because Charley hears nothing, his performance drops off to point D (attention). Then up to E (extinction). And down to F (attention). See? A veritable roller coaster.

Remember our earlier equations, with reinforcement equaling good attention, punishment equaling bad attention, and extinction equaling no attention at all? Not surprisingly, most people's preferences lie exactly in that order. Their first preference is to get good attention, their second preference is to get bad attention, and their third choice is to receive no attention at all. Some attention, even if it's bad, is better than no attention at all. If someone can't get good attention from us, they'll take bad. In this situation, old Charley is receiving negative attention when he's down and no attention when he improves. And when he receives no attention even when he improves, it's just like having no one laugh at his jokes at a cocktail party. It's very discouraging, and it extinguishes the improved behavior. Fortunately, there is a simple break-out technique for this roller-coaster pattern. You merely reinforce the individual when he moves from "acceptable" toward "good." Actually, he doesn't even have to reach "good" before you reinforce him. *Shaping* refers to this recognition that improvement has taken place.

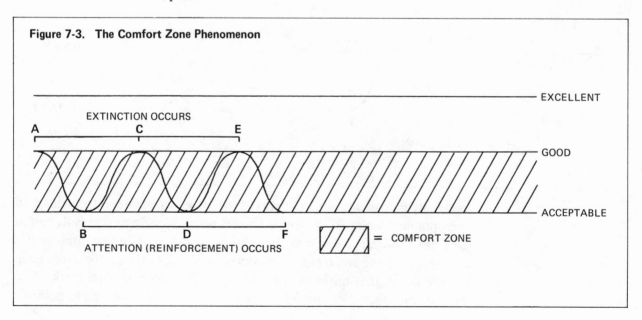

Figure 7-3. The Comfort Zone Phenomenon

The roller-coaster performance pattern can take another form. Think of the salesman who makes a little effort for a while, then slacks off. Then makes another little effort, then slacks off. It's up and down, up and down, up and down, all within the confines of what is called a "comfort zone," illustrated in figure 7-3. This salesman's psychological comfort zone is defined in terms of those points where the salesman alternately receives reinforcement and extinction. In this form of roller-coaster performance, the parameters of the comfort zone are the levels at which the heart-to-heart talk takes place and where the performance peaks and then plummets.

Moving former high producers from their present comfort zone to a higher level is simply a matter of charging their Self-Starting Mechanism. No salesman has a constant performance level; it might average pretty close to constant, but the actual numbers vary at least a little (and sometimes a lot) from period to period. You should simply wait until performance rises a little, either as a result of a heart-to-heart talk, a little extra work, or some other variable. As soon as performance rises slightly, from the merely acceptable level to an acceptable-plus level, you should reinforce that individual. Say something like, "Mike, I notice sales have gone from eighty to eighty-three. I really appreciate the effort behind that improvement. We're making good progress now, the kind of progress that's the mark of a real pro."

Mike's performance will probably continue to improve and then perhaps slack off just slightly. Ignore or make little of this slacking off. Then, when the next surge occurs, reinforce it. In figure 7–4, the extra-heavy lines represent those times when reinforcement is applied, and the lighter lines indicate

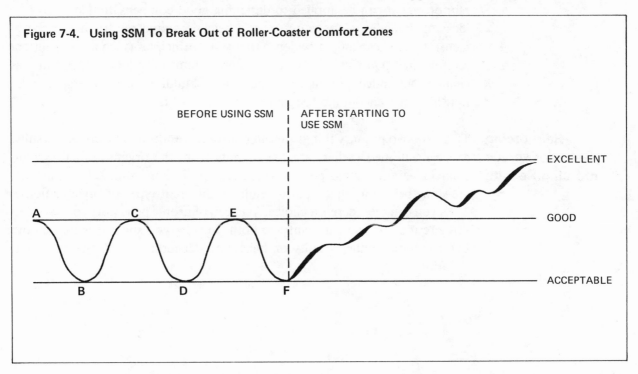

Figure 7-4. Using SSM To Break Out of Roller-Coaster Comfort Zones

when very little attention should be paid to an employee. By applying the techniques of reinforcement and extinction at the suitable times, you can move an employee from his or her comfort zone up to a higher level. I've known countless managers who've used this combination of techniques to move salesmen and other personnel up to higher levels. Within a very few months, the new zone becomes both comfortable and more productive.

This approach works because most employees do not live by bread alone. That is, everyone requires a *psychological*, as well as a monetary, income, and the Self-Starting Mechanism contributes to this psychological income. Improvement earns psychological income, and few of us, regardless of our financial situation, can ever get enough of it. Merely by providing psychological income at opportune times, you can help your subordinates raise their performance to a higher level. Once individuals reach this higher level, you can cut back to the intermittent schedule of reinforcement I described earlier.

One reason intermittent reinforcement works is that, as the individual builds up momentum at the newer level, he begins to reinforce himself. Actually, reinforcement flows from the job or the task, and the person performing it is able to say to himself, "Nice job." When these naturally occurring reinforcers start to take over, the Self-Starting Mechanism is solidly in place.

It is important to point out here that I'm talking about non-economic reinforcers, not economic reinforcers. I'm not, in other words, talking about compensation or bonuses. Although many of the principles of feedback and reinforcement can be applied to designing good compensation systems (the ideas of immediacy, focus on specific behaviors, and reinforcing improvement), there's also ample evidence that some principles (such as intermittent reinforcement) do not apply to economic reinforcers. Our focus in this chapter and, indeed, in the whole book is on building the interpersonal relationships that encourage people to become Self-Starters.

**Reinforcing Behavior versus Reinforcing Results**

There are two primary things we can reinforce: results and behavior. Results, as we mentioned earlier, are the outputs from the organizational system; behaviors are the things people do to accomplish those results. Here, briefly, are some behaviors that lead to results in different types of organizations.

As you can see, there's a choice. You can reinforce behavior, you can reinforce results, or you can reinforce both. Ideally, you should reinforce both but emphasize either results or behavior, depending upon the particular situation.

**TABLE 7-1**

**HOW BEHAVIOR LEADS TO RESULTS**

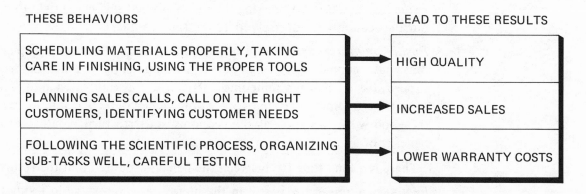

| THESE BEHAVIORS | LEAD TO THESE RESULTS |
|---|---|
| SCHEDULING MATERIALS PROPERLY, TAKING CARE IN FINISHING, USING THE PROPER TOOLS | HIGH QUALITY |
| PLANNING SALES CALLS, CALL ON THE RIGHT CUSTOMERS, IDENTIFYING CUSTOMER NEEDS | INCREASED SALES |
| FOLLOWING THE SCIENTIFIC PROCESS, ORGANIZING SUB-TASKS WELL, CAREFUL TESTING | LOWER WARRANTY COSTS |

To give you an idea of how this technique works, I offer the following situations and suggestions for appropriate reinforcement. Reinforce *behavior* when

1. the person is new to the job or is learning a new skill.

> *Example*: A new salesman has asked the right kinds of questions and has done the right kinds of things during a sales call.
>
> *Positive Reinforcement*: "Bill, I like the way you handled that call. You related well to the buyer, you helped him identify his needs, and you used good questioning techniques. Even though he didn't buy, you obviously know what kinds of things will eventually pay off on the bottom line.

> *Example*: An experienced department head is trying out a new delegation technique.
>
> *Positive reinforcement*: Mary, I noticed you trying out some of the new techniques you learned during the seminar. In particular, I noticed you working on a list of priorities with some of your key people. That's the mark of a good department head.

> *Example*: The director of marketing has tried a new approach to the annual dealer meeting and it seems to be going well.
>
> *Positive reinforcement*: Bill, the new approach is not only forward-looking and creative, but the dealers are just eating it up. That kind of ingenuity helps keep us on top.

2. Outside conditions prevent the employee from obtaining good results, even though he or she is doing all the right things.

> *Example*: A general foreman is working hard with his foremen and their crews to adapt to a model change, but the line still isn't running smoothly.

> *Positive reinforcement*: Jim, I don't like the fact that things aren't running smoothly any better than you do, but you're doing all the right things. Just hang in there and things will turn around.

> *Example*: A salesman is making the right calls and saying the right things but the economy is adversely affecting sales results.
>
> *Positive reinforcement*: Carl, I noticed that your call frequency is up and that you're contacting our high potential accounts, but overall sales have slipped. I know that it's sometimes difficult to stay motivated in the face of tough economic times, but you're doing a hell of a good job. Keep up the good work. As soon as the economy starts to turn, you'll see the benefits of all the spade work you're doing now.

3. There is a long time lag between the behavior desired and the results.

> *Example*: A researcher is still in the literature-search stage in trying to develop a new process.
>
> *Positive reinforcement*: Mary, I know a lot of no answers come up as we move through some of these steps, but eventually we'll reach the end of the tunnel *and* the right answer, even though both may seem pretty remote at this point.

> *Example*: A salesman is calling on a high-potential account that is difficult to crack.
>
> *Positive reinforcement*: Tom, I know you haven't opened that Hentschel Instrument account yet, but the tenacity and persistence you're showing will pay off, not only on that account but on others as well.

In each of these situations, a specific behavior or set of behaviors is reinforced. This, of course, increases the probability that these behaviors will continue, even though the individuals haven't yet experienced the satisfaction of seeing their particular task completed or accomplished. In each situation, of course, we are presuming that what we saw was the correct behavior and would eventually lead to results in this or some similar situation.

On the other hand, you should concentrate on reinforcing results when:

1. Everything is running smoothly.

> *Example*: A general foreman has been doing a good job of maintaining yield.
>
> *Positive reinforcement*: Hey, Mike, I see that our yield is still clipping along at 97–98%. Keep up the good work. That helps make everyone's job easier.

> *Example*: A salesman on the inside order desk is keeping average line items per order at a high level.
>
> *Positive reinforcement*: Steve, I don't know how you do it. Our chart shows you still average ten line items per order. That's just super.

2. Results have improved.

> *Example*: Sales have improved slightly but steadily over the last few months.
>
> *Positive reinforcement*: Mary, your district has improved every month for the last four months. Keep doing whatever you're doing to motivate your sales team. It really works.

> *Example*: Efficiency in department 72 has gone from 93% to 94%.
>
> *Positive reinforcement*: Nick, the latest report shows your department has moved from 93 to 94%. I appreciate the amount of effort and attention to detail I know that takes.

3. You want someone to make a mental connection between something he or she did and the results achieved.

> *Example*: Someone tried a new way of scheduling materials, and line shortages have decreased.
>
> *Positive reinforcement*: Nancy, that new material scheduling idea of yours seems to be really paying off. Line shortages have gone from an average of four a day to an average of less than one a day.

> *Example*: A salesman does a particularly good job of identifying a customer's needs. When the customer places an order, he tells you it's because the salesman was so good at identifying the customer's needs.
>
> *Positive reinforcement*: Frank, Bill over at Fox Products just placed an order for three dozen of our long-eared flamzels. He said the main reason was because you'd done such a good job of helping him identify his needs.

In each of these situations, the individual had done the right things (engaged in the right behavior) and obtained the desired results. The emphasis in reinforcing was thus placed upon those results. Chances are that the recipient of the reinforcement probably will continue to practice those behaviors that led to the positive results.

**Who Decides What's Reinforcing**

This is easy enough to decide. The person who is the recipient decides what's reinforcing and what's not. However, while this is easy to decide, it also seems to be easy to forget. Too frequently we attempt to reinforce someone with what *WE* would find reinforcing. Astute managers realize the importance of determining what reinforces other people and continually try to put themselves in the other person's shoes.

Kevin O'Donnell, President of Sifco Industries, is one such individual. Mr. O'Donnell notes that what motivated him in 1941 will not fly today. He points out that today's employee has a different mind set, but also has more education and talents. People entering the work force today want more to be treated as individuals. They're looking for and are motivated by challenges.

This means, of course, that we have to learn what makes the other person tick by getting to know him.

Carolyn Tomacek, Vice President for Personnel at CNA Insurance Company, helped her company's branch managers understand the importance of getting to know their staff. In a meeting with CNA's branch offices, she gave each branch manager a lime. Then she said, "this is your own personal lime; keep it with you. It will cost you a buck if you don't have it on you at all times. You can do whatever you want with it; you can sleep with it, you can massage it, you can write on it." According to Carolyn, one guy cut his lime in half and ate it. At the end of the three-day workshop, she took all the limes back and put them on the table. Then she asked them to come up and pick out their limes. To those that could identify their limes, she said, "If you can only get to know your people in as short a time as you got to know your limes, you could be a much better manager than you already are."

Her point is well made. We have to learn what reinforces the other person if we're going to help that individual become a Self-Starter.

## In General, Be Specific

To be most useful, reinforcement should be specific. Generalized "warm fuzzies," "attaboys," or nonspecific "positive strokes" are not particularly meaningful reinforcers. The human tendency is to be very general about what's right ("Overall, you did a good job on that report, Bill . . .") and very specific about what's wrong (". . . but the lead paragraph was too short, the punctuation was lousy, I don't think your conclusion was sound, and it wasn't long enough."). This general approach has several disadvantages. First of all, when the interaction is basically negative rather than positive, people begin to assume that all interactions with their supervisors will be negative. And that conditioning tends to taint the quality of the entire relationship. If all of an individual's interactions with his supervisor are negative, that individual will tend to retreat from interactions. You can't develop Self-Starters if you can't interact with them.

The second problem is that, while people learn very quickly what's wrong with their work, they never learn what's right with it. They don't learn how to capitalize on their strengths. They might learn five things that are wrong, but they never learn five things that are right. Because they don't know what's right with, say, a particular report, they have no model to follow; they have nothing to imitate or emulate the next time they prepare a report. Thus, they always depend upon their supervisor for guidance and advice, and it's extremely difficult to become a Self-Starter when you're always dependent upon someone else.

The third problem with vague reinforcement is that it conditions people to hear only "it's good, but . . ." types of statements. Think how often we hear statements like the following:

• Overall, it's a good report, Mary (*but* I noticed that the introduction was too short, there was no conclusion, and you didn't have a paragraph on the cost-benefit ratios).

- Well, I'm glad you got the order, Mike (*but* are you sure you didn't leave any money on the table by giving in on price; that it's signed, sealed, and delivered; that you got enough front money for a deposit; and that they will really follow through on the order?).

- It's a nice tie (*but* it's too long, too short, too narrow, too wide, too loud, too quiet, too colorful, or too dull).

People have learned to ignore everything that comes before the "but" or "however" and to listen to everything that follows because that's the real meat of what's being said. As a result of this conditioning, many people have learned not to accept compliments or reinforcement. Not because they don't want to, but because they're so used to someone letting them have it with the "mean barrel" after they've fired the "good barrel." The best way to avoid this is to be just as specific about what was right with the work as what was wrong with it.

When an employee turns in a good report, too often the supervisor says something like, "I was wondering where the hell this was." How much better it would be for all concerned if the supervisor said, "Hey, this is a pretty good report." And how great if he said, "Bill, this is a good report. It's concise, well-written, and to-the-point. This section right here is exceptionally well done because it ties the specifics into the big picture." Bill then knows exactly what's good about his report, and he can make the next one better.

But what if part of a subordinate's work is poorly done? When do you tell him about it? Do you tell him the good part first, then the bad part, or the good part, then two bad parts, then a good part? The best way to handle this is to review the work, section by section, with the employee. If there are five sections to a report, for example, go through them in order. And say something like, "Sally, I'd like to give you some feedback on this report. Section 1 looks good, it's concise and it contains the required information. I feel section 2 could be improved if it looked a little more like section 1 and had some of the key points underlined, as well as a short summary paragraph at the end to tie the whole section together. Sections 3 and 4 are just as well done as section 1. They're both concise, but all the required factual information is there; in addition, they each have a summary paragraph at the end. Section 5 is perhaps the best section in the report. Not only is it concise and well-written, but it helps tie all the specifics into the overall picture."

In any situation where you want to discuss several parts of the same piece of work, go through the items in the order in which they appear. Otherwise, the person whose work you're assessing tries so hard to figure out what you're talking about and why you picked the sequence you did that he can't concentrate on what you have to say about each part of the assignment.

**To Reinforce or Not to Reinforce**

"Hold on a minute," you say. "If people were really Self-Starters, I wouldn't have to reinforce them as much as you're suggesting." That's true. If everybody was a *natural* Self-Starter, you'd hardly need to use as much reinforcement as I've suggested. However, not everyone *is* a Self-Starter, at least not naturally, and it takes extra reinforcement to get people to the point where they become Self-Starting. At the same time, people who are already Self-Starters are not necessarily Self-Starters in every aspect of their personal or professional lives. So extra reinforcement is necessary to get them to improve some specific behavior(s). Once an individual gets up to speed, however, the amount of reinforcement can be greatly reduced, and then only occasional reinforcement is necessary to maintain that Self-Starting behavior.

Skeptics often pose another question about reinforcement. It goes something like this: "I'm paying people to do a good job. Therefore, they should *do* a good job. Shouldn't that paycheck be reinforcement enough?" Unfortunately, this statement usually ignores the facts of the situation, as you'll see in the following exchange.

"Tom, I don't know if I should have to reinforce people for turning in good reports. I pay them for turning in good reports; therefore, they should turn in good reports."

"Are people turning in good reports now?"

"No, most of the reports they turn in are pretty poor."

"Are they getting paid?"

"Yes."

"Well, it sounds to me like you're paying them for not turning in good reports."

Obviously, no one *intentionally* pays people to do mediocre work, but that's essentially what happens in too many organizations. People are, in essence, getting reinforced—paid—for not performing well. Distasteful as this arrangement is, it's one we must confront and deal with. Here's how. First, we must remember that people have two types of income needs: economic income and psychological income. And psychological income can be just as important—often more so—than economic income.

I have been particularly struck by the importance of psychological income when I've introduced SSM techniques to commission salesmen. Since these salesmen are paid only for what they produce, you'd certainly think that they would be Self-Starters. And many of them are, but some are not, and almost all of them could improve their Self-Starting abilities to some degree. Sales managers who know how to use the Self-Starting Mechanism with commission salesmen have produced increases in results as high as 18%. Commission salesmen have changed from low producers to high producers and from high producers to even higher producers. Why? Because their managers have learned how important psychological income is to most people. Furthermore, they've learned to distribute that pscyhological income so that both individuals and organization have benefited enormously.

**How to Increase Psychological Income**

There are different ways to deliver psychological income. First of all, there is the face-to-face encounter. Of all the options, this is usually the best, because it fosters interpersonal contact, and it's much more personal than a written communication. Compare, for example, the motivational impact of receiving a plaque through the mail with the heady experience of receivng a plaque from a higher-up, shaking his or her hand, and being told, "You should feel really proud of your accomplishments."

The telephone offers the second option for delivering reinforcement. A phone call is appropriate when the person whose behavior or accomplishment you want to reinforce is not geographically close to you. The call needn't be long; in fact, it's probably better to keep it short and to discuss only the specific behavior or accomplishment you want to reinforce.

The third way to deliver reinforcement is by means of the written word. Here we have two choices: typewritten or handwritten. A combination seems to work best for most organizations. I've watched people receive written reinforcements of all types, and I'd say that a typewritten letter with a handwritten note at the bottom or a letter that's handwritten throughout is the most effective mode of conveying written reinforcement.

A typewritten letter with a handwritten note at the bottom has both an "official" quality and a personal touch. A completely handwritten letter is, of course, more personal, but in some organizations, it's less valuable because it lacks an "official" air. Least effective is a letter that is simply typewritten and signed by the sender. You'll have to judge you own organizational value system and decide which method is most appropriate.

Just as important as the *type* of reinforcer is the *way* reinforcement is delivered. Each individual responsible for reinforcing behaviors must adapt the technique to his or her own personal style. All of us have known managers who, like John, the gruff foreman, have overdone reinforcement to the point where it appears insincere and actually turns people off.

The key word in the preceding paragraph is *appear*. One question that I frequently hear is, "Isn't it important to be sincere when you reinforce somebody?" The answer is, "No, it's not." I wish it were because I don't like the fact that you can be both insincere *and* convincing when you reinforce somebody. But, in reality, that's the situation. The reverse, however, is also true. If you're sincere in your reinforcement and *appear* to be insincere, it won't work. However, it's also true that the probability of *appearing* sincere is greater if you truly mean what you're saying.

**Criteria for the Best Reinforcers**   The ideal reinforcer for supporting behavior is of value to the individual, is under the manager's control, is immediate, is reusable, and is of low cost to the organization. That's why I've emphasized the use of social reinforcement for recognition of a job well done. As you can see from figure 7-5, it meets all the criteria. It also quickly gets people to the point where more and more naturally occurring reinforcers take effect.

**Figure 7-5. Criteria for Selecting Reinforcers**

| | VALUE TO INDIVIDUAL | UNDER MANAGER'S CONTROL | IMMEDIATELY AVAILABLE | REUSABLE | COST TO ORGANIZATION |
|---|---|---|---|---|---|
| SOCIAL | High | Yes | Yes | Almost Always | Very Low |
| NATURALLY OCCURRING | High | No | Yes | Yes | None |
| PERSONAL GROWTH | High | Usually | Usually | Sometimes | Medium |
| JOB CONTROL | High | Often | Sometimes | Sometimes | Medium |
| STATUS | High | Somewhat | Sometimes | Sometimes | Medium |
| ECONOMIC | High | Somewhat | Usually Not | Yes | High |
| JOB ENVIRONMENT | High | Somewhat | Sometimes | Seldom | Usually High |

However, other types of reinforcers are also available; these are things that occur naturally during the job tasks, that involve personal growth or development, that give an individual more job control, that give status, that affect the job environment, and/or that are tangible, material rewards. The following list of reinforcers, identified according to type, should start you thinking about whom to reinforce and how. The *why* is simple: because it makes good sense and builds Self-Starters.

### ▶ Social

Recognition of a job well done.
- Praise
- Smile
- Listen and do not interrupt
- Nod approvingly
- Look directly into eyes (attending behavior)
- Invite to lunch
- Buy a cup of coffee
- Praise in front of peer or visitor (careful not to embarrass)
- Integrate ideas into a bigger idea or program
- Use suggestions and recommendations
- Request comments, suggestions, etc.
- Use individual's ideas and acknowledge it publicly
- Letters of commendation
- Give awards
- Write up efforts in publication for organization
- Recognize achievement privately, just between superior and subordinate

### ▶ Naturally Occurring
- Feel satisfaction in a job well done
- Feel a sense of accomplishment
- See an individual or team goal accomplished
- See a new idea implemented

### ▶ Personal Growth
- Give subordinates accurate and current information
- Consult individual on specific problems, where he/she has special competence
- Involve in group problem solving
- Involve individual whenever a decision is going to be made that affects him or her
- Allow anyone who feels he/she can contribute to a decision to do so
- Request individuals who are thought to have relevant expertise to participate in decision making
- Participation in setting goals and objectives
- Placing responsibility for setting and adherence to group norms
- Task force involvement
- Representing department at meeting
- Go to trade show
- Attend seminar
- Join professional association
- Perform desirable task delegated by boss
- Learning new skill

### ▶ Job Control
- Permission to make adjustment to equipment
- Changing procedure on own
- Flexible working hours
- Setting pace of work
- Time off when job is complete
- Schedule own work

### ▶ Status
- Assign a new title
- Business cards
- Print personalized stationery
- Order bigger desk
- Assign a private office
- Allow/hire own secretary
- Give special dining privileges

### ▶ Economic
- Give or increase salary
- Merit increases
- Bonus
- Commission
- Fringe Benefits

### ▶ Job Environment
- Assign more work space
- Order new paint
- Reduce noise
- Install air conditioning

Now that we have examined the use of reinforcement as a form of feedback, let's revisit our ABC model from page 106. Here are some samples to help tie the ABC's together with reinforcement, extinction and punishment.

| ANTECEDENT | BEHAVIOR | CONSEQUENCE | PROBABLE OUTCOME |
|---|---|---|---|
| *1. Employee is encouraged to record production output more carefully* | *Employee meticulously records production output—has some production rejects* | *Supervisor ignores employee altogether* | *Employee eventually stops recording work level unless specifically reminded. Quantity and quality probably slip.* |
| *2. Employee is encouraged to record production output more carefully* | *Employee meticulously records production output—has some production rejects* | *Supervisor chews employee out for production rejects* | *Employee becomes "creative" in reporting production* |
| *3. Employee is encouraged to record production output more carefully* | *Employee meticulously records production output—has some production rejects* | *Supervisor compliments employee on accuracy in reporting and notes any improvements in quantity or quality of output* | *Employee continues to record information accurately and works on improving both quantity and quality of work* |
| *4. Employee is encouraged to record production output more carefully* | *Employee meticulously records production output but has a large number of rejects* | *Supervisor compliments employee on accuracy and uses neutral question (page 182) on suggestions for improvement* | *Employee continues to report accurately and seeks ways of improving quality of work* |

In all four situations, the antecedent was the same and in all but the fourth, the behavior was the same. But in each, the consequence was different and *the probable outcome was different as a result of that difference in consequence.* This is because while antecedents start behavior and even continue it for a short time, *only consequences insure the continuation of behavior over sustained periods of time.* The basic rule is: if the behavior leads to positive consequences, it will continue. If it leads to no consequences or negative consequences, it will diminish, or cease. Improper use of positive or negative consequences explains many of the performance problems that exist in today's organizations. Here are just two quick examples using the ABC model.

| ANTECEDENT | BEHAVIOR | CONSEQUENCE | PROBABLE OUTCOME |
|---|---|---|---|
| *1. Department Head told to cut budget* | *Department Head cuts budget by $15,000* | *Budget is reduced by $20,000 for the following fiscal year* | *Department Head will pad budget in the future to guard against the effect of any cuts* |
| *2. Employee told to get the work out* | *Employee increases production and skimps on quality* | *Supervisor smiles, and plant manager receives bonus for high production* | *Decreased quality and increased quantity* |

Thus, antecedents (high expectations, clear cut goals, and well thought out action plans) to start behavior (what people do to ensure that necessary performance levels are reached), and consequences (specific, well-timed, reinforcement, shaping) to ensure that the desired behavior continues. Where possible, use graphs as a basis for reinforcement (Chapter ten), and use the steps in chapter eleven when employees need counselling.

# 8 | How to Stop Counterproductive Behavior

There are two basic ways to get rid of behaviors you don't want. First, you can simply tell someone not to do something again. While this may stop someone from doing something, it doesn't always ensure that the person will stay stopped. Nor does it insure that he or she will do the right thing. Second, to ensure that the behavior you don't want doesn't occur regularly, don't reinforce it. Remember, if a behavior isn't being positively reinforced, it either has to be punished or extinguished.

To review, reinforcement (good attention) is something positive that happens as a consequence of a behavior. Punishment (bad attention) is something negative that happens as a consequence of a behavior. And extinction (no attention) means there's no feedback, either positive or negative, for a behavior. Thus, to diminish the probability that a behavior will occur again in the future, it must be followed with either punishment or extinction.

Let's look at punishment or discipline first as a basis for stopping behavior. First of all, punishment is something the individual *perceives* as being negative and something that must occur *after* a behavior takes place. Saying to somebody "I'll fire you" is a *threat* of punishment, not actual punishment. The actual punishment occurs when the person is indeed fired. But only if that person perceives not having a job as negative is the action truly punishing.

Saying to someone "I don't think you can do the job" is not punishment; such a statement creates negative expectations, but it's not true punishment. The actual discipline or punishment occurs when the person fails and gets chewed out for not meeting performance standards. Punishment certainly isn't torture or physical abuse; it's a specific technique for stopping a behavior. And it's generally counterproductive to the development of Self-Starters.

**Punishment Has Its Place**

Punishment or discipline is not always undesirable. In fact, there are several advantages to using it. First of all, it works—at least in the short run. Usually, you can get somebody to stop doing something by using punishment or discipline. Only a fool (and there are some) would continue to do something that consistently led to punishing consequences.

Second, you can stop behavior with punishment when it's necessary. This is particularly valuable in emergency, dangerous, or high-risk situations. In theory, of course, the best way to get a desired behavior is to reinforce that behavior when it occurs. But, in some situations, it just doesn't make sense to do that. Imagine, for example, that you want somebody to touch two buttons on a press in order to bring the press down. However, the employee might have wired those two buttons together so that it doesn't take as much time to do the job. Theory would say that you wait until the person starts doing the job right and then you reinforce that behavior. But common sense says that you tell the person, in no uncertain terms, that short wiring is unacceptable behavior and one that calls for dismissal if it continues.

Here's another example. Theory says that if a salesman isn't submitting reports on time, you wait until he submits the reports on time, and then you reinforce that behavior. But common sense says you tell the salesman to stop submitting reports late and to get them in on time. Common sense also says that when they come in on time, you reinforce that behavior, which is something we frequently forget to do.

Theory says that if sales are dropping, you wait until they increase, and then you reinforce the sales manager for getting sales back on target. But common sense, as well as good business practice, says that if sales start to drop perceptibly, you call in the sales manager and express your concern over the slide in sales. The expression of concern might take one of several forms; probably it's some type of rational discussion in which you make clear that a negative consequence will follow any undesired behavior. After all, an alarming drop in sales is a high-risk situation and one that you want to reverse quickly before it gets out of hand.

The third situation in which discipline and punishment are appropriate is where it's necessary to "get the mule's attention." It's tough to attract and hold the attention of some individuals, and sometimes the best way to get them thinking about their job performance or the accomplishment of a specific task is to hit them, figuratively, with a two-by-four. Once you have their attention, you can then begin to work with them in a more constructive manner.

Bob was the sort of "mule" we're talking about. He had recently been promoted from the field operations to the home office of a large insurance company. In his new position, he became arrogant and, at the same time, lackadaisical. His relationships with people in the field changed, and his behavior was not at all conducive to building strong bonds between the home office and its branch operations. When people called in from the field for information, he was curt on the phone. Often, he returned calls days after he said he would. His office wasn't sending information out on time; and when people from the field complained, he cut them short with comments like, "Look, I'm at the home office now, and I've got more important things to do than respond to your every little wish."

Of course, it didn't take long for reports of this type of behavior to get back to Bob's boss, who called Bob in and laid it on the line. He told Bob that his behavior was totally unacceptable and that if he really was the fast-track person he had been identified as, he'd realize the hazards of his new attitude. The boss told Bob that the home office was, in fact, there to serve the field and that he hoped Bob's promotion hadn't gone to his head. Then he listed in detail the offending behaviors that had come to his attention and, in each instance, stated what an acceptable behavior would be. He concluded the lecture (it clearly wasn't a discussion) by stating that he had a meeting and that he wanted Bob to use the next two hours to think about what he'd said. He asked Bob to be back in his office at 3:30 to discuss the issues.

Needless to say, the boss's approach grabbed Bob's attention, and, after two hours of soul searching, Bob had to admit to himself that his boss was right. The promotion *had* gone to his head: he'd become both arrogant and lackadaisical. At 3:30, he was back in his boss's office, and this time, Bob did the talking. He said that his boss was right and that he, Bob, was wrong. He agreed with the identification of the undesirable behavior and the explanation of the acceptable behavior. Furthermore, he stated that he was going to work on repairing the relationships that he had damaged with the field operations. He concluded by asking his boss, "How does that sound to you?" The boss replied that it sounded fine, and, with that, the conversation was over.

In this instance, discipline worked. Somebody had to get Bob's attention, and it seemed that the only way to get it was to hit him over the head with a verbal two-by-four. Once the boss got Bob's attention, Bob altered his behavior and eventually corrected the situation. Bob's boss also reinforced Bob's acknowledgement of his mistakes, and this helped Bob grow as a Self-Starter.

A fourth advantage to using discipline is that it can relieve tension. If something goes wrong and we're disappointed or angry about it, calling somebody into the office and bellowing at him or her might relieve some of our tension and frustration. Unfortunately, the person upon whom we vent our anger is hurt by our outburst. We feel better, but the recipient of our anger feels worse—and the disagreeable situation probably won't change much. There are some instances, such as the case of Bob, where letting off steam makes sense. But if you're using excessive amounts of discipline or punishment, you should ask yourself if you're doing it because it really helps the individual you're disciplining or if you're doing it because it reduces your own tensions and frustrations. If the latter is the case, you should seek another outlet for your hostility.

## Punishment Also Has Its Price

Admittedly, there are advantages to discipline and punishment, but there are also a number of disadvantages. First, although punishment frequently works in the short run, it almost never works in the long run. People get used to the level of punishment, and after a while, it has relatively little effect on their behavior, either on or off the job. Just as the child whose parents yell at him or her frequently *habituates* to that level of punishment, employees likewise become used to punishment from their supervisors or managers.

A second disadvantage of punishment is that it doesn't teach new skills or behaviors. True, you can stop someone from doing something wrong with punishment, but that doesn't necessarily mean that you can get somebody to do something right. To get someone to do something right, you must communicate your expectations about what's right in a positive fashion, establish goals and action plans if necessary, and then step aside and let the behavior occur. If, for example, somebody fails to turn in a report, you can stop him or her from engaging in that particular poor behavior by using discipline.

Imagine that a director of manufacturing yells at one of his general foremen every time the foreman does something wrong. If you tell the director of manufacturing you don't want him to engage in that behavior, you can stop him from yelling at his general foreman's every mistake. However, that doesn't ensure that a positive approach to staff development *will* take place; it merely means that a particular approach (yelling every time someone does something wrong) *won't* take place. And it doesn't ensure that the director of manufacturing will engage in the right behavior. Quite the contrary; he may well substitute one poor behavior for another.

A third disadvantage of punishment is that it frequently eliminates not only the behavior we're seeking to eliminate but a number of associated behaviors as well. Let's look at a sequence of events to see how this happens.

*Step 1.* A regional sales manager makes an error on a report, which is later forwarded to company headquarters.

*Step 2.* Approximately two weeks after making the error, the regional sales manager finds the error on his own.

*Step 3.* He reports the error he made to the national sales manager.

*Step 4.* The national sales manager berates the regional sales manager for such a dumb mistake.

*Step 5.* The regional sales manager learns not to report his mistakes to the boss.

One characteristic of Self-Starters is that they own up to their mistakes. They then do their best to correct them. If, however, someone gets reprimanded each time he points out an honest mistake he made, he'll learn quickly, either consciously or subconsciously, not to tell other people about such mistakes. Remember, the Self-Starting Mechanism is a *behavioral* approach to motivation and development. In the preceding sequence, there are actually two behaviors we can deal with: first, the individual made a mistake, and, second, he told someone about it. Now, if we treat those *two* behaviors as *one*, the individual will learn not to tell us "bad news." If, however, we're able to deal with each behavior as a separate issue, we can encourage people to do two things: tell us about their mistakes and do something about the mistakes they find.

Thus, the correct sequence of events should look something like this.

*Step 1.* A regional sales manager makes an error on a report, which is later forwarded to company headquarters.

*Step 2.* Approximately two weeks after making the error, the regional sales manager finds the error on his own.

*Step 3.* He reports the error he made to the national sales manager.

*Step 4.* The national sales manager deals with the two behaviors separately by saying to the regional sales manager, "Well, Al, I guess I can say two things in response to that. First of all, I'm glad you found the mistake before it went any further and, second, I'm glad that you brought it to my attention. As you know, mistakes like these are very costly to us, and I'd like to see what we can do to prevent this type of error in the future. Now, what can we do to make sure that it doesn't happen again?"

After discussing the corrective action with the regional sales manager, the national sales manager might conclude by saying: "It sounds like we've got this situation in hand so it won't occur again, Al. That's good, and I want you to know that I appreciate your taking the time to bring these types of errors to my attention."

Too frequently, we "shoot the messenger" in our organizations. When we discipline the bearer of bad news, people learn quickly that it doesn't pay to deliver such news. That's why so much information at the top of an organization is filtered or edited. When the upper levels of an organization receive filtered, late, or incomplete information (good information with bad parts left out), they start making poor decisions. Yet we managers frequently have no one to blame but ourselves because we're the ones who started the "shoot the messenger" syndrome. Separating the two behaviors—making the mistake and then telling somebody about it—is not difficult to do, but it's imperative that we do it if we wish to help people grow into Self-Starters.

A fourth disadvantage of punishment is that it leads to escape and avoidance behavior. If people are able to pinpoint the source of punishment, they learn to avoid that particular situation. Sales manager Ken found this out the hard way over a period of several months. Reporting to him was a team of thirteen sales representatives, who spent most of their time in the territory calling on accounts. About once every two months, Ken would travel with one of his representatives to see how things were going and what could be done to boost sales. He also used that time as an opportunity for coaching one of his staff or perhaps chatting with a couple of key accounts. Eventually, he noticed that sales weren't exactly where he wanted them to be, and he realized that the guys in the field weren't "hitting the ball" enough of the time. So he decided to lean on them a little bit to get them running faster.

Ken usually received the weekly sales-call reports from his staff on Monday or Tuesday, depending upon the mails. On Tuesday and Wednesday, he usually checked with his sales representatives by phone to see what was going on. He decided to use those phone conversations as an opportunity to spur his salesmen on. Accordingly, he began his program of "motivating the troops" during his Tuesday and Wednesday phone conversations but only after he had received their sales-call reports. During those phone calls, he would point out areas in which the salesmen had been deficient: he would note that perhaps they weren't making enough calls, that they could have made more calls on higher potential accounts, or that not enough calls were resulting directly in business. The type and amount of pressure he applied depended upon the individual and what his field sales-call report looked like.

Shortly after Ken instituted this approach, he noticed that a distressing thing was happening: more and more of the field sales-call reports were coming in late. At first, they were just a day or so late, and then one individual didn't even submit his until Wednesday of the following week. It became more difficult for Ken to do his "leaning" because he lacked the information necessary to determine whether or not somebody had made the right type of calls. What was occurring, of course, was a clear-cut demonstration of the power of positive and negative feedback. You see, the field sales-call reports had become the basis of Ken's pressure. And the salesmen had learned, either consciously or subconsciously, that if the regional sales manager lacked certain information, he couldn't lean on them. Thus, the reports continued to come in later and less frequently.

After several weeks, Ken called a regional sales meeting and told everybody that completed reports should be submitted on time. Immediately after the meeting, completed reports started coming in on time.

But now a new problem developed: Ken couldn't get in touch with his staff on Tuesdays; nor could he get in touch with some of them on Wednesdays. In fact, it was becoming more and more difficult to reach any of them at any time. They either "got back to the hotel late," or they "left early," or they "forgot" to tell him which hotel they were staying at, or they "changed around call plans" so they weren't calling on the usual accounts at the usual times.

Coincidentally, Ken happened to be attending one of my seminars soon after this second problem materialized. When he described the situation during one of the discussion periods, I recognized it as a typical case of escape or avoidance behavior. Clearly, the sales representatives were avoiding those behaviors that caused them grief. In this case, that meant avoiding contact with Ken. Fortunately, it was pretty easy to turn the situation around. I suggested that Ken use a simple, three-step process. First, he had to stop using the field sales-call report primarily as a basis for punishment and discipline. Second, he had to start providing positive reinforcement just for submitting the reports on time. And, third, he had to provide further positive reinforcement for increases in the type of behavior he wanted instead of looking for things to criticize; in other words, he had to concentrate on those areas that *showed improvement*, even if they weren't up to the standards he ultimately hoped to reach.

Three weeks after Ken initiated this process, the reports were coming in on time. And three months after that, sales were back up to what he had previously identified as a reasonable target level; within five months, they were 7% above that level. But, perhaps best of all, Ken found that his interpersonal relationships with his sales representatives had improved almost 100%.

The deterioration of interpersonal relationships is a frequent by-product of excessive punishment. If every interaction an individual has with his or her supervisor is negative, the individual soon comes to view the whole relationship as negative. Unfortunately, our tendency to "manage by exception" encourages us to focus upon those events that aren't going well. When managers become preoccupied with below-standard performance, they tend to overlook performance that's improving. But there is a more positive form of management by exception and that is to identify the performance that is below the acceptable standard of a particular employee and to use the techniques described in chapter 11 to bring the performance back up to standard. As performance starts to improve, you can then use a second type of management by exception: you can note the fact that improvement has been made and reinforce this improved behavior. Thus, you will prevent an interpersonal relationship with a subordinate from deteriorating.

Perhaps the biggest disadvantage of punishment is that it frequently backfires on us. It has unintended and often undesirable side effects of which we are unaware before we administer it. Moreover, what we intend as punishment or embarrassment frequently ends up being reinforcing. One example that comes to mind occurs in my presence several times a month. I frequently have the opportunity to address sales meetings on the Self-Starting Mechanism. Most people in sales and sales management are very keen on plaques, prizes, and awards, and sometime during these meetings, these are usually given out to the appropriate individuals. The sequence of awards might go something like this:

1. "The first award we want to give out tonight goes to Chuck Jones. Chuck received the largest single order from any customer during the course of the year. Chuck, come on up and receive your award." (Loud clapping and cheering while Chuck receives his award)

2. "The second award of the evening goes to Kathy Carey. One of Kathy's accounts did more dollar volume with our company than any other account during the course of the year. Kathy, come up and receive your award." (Loud clapping and cheering for Mary)

3. "This third award is given each year to the individual who had the largest percentage increase in sales over last year. The award this year goes to Brent Samuelson. Let's have a big round of applause for Brent when he comes up to receive his award." (Loud clapping and cheering for Brent)

4. "Now this last award is given out each year to the person who's been late to more sales meetings than anybody else during the course of the year. It's designed to encourage him or her to be on time during the coming year. The award this year goes to Harry Smith." (Loud clapping and cheering while Harry walks up to receive his award)

Obviously, Harry is being unintentionally reinforced for the wrong behavior. All that clapping and cheering probably represent more attention and reinforcement than Harry normally receives. Clearly, the intention was to punish Harry, to embarrass him into coming to the meetings on time, but the probability of his being late the following year is actually increased rather than decreased. It's no surprise to me when I learn that the same people have won it year after year. And why not? Winning it gives Harry more attention than he's had all year, and, rather than being ignored, he'd prefer *some* attention to no attention at all.

Here's another example of punishment gone awry. A firm had trouble getting its supervisors to keep their work areas clean. If management put a lot of heat on, supervisors would urge everyone to clean up his or her individual work area. But without that heat, the supervisors didn't do a very good job. Because they weren't *Self*-Starters, they would start only under pressure.

Then management hatched an idea. To encourage the supervisors to keep their work areas clean, they would present an award each week to the supervisor whose department was the sloppiest. This trophy, a plywood cutout of a pig, was called the pigsty award. A joint committee, consisting of someone from management, a union official, and an hourly rated employee, who was also a union member, decided which department would receive the pigsty award. Each week, the three people on the committee would tour the plant, looking for the department with the worst housekeeping. When they concluded their tour, they would vote on which department would receive the pig. Then they would go to the "winning" department to make their presentation.

Within several weeks of initiating the award, the inevitable happened: the award became coveted. The department that had to relinquish the award would boo, hiss, whistle, and catcall when the committee came to reclaim the pig. And as the committee moved through the plant, each department would try to coax the threesome over to its work area in hopes that it would get the award. When the award was finally presented to the supervisor whose work group had the worst housekeeping, the "winners" would clap and cheer, obviously pleased to have been singled out for this dubious honor. As departments consciously competed for the award and subconsciously let their housekeeping slip to increase their chances of winning it, their work areas became messier and messier.

Fortunately, the solution to this ludicrous problem was relatively simple. Since the pig was now a coveted object within the value system of the plant, I suggested that management capitalize upon that existing value system. How? By spray-painting the pig gold and renaming it the Golden Pig Award. The committee did just that and started presenting it to the department with the *best* housekeeping. Within a month, all the work areas were cleaner than ever before.

Excessive absenteeism is a problem frequently "solved" with discipline, which generally backfires disastrously. Most plants have disciplinary procedures for dealing with people who are absent and/or tardy to excess. However, these procedures are essentially useless. For example, how do you punish someone for taking too much time off from work? By giving them *more* time off from work? Hardly. After all, that's probably just what such laggards are looking for. A better way to punish people for excessive absenteeism is to move them along through the disicplinary process but to make the time off only a "paper penalty."

Suppose, for example, that a plant has a disciplinary process that handles excessive absenteeism or tardiness this way: a verbal warning, a written warning, one day off without pay, three days off without pay, five days off without pay, thirty days off without pay, and finally, dismissal. Now, part of that system is okay. Somebody who is absent excessively should receive the verbal warning. If it continues, the individual should be given a written warning. However, when excessive absenteeism occurs the third time, the person should perhaps receive a "paper penalty," not an actual day off. The person should be told he or she is receiving a "disciplinary day off" but that the discipline will be on paper only; that is, it will go on the employee's record, but he or she is expected to report to work the next day at the regular time. The same paper penalties should be administered for three days and five days, if necessary.

The results of this approach are remarkable. I've seen a supervisor give an employee a paper penalty, then watched as the employee grew livid and demanded, "You've *got* to give me the time off! You can't do this to me!"

Why? Because employees guilty of excessive absenteeism frequently look forward to the time off. They may even have caused the situation or aggravated it in order to receive that time off. By moving them through the disciplinary process and, at the same time, making them show up for work, you accomplish two things: you administer meaningful punishment and you get a day's work for a day's pay.

(One word of caution here. If you plan to use this technique, check first with your union representative, arbitrator, or labor attorney to make sure you're doing something sanctioned by your labor contract or local practices. Arbitrators have, on occasion, ruled that all the penalties cannot be on paper, that the individual must feel the "pain" of the disciplinary process prior to discharge. Thus, you might be able to give offenders one day off, three days off, and perhaps five days off *on paper*; but then perhaps you must actually give them the thirty days off so they will feel the "pain" and, thus, make the disciplinary process valid.)

As you can probably tell, one of the big problems with punishment is its unpredictability. Determining exactly how people are going to react to negative feedback is difficult, and we often find ourselves getting exactly the opposite—and wrong—effect. Sometimes people will fight back directly. Other times, they will fight back indirectly; we can't see them retaliate, but they eventually stymie us with another bizarre behavior pattern. It might take days, weeks, months, or even years, but people who've been punished have subtle—and not so subtle—ways of getting back at those who dished out heavy doses of punishment.

This is especially true in sales, particularly sales within the insurance business. For the first few years of his career, an agent works for the general agent of the company. After an agent becomes successful and established, however, almost the reverse is true. Organizationally, it looks like this:

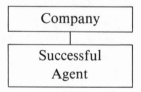

In practice, however, it looks like this:

The company almost works for the agent. If someone in the company punished the agent severely during his first years in the business, the agent will no doubt remember. And in small but insidious ways, he'll begin to get back at the company for those early doses of punishment. Usually, the agent knows what the limits are, and he'll seek his vindication right up to the edge of those limits.

## Guidelines for Punishment

My point is, there are both advantages and disadvantages to negative feedback or punishment. And if you're beginning to think that the disadvantages outweigh the advantages, you're right. However, there *are* situations that practically demand negative feedback. So if you're going to use it, I suggest you follow certain guidelines to minimize your risk and maximize the probability that you'll get what you want.

First of all, make sure that the negative feedback is immediate. Because if it's not, it probably won't work. The more immediate the punishment, the more powerful it is. In fact, it should occur at almost the same time the behavior you're trying to stop occurs. Waiting won't change the behavior pattern of the offender. But if the behavior wasn't important enough for you to say something when it originally occurred, then don't say anything about it long after the fact. Wait until it happens again, and then immediately deliver the negative feedback. Just as with positive reinforcement, immediacy is considerably more important than intensity. Unfortunately, when negative feedback doesn't seem to be working, we usually try to increase the intensity of it rather than making it more immediate. But this is a step in the wrong direction; the thing to work on is increasing the immediacy and then worry about the intensity.

Second, punishment must follow every occurrence of the undesired behavior. One problem with negative feedback, of course, is that, when it stops, people naturally assume that they must be doing the right thing. The fact is, though, that they're frequently not doing the right thing at all; it's just that the person who administered the negative feedback has stopped dishing it out. The minute the "pain" stops, the offenders adopt whatever behavior pattern they're currently engaged in, and, frequently, that's not the behavior pattern we're looking for. Actually, the punishment may have stopped simply because the manager or supervisor ran out of steam or had to expend energy elsewhere. So unless you can be sure that somebody's going to receive the negative feedback every single time he or she does something you consider wrong, it's better not to use it at all.

I've combined these first two guidelines to formulate what I call, for lack of a better term, Connellan's Rule of Negative Feedback: A well-timed and well-aimed beebee has greater impact than a poorly timed, poorly aimed howitzer. Nowhere is this truism more evident than in our criminal justice system. While the intensity of the punishment certainly plays a role, the immediacy and certainty of the punishment are woefully lacking. Rather than debating about whether life imprisonment or capital punishment is more effective, people should concentrate on how to make the punishment more immediate and more certain.

Third, don't threaten somebody with punishment if you have no intention of following through on it. Idle threats of punishment do more harm than good in developing positive behavior patterns. Don't be like the little boy who cried "Wolf!" so many times that he lost his credibility. *If you point the gun, be prepared to pull the trigger*. However, the best way to not to have to pull the trigger at all is to make sure that you follow up on small threats of disciplne. In other words, if you shoot somebody with a beebee, he'll begin to believe that you mean business, and you may never have to follow up with the howitzer or the cannons.

Fourth, if you do use negative feedback, try to keep a positive-negative ratio of at least three to one—that is, three instances of positively reinforcing someone for something for every one instance of disciplining or punishing that person. There are a couple of reasons for maintaining this ratio. First of all, it helps develop a stronger interpersonal relationship and keeps that relationship from deteriorating when negative feedback must be used. Moreover, it more closely approximates actual job behavior. Very few people do everything wrong. In fact, very few people do very much wrong at all when you look at their overall behavior patterns on the job. For every single thing that someone does wrong, he or she probably does ten or twenty things right. So acknowledging some of the better things they do is only common sense. Besides, it helps develop people into Self-Starters and keeps them that way.

My fifth point about giving negative feedback is: Do it in private. Actually, there are two reasons for this. First, there's no confusion about who's receiving the negative feedback. When the boss and a subordinate sit down in a room and the boss says that something is wrong with a certain performance level, there should be no question in the subordinate's mind about whom the boss is talking to. But when the boss addresses a meeting of employees and reprimands one and all for not maintaining an acceptable performance level, everybody looks around and tries to figure out to whom the boss is talking. Generally, each and every employee will conclude, "At least he's not talking to *me*."

A second reason for delivering negative feedback in private is that it minimizes the amount of tension that naturally is generated by a chewing out. As we've seen, punishment frequently backfires on us and even serves as a kind of reinforcement. Remember the salesman who was given an award for being late to more meetings than anybody else? The attempt to embarrass him into coming to meetings on time backfired and resulted in continued tardiness. However, had his sales manager sat down with him and said, "Look,

I don't want you to be late again to any meetings'' and then had reinforced him when he came on time, the behavior pattern probably would have changed.

Sixth, when disciplining, it's important to talk about behavior rather than the individual. Instead of telling the offender that he's deficient in a general way, talk to him about the specific troublesome behavior. For instance, talk about the timeliness of particular reports that have been late rather than the fact that the person seems unable to do anything on time. This specific approach diminishes the personal-attack aspect of the punishment without diluting the actual negative feedback.

It also objectifies the cause of the punishment and, thus, helps keep the interpersonal relationship from deteriorating. Instead of saying, "Because you've been late three times this month with the report, I'm going to really let you have it," say, "The fact that your report has been late three times this month forces me to take this action." This puts you in the position of an "agent" of the negative consequence rather than the actual "creator" of that consequence. Emphasize the fact that because someone has't performed up to expectations, you are compelled to provide the negative consequence.

Finally, if the punishment *does* work, if the individual's performance turns around and his or her behavior improves, remember to reinforce it. Once a behavior gets righted around, we too often forget to acknowledge and reinforce it. But the turnaround is only temporary without reinforcement. If we fail to "applaud" the improvement, we'll soon find ourselves burdened with a roller-coaster performance pattern.

"Well," you say to yourself, "*I'm* the one who caused the performance to improve. I told her she wasn't doing a good job and that she'd better start doing a better one. And, as a result of that discussion, her performance improved. Why should I reinforce her improvement when I'm the one who caused it?" The best answer I can give you is: Do it because it works. Even if you instigated the turnaround in performance, make sure that you reinforce that improvement. When behavior is reinforced, it is strengthened, and chances are good that it will improve further in the future. Once a behavior is strong enough, it will sustain itself. And self-sustaining behavior is a key feature of the Self-Starting Mechanism.

**Extinction is Surprisingly Effective**

Another way to stop behavior is to withhold or withdraw reinforcement that previously supported that behavior. The technical term for this technique is *extinction*.

Imagine what would happen if O. J. Simpson were to run down the field and score a winning touchdown after eluding seven potential tacklers and reversing his field three different times. The stands would erupt in pandemonium. People would clap and cheer and stomp and shout. Talk about positive reinforcement! Now, imagine O. J. performing the same amazing feats—and being greeted by stony silence. That's a pretty dramatic example of extinction and a pretty effective one. Imagine how O. J. would feel. For that matter, imagine how you or I would feel. When you think about those feelings, you can see why withholding reinforcement is a very powerful way of stopping a behavior.

Reinforcing the right behavior and extinguishing, or minimizing the amount of attention paid, an undesired behavior are two techniques that form a powerful behavior-change combination. But the second technique, extinction, isn't used very often. Perhaps that's because it's somewhat misunderstood. To a purist, extinction means ignoring behavior altogether. However, that approach isn't practical in most organizations. It's possible under closely controlled conditions, such as in a laboratory or a clinic. But on most jobs, it's pretty difficult to completely ignore inappropriate performance. Thus, the closest we can come to extinguishing behavior is to pay a minimal amount of attention to nonperformance or below-standard performance. For example, extinction might take the form of leaving out of meetings those people who didn't submit their reports on time; or ignoring people who come to meetings late, rather than joking about it; or not laughing at someone whose antics disrupt the office routine; or not engaging in arguments with someone who is extremely contentious.

Both the arguer and the office clown provide good examples of how extinction can work. If Louie, who is always disrupting the office routine with his jokes and tricks, isn't reinforced by peers, supervisors, and subordinates with laughs, smiles, and attention, he'll eventually stop telling jokes and playing tricks. The same thing will happen with Clyde, the argumentative guy who likes nothing better than to pick a fight. It takes two to argue, and if nobody will argue with Clyde, his disagreeable behavior will eventually disappear.

It's important to note, however, that *eventually* is a key word here. Because initially, the duration, intensity, and frequency of the offending behavior will increase after you attempt to extinguish it. In the case of the argumentative person, for example, it would seem that if the technique of extinction is valid, the arguments would cease immediately. But that won't happen. Instead, Clyde will try even harder to argue once he senses that his behavior isn't being reinforced. Why? Because he misses the customary reinforcement, and he wants desperately to get it back again. Arguing always earned Clyde reinforcement in the past, so his instinctive reaction is to argue longer, more intensely, and more frequently in an effort to be reinforced once again.

The same thing will happen with Louie, the office clown. His antics were reinforced in the past. Now that they're not, he'll spend even more time telling more jokes in an effort to maintain the same level of reinforcement. However, as his behavior continues to be extinguished (not reinforced),

Louie will eventually get the point, and his raucous behavior will decline, as illustrated in figure 8-1.

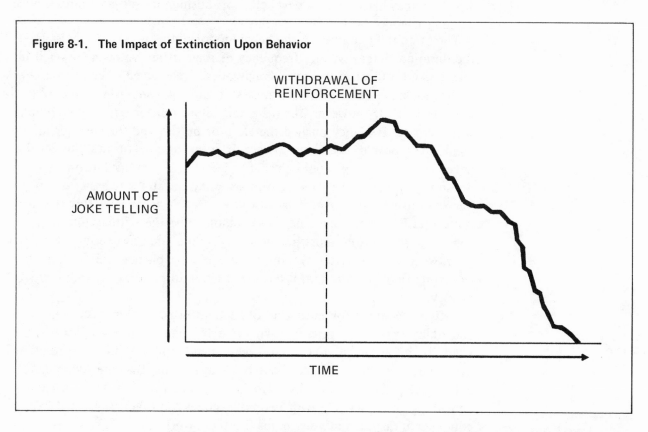

**Figure 8-1. The Impact of Extinction Upon Behavior**

WITHDRAWAL OF REINFORCEMENT

AMOUNT OF JOKE TELLING

TIME

The same type of thing occurs with the elevator-button-pushing syndrome. Let's imagine that we turned Nancy loose in a six-story building with no other tenants but with three elevators. For the first month, Nancy, who stays on the second floor, has an elevator at her disposal any time she wants it. She pushes a button, and, bingo, the elevator is right there. However, at the end of the first month, several other tenants move into the building and occupy the top four floors; Nancy is still the only person on the second floor, and the first floor consists of small shops. The first day the new tenants are in the building, Nancy goes to the elevator and punches the button. For the first time in four weeks, the elevator doesn't come right away. In behavioral terms, a behavior (punching the elevator button) that was previously reinforced is no longer being reinforced. So Nancy begins furiously punching the elevator buttons—harder, faster, and more often. But the elevator still doesn't come. Nancy tries several more times. Still no luck.

At this point, she reaches a critical juncture. If the elevator happens to arrive after one of these outbursts of button pushing, Nancy's behavior of pushing the button several times in succession and then waiting a moment and pushing it several more times will have been reinforced. Thus, the next time Nancy approaches the elevator, she will push the elevator button several times in succession because that's what seems to bring the elevator. In other words, Nancy has learned a new behavior: pushing the elevator button once no longer works, so you have to push it several times.

The same thing applies to the behaviors of both Louie and Clyde. First, the duration, intensity, and frequency of their offensive behaviors will increase. And if those exaggerated behaviors are reinforced, they will stabilize at the new higher levels, just as Nancy's elevator-button pushing stabilized at a higher level. If, however, the behaviors aren't reinforced, they eventually will decrease. If Nancy pushed the elevator button and the elevator didn't come, she'd push it several more times. If, after repeated pushes, the elevator never arrived, Nancy would probably learn that furious button pushing doesn't work. Then she'll either stop using the elevator altogether or will go back to pushing the elevator button just once. So what does this elevator-button-pushing syndrome show us? Simply this: the withholding of reinforcement (extinction) must be virtually absolute and unwavering. If it's erratic, we might inadvertently reinforce the undesirable behavior and, instead of getting rid of it, find that it has increased in intensity, duration, and frequency.

A final technique for getting rid of behavior we don't want is to reinforce something that is incompatible with that behavior. For example, because Clyde is the argumentative person who spends most of his time needling everybody, we can reinforce those behaviors of his that are incompatible with arguing. If you walk by Clyde's desk and find him busy discussing something constructively with two colleagues, you might say, "I'd like to compliment the three of you on this fine team work. I'm glad to see you putting the effort in to get things back on track." By reinforcing Clyde's cooperative behavior, you've probably quashed the probability of his arguing with at least two other coworkers. We could decrease the probability even more by catching Clyde when he's alone and saying, "Clyde, I just want to take a minute to tell you how much I appreciated your working closely with Todd and Mary. I know it's sometimes difficult to do the amount of team work necessary to make things flow smoothly, but that's the mark of a top-notch advertising man. And it's the kind of behavior I can count on from you because of your leadership position within the company." A statement like this further decreases the probability of Clyde arguing with his colleagues in general and with Todd and Mary in particular.

In sum, there are two primary ways to get rid of undesirable behavior. One is *punishment*, which works when it's used judiciously but which does have many disadvantages. The other is *extinction*, which entails reducing the amount of attention paid to an undesirable behavior or ignoring the behavior altogether. In actuality, a combination of these two primary methods and variations of them can and should be used to stop behavior that is counterproductive to the growth of Self-Starters.

# 9 | Feedback as Information

This chapter introduces the informational aspect of feedback. To properly position the feedback factor into the Self-Starting Mechanism, let's go back and complete the systems model we began in Chapter 5. If you look at figure 5-2, you'll see an incomplete model of a management system, one that lacks feedback. The completed model in figure 9-1 shows how feedback fits in.

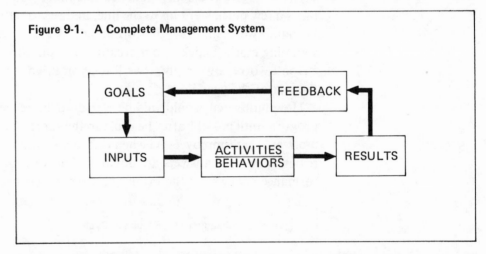

**Figure 9-1. A Complete Management System**

Now, let's see what actually happens when there is *no* feedback. Frequently, we'll say that somebody on the job "isn't motivated" or "doesn't seem to have his heart in the job" or "isn't a Self-Starter." Yet that same individual can leave the job and go out and play three sets of tennis and two games of racketball. What's more, he plays league hockey three nights a week, watches football all weekend long, and used to play rugby. Obviously, a person who isn't motivated on the job can be highly motivated by sports. One reason, of course, is that participating in sports means assuming specific responsibilities and meeting definite goals.

What happens when we translate our systems model into sports? Let's suppose that you and I are teaching someone to bowl, making sure that he's doing the right thing. Let's also suppose that we coaches have neglected to put any pins at the end of the bowling alley. When our pupil lines up with the ball and lets it go, the ball simply rolls off the end of the alley. He releases the ball several times, and each time it just disappears into nowhere.

How motivated will our pupil be by this experience? Not very. Why not? Because this bowling game lacks pins, and pins represent the goals in our systems model. The result is simple: no pins, no motivation.

This time, let's put the pins (goals) in and cut off the feedback. Our pupil lines up the ball in hopes of getting a strike. He takes a few quick steps to the line and releases the ball. However, as the ball leaves his hand, we coaches draw a big curtain across the alley, and all our novice bowler hears is a loud crash. The ball comes back up again and the curtain is drawn back. Again, the bowler lines up his shot, runs up to the line, and releases the ball. But as soon as he does, the big curtain is drawn across the line, and all he hears is another crash.

How long do you think that fellow would continue to bowl? How motivated would he be by this game? Probably not very. Suppose he finally says to us, "Look, I need a little feedback on how I'm doing." "Okay," we say, "we'll give you some feedback this time." So our bowler lines his shot, takes a few quick steps up to the line, and releases the ball. As the ball leaves his hand, we again draw the curtain across the alley, and again there's a resounding crash. Quickly, our frustrated pupil asks, "Well, how did I do?" "Don't worry," we reply, "we'll tell you in your performance appraisal at the end of the year."

How motivated would this bowler be if he received no feedback on his progress until months after he took up the sport? Or, more to the point, how motivated can employees be when they only receive feedback at performance review time? The answers are obvious. And yet, too frequently, annual performance reviews are the primary source of feedback on the job.

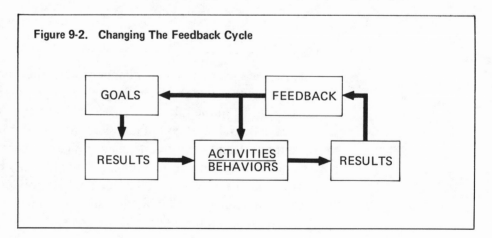

Figure 9-2. Changing The Feedback Cycle

Fortunately, we can correct that. We can shorten the feedback loop so it goes directly to the person at the time he does something. Figure 9-2 illustrates this process, which gives us the opportunity to provide feedback more frequently and more immediately.

Now, let's return to our bowler. This time, he takes a few quick steps up to the line, releases the ball, and again we draw the curtain. As the ball strikes the pins, there is a loud crash, and the employee turns to us and says, "Okay, tell me *right now* how I did." "Well," we say, "you got four." "Which four?" "Don't worry about the details; just keep your shoulder to the wheel."

We coaches *did* provide timely feedback this time but something was lacking: specifics. Both in sports and on the job, people need not only timely feedback but *specific* feedback on how they are doing. Just as people would lose motivation in sports without feedback, people lose motivation on the job without feedback. And without motivation, they'll never reach the point of seeing what kind of a job they can do without help from anyone else.

Remember, there are two aspects to feedback: the information aspect and the applause aspect. An athlete is fortunate enough to have both sources of feedback. That's why sports are so motivating. Athletes have service lines, foul lines, and yardline markers, all of which represent the information aspect; clapping, cheering, and yelling from the fans constitute the applause aspect. Remember, too, that once people become Self-Starters, they provide much of their own applause. But even Self-Starters need some applause from outside that internal source. In this chapter, I'm going to show you how to construct an effective feedback system for your employees, one that will motivate them and make their jobs more rewarding.

We know that feedback consists partially of information. It's the communication about performance, either past or present, that lets people know exactly how they're doing. Presumably, employees will process this information so that it will influence their future performance. On the job, feedback can come from field sales-call reports, quality audits, monthly budgets, computer printouts, the boss, the customer, and many other sources.

A complete organizational system consists of five things: goals, inputs, activities or behaviors (processes), outputs or results, and feedback. An organizational system with these five elements is called homeostatic. Such a system not only has feedback loops but it can adapt its processing activities and change its goals in order to seek a new direction.

The term *homeostatic* refers to the process of maintaining balance through self-regulation. Most home heating systems are controlled by self-regulating thermostats, and their operation illustrates how feedback can affect an entire system. Inputs in the form of oxygen and fuel are injected into a furnace, where they are processed. The results or outputs, in the form of heated air, are released back into the room. Within the thermostat, a feedback mechanism regulates the furnace so that it shuts on and off to maintain the desired temperature within the room. Without that feedback loop, we have only a *ballistic* system. A ballistic system has goals, inputs, processes and activities, and outputs or results, but because it has no feedback loop, it's unable to correct its course or change its target.

A good feedback system, one that will motivate employees and help make them Self-Starters, requires seven major elements. I'll describe each in some detail in the remainder of this chapter. I suggest you use the headings of the following seven sections as a checklist to determine how your own information system measures up.

## Feedback Should Be Related to a Goal

Virtually all human behavior is goal-directed: people are always moving toward some sort of goal. If a feedback system relates to the goals people are striving for, they will be able to measure their progress. And once they can do that, they can identify those behaviors that lead to goal accomplishment and those that do not, and they can separate the two. This behavior identification is particularly important for new employees, who, during their initial learning period, are trying to decide which types of behaviors will maximize goal accomplishment, which will minimize goal accomplishment, and which will actually detract from goal accomplishment. Providing feedback in relation to a goal helps shorten the learning curve by 20 to 30% for a new employee.

Feedback on the job is analogous to yardline markers on a football field. Just as yardlines markers wouldn't make much sense without a goal line, feedback or information on the job that doesn't relate to some goal doesn't make much sense either. Every well-implemented goal-setting system also has a carefully conceived feedback system.

Let's look at one organization that was having problems with its sales and, as it turned out, with its feedback. Annual sales targets were established every year from the top to the bottom of the organization, which was running at 80% of its target. Feedback in this company took the form of quarterly progress reviews (for some employees) and annual performance reviews (for most of the employees). Although there was information in the system about how people were doing on a monthly, weekly, even daily basis, this information wasn't used to design a good performance feedback system that the employees could rely upon on a regular basis.

To improve sales, management first decided to shorten the goal-setting cycle to once a month for all employees who were performing adequately, to weekly for employees whose performance was below standard, and to daily for employees whose performance was considerably below standard. Information about how each individual, district, division, and the overall company were doing was provided on a weekly basis to everybody within the organization. Every time an employee hit his target or didn't hit his target but simply improved, he was positively reinforcd (applauded). Within six months, the company had moved from 80% of its target to over 130%.

At another company, a distributor decided to use the Self-Starting Mechanism to improve sales. He communicated positive expectations about performance and performance opportunities in the sales area to every member of the sales team. He asked his sales manager to set up specific dollar volume goals for each salesman, and action plans were developed to reach those goals. Feedback on a weekly and monthly basis was provided to the sales manager and to individual salesmen. When employees hit their targets, they received a lot of applause.

Unfortunately, toward the end of the year, the president found that the company was teetering on bankruptcy. Sure, people were hitting their goals, but they were the *wrong* goals. As in many organizations, this one offered some products that were easier to sell than others. In this particular organization, the products that were the easiest to sell and had the highest dollar value also had the least amount of margin. Thus, while sales were going up, gross profits were going down.

The next year, the president changed the program around. Because the company was seeking gross profits, he asked the sales managers to establish a gross-profit goal for each salesman. This meant providing salesmen with more information than they previously had about high-margin items. In the past, the salesmen had been paid a commission on dollars of revenue they generated; but the new commission system paid the salesmen a commission based upon the gross profit dollars or gross margin dollars they generated. During the second year, sales leveled off; they increased by only a few thousand dollars, which, in a $6 million company, isn't very much. But after the SSM had been in effect two years, profits were double what they were two years before.

This company's success story dramatically illustrates that not only should feedback be goal-related but that it should be related to the *correct* goal. The goal should be built into the reporting system. If you issue weekly or monthly reports, make sure that the goal itself is described in the report so that employees can see, on a constant basis, how they're doing in terms of goal progress.

It's also important to be specific about the goal you're shooting for. One restaurant used the Self-Starting Mechanism to improve hospitality and decided to take it one step further to improve some of its cost-effective measures. The first thing management decided to tackle was "cutting yield." In most restaurants, this is expressed as the dollar cost of the meat as a percent of the dollar cost of the sale of that particular meat. In this particular restaurant, the percentage was a little too high, and management wanted to reduce it from 33½% to 31%. They explained their target to the people responsible for controlling the yield. They communicated positive expectations about the ability of those employees to meet the target and actually installed a graph in the kitchen area to keep track of how they were doing.

The first week the graph was posted, cutting yield fell from 33½% to 31½%. Naturally, management dished out a lot of reinforcement and applause, telling everybody what a good job they had done and commending them on their progress. Unfortunately, management neglected to tell the kitchen crew that a cutting yield very much **below** 31% wouldn't be acceptable. When, during the second week of the program, cutting yield fell to 29%, the restaurant management realized that customers weren't getting their money's worth. So they returned to the kitchen crew and explained that they wanted a cutting yield somewhere betwen 30% and 31%; below 30% wasn't fair to the customers and above 31% was costing the company too much money. To illustrate this range, they drew a band running between 30% and 31% on the graph in the kitchen and labeled it "Goal Area."

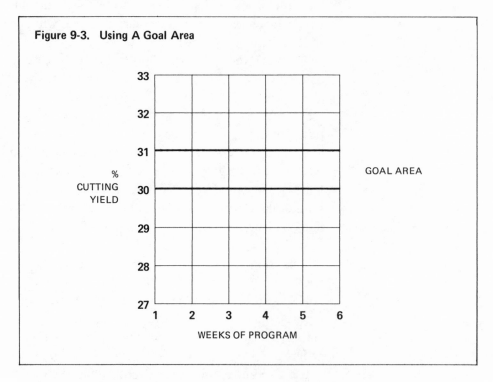

Figure 9-3.  Using A Goal Area

Establishing a "goal area" is a good tactic to use in providing feedback against the goal when performance is not exactly where it should be. Let's say that quality is currently at 52%, and we would like to get it up to a realistic target of 85%. As you can imagine, a work group that is batting along at 52% is going to flinch when it sees a goal line way up at 85%. That's why supervisors should carefully explain to their subordinates that, although they would like to end up at 85% eventually, they first would like to get up to 60%. As progress is made and the work group reaches the initial target of 60%, supervisors should provide ample reinforcement, applause, and feedback. When the work group consistently performs above 70%, the bottom of the goal area can then be moved up to 70%.

But that bottom line should not be "snapped" up to whatever performance plateau the work group has reached. Instead, it should be moved up slowly so that employees will still feel comfortable about being within the goal area. Thus, two things are important in moving that bottom line up. First of all, you must explain in advance that it will be moved up. Second, you must make sure that it isn't moved up to exactly where the group is functioning now. What you want to avoid is the rubber-band effect wherein employees feel that, every time they take a giant step forward, a rubber band is going to snap up behind them. Fear of this figurative snap encourages people to take shorter and shorter steps. If, however, the minimum goal line is moved up gradually and never really snaps too hard, people learn to adjust to it. They realize that improvement is important, and, as long as they don't feel unduly pressured, they'll continue to help the company improve.

**Feedback Should Be Self-Administered**

Individuals are much more likely to believe information about their own performance when they measure it themselves. This is particularly true when performance is below standard.

In one manufacturing company I worked with, for example, there was continual fighting between quality control and the manufacturing operation. The quality control department conducted a daily audit of overall plant quality and assigned defects back to individual departments. But none of the departments believed the information that quality control fed back to them. And complaints about quality control were rampant: "Those guys think this place is run so they can point out defects," "They think the plant is run so they can shut the line down," "Hell, you can audit a product right down to nothing if you keep looking for defects the way those quality control guys do." As a result, most of the organizational energy was directed toward trying to prove that the "other guy" was wrong. Instead, that energy should have been channeled toward self-management, self-development, and the other positive pursuits that make individuals Self-Starters.

One of the things I did to try to correct this lose-lose situation was to change the feedback system so that individuals audited their own performance right in their work groups. Each day, a supervisor and one of the hourly rated employees would spot check five or six "products" from that particular work group. They analyzed each product against a list of items to be checked later by quality assurance. Within a week after we introduced the spot checks within each work group, quality started to improve. As people checked not only their own work but that of their peers and colleagues, they began to see where improvements could be made in the quality of the products. They noticed defects that they had missed before, and, what's more important, they began to accept those defects as their own. In other words, *they began to accept responsibility for their own performance*. Both supervisors and hourly rated employees who had been complaining about quality control suddenly began to work on improving their own quality.

When I asked one of the hourly rated employees why he thought quality was improving, he said, "Those cats over in quality control used to just pick some units off the line, look at them, mark everything that was wrong, and send the supervisor a note that told him what a lousy job he'd done on quality for that day. Actually, I guess the note went to the department head, who would then come down and yell at the supervisor. Then the supervisor had to yell at somebody, so he'd turn and yell at us. I think that most of the defects they were picking out had happened further down the line, where somebody made a ding or a scratch in the product. Most of those defects were probably caused by somebody else and just charged back to us because everybody picks on us.

"This new system is pretty good though. We take turns, and every day a different person goes around with the foreman and checks the products. This way we can tell right away how we're running, and if something isn't right, we can correct it. We know when things are right and when they're wrong because we're doing the checking ourselves. Hell, we know more about making a good product than those guys in quality control.

"We used to bitch a lot to the quality control staff. Well, we still do, but we don't need them as much anymore, except to help us when something has gone wrong that we can't seem to fix here. We're doing a better job now, and we're all kind of motivated by that."

Supervisors for the various work groups were equally enthusiastic about the new system. In fact, one of them told me, "I used to have to spend a lot of time supervising my work group pretty closely. We did have some quality problems, and it seemed that the more defects we had, the worse we became. With this new program, I don't have to spend so much time convincing employees that they made mistakes. They can *see* them. Now when they do something wrong, they know it, and they can correct it themselves. I don't have to spend as much time supervising them because they supervise themselves. When somebody has a problem with a particular operation, he gets some good-natured joshing and, if he needs it, some help in straightening out the difficulty. The group is working together better as a team, and it's made my job a hell of a lot easier."

As you can see, the Self-Starting Mechanism is beginning to take hold in this situation. Hourly rated employees are checking their own quality and actually supervising themselves. Supervisors who use the Self-Starting Mechanism in their work groups find that their job takes less energy, and they're able to accomplish more because they don't have to control the people in the work group, who now are essentially controlling themselves. Supervisors no longer have to be dictators; instead, they can serve as coaches and facilitators and use the techniques of the Self-Starting Mechanism to further enhance their role as leaders.

The technique of self-administering feedback also works well for top management. The president of one company told me how he used to call in his director of manufacturing for "fireside chats" to discuss the manufacturing operation, even though he already knew how production was going and how it compared to the previous two weeks. When he called the director of manufacturing in, he would sit him down and say something like this: "I see where unit costs are up 3% over the last month. What seems to be causing that?" Invariably, the director of manufacturing would become defensive and would try to justify the increased costs.

But then the company president learned about the Self-Starting Mechanism. Of particular interest to him was the idea of self-administered feedback, which he promptly adopted for his own use. Now, when it's time for a fireside chat, the president summons the director of manufacturing and asks *him* to report on what's happened and how it's affecting each area and the efficiency of the total manufacturing operation. According to the president, the tenor of the meetings has changed considerably since he began doing this. The director of manufacturing has stopped being defensive and has started explaining, for example, not only how costs have increased over the last month but what steps he and others have taken to get costs back to where they should be.

In other words, the manufacturing director has begun to acknowledge ownership of his problems. The more people measure their own performance, report on their own performance, and administer feedback to themselves, the more likely they are to recognize that they own particular problems and the less likely they are to assume that somebody else owns those problems or is responsible for solving them.

So impressed was the president with the success of self-administered feedback that he began applying the principle to his staff meetings. He was very careful to ask people to report on how they were doing and what kind of progress they were making. And he saw to it that they "graded" themselves on their achievements or lack of them. By changing his own behavior, this executive changed the behaviors of his entire staff. And this small change went a long way toward developing more Self-Starters on his organizational team.

## The Measurement Unit Should Be Positive

As a general rule, people react more positively to positive measurement than to negative measurement. Changing the measurement unit often changes the focal point of a discussion. One quality control department, for example, was asked by the director of operations to change its measurement system from negative to positive. As soon as the people in quality control stopped measuring and talking about *rejects* and started concentrating on *yield*, the whole outlook of the department changed for the better. "Not only did it change our internal outlook," recalls the quality control manager, "it also changed how we interrelated with other departments. We used to be forever fighting with other departments about their high reject rates. Now, instead of dwelling on the reject rate, we're able to sit down and talk with them about what we can do to get the yield up to where it should be. It's a very small change but one that seems to have a great impact throughout the entire department.''

His experience is not an uncommon one. In many organizations, people are finding that changing a negative measurement unit to a positive one increases employee motivation and makes employees more eager to seek out and act upon opportunities and problems that may arise. It's no accident, incidentally, that we talk about a professional baseball player batting 300, not about his missing 700. And just as a positive measurement unit produces a higher level of motivation in sports, the use of positive measurement units in business produces higher levels of motivation.

Management of an engine plant carried this concept one step further and found out that not only does changing negative to positive measurements work at the high levels of an organization, it also works at the lower levels. People we normally wouldn't think of as being Self-Starters can become more Self-Starting when they are exposed to a positive feedback system. This particular plant had been running about 14% rejects at final test: that is, out of every 100 engines that came down the line, 14 needed repair work and had to go into the repair area after they had been tested. Intrigued by some of the results his staff experienced when using the Self-Starting Mechanism to increase positive feedback, the supervisor of operations placed a big graph that read ''Good Engines to Test'' at the end of one of the engine lines. Every time the ratio improved, management reinforced the workers involved. As a result, good engines to test on that particular line climbed from 86 to 94%.

In another situation, Harold, a company president, was determined to introduce the Self-Starting Mechanism in as many areas as possible, and circumstances dictated that he should start with the organization's lead typist. According to the office manager, Alice did a good job, but she was frequently tardy or absent from work. Harold asked the office manager if he had talked to Alice about this performance problem. ''Yes,'' he said. ''I sat down and talked with her about her tardiness and absenteeism, and we tried to find ways to get it down to a reasonable level. But she was pretty defensive, so we didn't make much progress.'' At this point, Harold explained some of the principles of the Self-Starting Mechanism to the office manager. Then he asked him to prepare a graph that measured the number of hours worked from zero to forty along the left-hand margin and listed the Friday dates of several weeks across the bottom. The next step was to show Alice the graphs. After the office manager explained its purpose, Alice agreed that a reasonable goal to shoot for was thirty-nine hours or more per week present on the job. And, with that agreement, the measurement unit of Alice's performance changed from negative (absenteeism and tardiness) to positive (attendance).

Every week thereafter, when Alice made progress in the right direction, she was positively reinforced, or applauded, by the office manager. The result? Within seven weeks, she was consistently present and on the job more than thirty-nine hours a week. As far as I know, she still is. For Alice, measuring performance in positive terms and then being reinforced for that improved performance turned the tide in the right direction.

## Feedback Should Be Immediate

The more immediately the feedback is administered, the sooner performance problems can be tackled before they get out of hand. Therefore, you should shorten the feedback cycle wherever you can. Depending upon the level of the organization and the type of work being performed, even hourly feedback is often appropriate; it would be particularly crucial in the case of manufacturing operations where numerous items are being produced. In a large factory, for example, where an employee might be turning out 500 or 600 parts per hour, hourly feedback on both quantity and quality of production can be important. I've found that, as hourly rated employees receive more immediate feedback on how they are doing, they begin to act as their own supervisors and take corrective action before a potential problem becomes a real one. In other words, they begin to be Self-Starters.

Most employees, from the president of an organization on down, want to do a good job. And the sooner they receive feedback about their performance, the better able they are to do that good job. That's because immediate feedback makes it easier to relate specific job behaviors to specific job results. If quality, for example, starts to fall off just slightly, the employee can quickly relate specific behaviors to the quality problem and then change those behaviors before job results deteriorate drastically.

In one situation I encountered, the employees at the inside order desks weren't asking for additional business. Sure, they were taking the orders, but they weren't asking for any others while they had the customer on the phone. Once a month, the branch manager would sit down with the people responsible for inside sales, show them the figures for the previous month on average number of line items per order, and ask them to try and do better the next month. Subsequently, these employees seemed to try a bit harder to get additional business over the phone, but there was no immediate attempt to measure this improvement.

Then the branch manager decided to change the feedback system. On a daily basis, the average number of line items per order was figured, and the average for all three inside salespeople was posted on a departmental graph labeled "Average Number of Line Items per Order." In addition, each person on the inside order desk was responsible for keeping a graph on how he or she was doing in terms of average number of line items per order. Almost immediately, the average number of line items per order climbed from 5 to 9.3.

After calculating for inflation and other factors, the branch manager estimated that the feeding back of information to the inside order desk increased the sales of those three employees by about 22%. Approximately 40% of the company's business came into the order desk, so the overall net increase in sales was approximately 8.8%. Thanks to the shortened feedback cycle, the inside order desk staff is now aggressively and consistently working to maintain that average number of line items per order or even to improve it. By looking closely at their job behavior and acting on the basis of what they saw, the three employees actually became Self-Starters.

"Yes," you say, "but sometimes you can't depend on that short a feedback cycle. What about a sales situation in which somebody has to call on a customer for two, four, six, even eight months before he gets an order? And only when he *does* get that order can we give positive feedback. How, in a case like that, can we possibly make feedback immediate?" For those of you who face that situation, I suggest you begin thinking about the sales call as a behavior change program on the part of the sales representative. What most sales representatives are really trying to do is to change the customer's buying behavior. They're trying to get the customer to buy from them and not from someone else. When the customer finally signs on the dotted line, the salesman knows he's scored.

Figure 9-4. A Feedback System in Sales

POTENTIAL KEY ACCOUNTS

| CUSTOMER RESPONSE STAGE | A | B | C | D | E |
|---|---|---|---|---|---|
| I.   NO | X | X | X | X | X |
| II.   I'LL LISTEN | | X | X | X | X |
| III.   I'LL CONSIDER | | X | | | |
| IV.   I'LL RECOMMEND | | | | | |
| V.   I'LL SPECIFY | | | | | |
| VI.   I'LL BUY | | | | | |

For the salesman in this sort of situation, we'll need a slightly different kind of feedback system. But before we design it, let's consider several behaviors that the salesman might expect to encounter in potential customers. Reactions to a sales presentation can range from "no" to "I'll listen" to "I'll consider" to "I'll recommend" to "I'll specify it" to "I'll buy." Now, I suggest that we take those customers' behaviors and put them into a matrix that looks something like figure 9-4. Across the top of that diagram, we'll list customers A, B, C, D, and E, each of whom represents a potential key account whose business we'd like very much to get.

With a simple visual aid like this, it's possible for sales manager and sales representative to establish clear-cut call objectives that are based on typical customer behavior. For example, at the beginning of the week, you, as sales manager, might sit down with one of your salesmen and define the call objectives for the week, based on your diagram. The objective for customer A might be "to get the customer to listen to me." For customer B, it's "to move the customer from 'I'll consider it' to 'I'll recommend it.'" And for customers C, D, and E, the call objective is "to move the customer from 'I'll listen' to 'I'll consider.'"

A system like this serves as a sort of football field upon which the sales representative can run. It also gives us an opportunity to applaud the rep when he gets the "first down" or even "gains a few yards." With many feedback systems, there is too long a time lag between the initial call and the final sale. Furthermore, when there's no established system for measuring the extent of customer behavior change, the salesman eventually gets discouraged and ultimately resigned to not making particular sales.

A similar problem exists in the research area. Someone might work on a project for three or four years before the payoff finally appears at the bottom line. So how do you develop Self-Starters and keep them motivated when the results of their efforts seem so remote? One way would be to break the research process down into several primary steps. Table 9-1 shows how these steps closely approximate the scientific process.

It's possible to break down each of these steps even further so that the substeps become a sort of sub-feedback system underlying the major feedback system. Under "Determining the Technical Possibility of the Project," for example, these substeps might be listed: "Conducting a Literature Search," "Developing a Working Model in the Lab," and "Testing the Strength of Different Materials." Each of these in turn might have an entire PERT chart, gant chart, or critical path laid out to provide a feedback system for those more directly involved in the development of the project. Obviously, this process doesn't shorten the cycle so that those involved receive hourly feedback. But it does make possible weekly or semi-weekly feedback, which gives people more opportunity to check their own progress.

**TABLE 9-1**

## FEEDBACK AND THE SCIENTIFIC PROCESS

1. DETERMINE THE OBJECTIVE OF THE IDEA.
   - Does it fit in with the company purpose?
   - Is it within the scope of the departmental mission?

2. TEST TECHNICAL POSSIBILITY OF IDEA.
   - Conduct literature search.
   - Develop working model.
   - Test material strength

3. DETERMINE FEASIBILITY OF IDEA.
   - Is funding available?
   - Will consumers buy it?

4. RUN A PILOT PROJECT.
   - Select a pilot color.
   - Run/test the idea.
   - Iron out "buts."

5. IMPLEMENT.
   - Establish an implementation strategy.
   - Obtain appropriate commitments.
   - Establish a check on milestones.

6. MEASURE THE WHOLE PROCESS.
   - Did it go as planned?
   - What should be changed in the future?

**Feedback Should Be Relevant**

The feedback system should measure a variable that is controlled by the individual who is receiving the feedback. Relevant feedback gives individuals a sense of control over those job variables that affect their job success. And because they receive feedback on the variables that affect their job success, they frequently are able to initiate self-correcting action and, thus, reduce the need for corrective supervision from above.

Relevance is determined largely by the goals established for each level of the organization. For instance, a plant manager might need a ten-day moving average of feedback on areas such as production cost and quality. But a department head in the same plant might be more interested in monthly feedback on the progress toward a particular goal. The supervisor in each work group is probably the most appropriate recipient of daily feedback. And an hourly rated employee should receive feedback on at least a daily basis; even hourly or two or three times a day would be appropriate if it's possible.

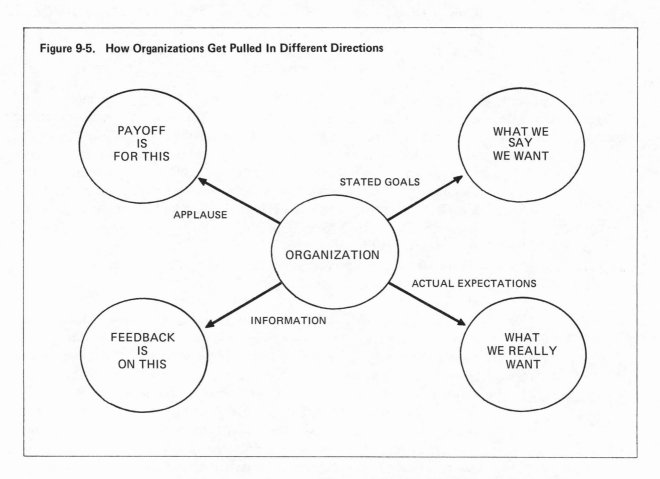

**Figure 9-5. How Organizations Get Pulled In Different Directions**

What too often happens, though, is illustrated in figure 9–5. The organization *says* it wants one thing, but it *means* it wants another; the feedback is directed one way, and the payoff goes in yet another direction.

For example, management might say, "We want high quality products." But what it means is, "We want high quality products, but we don't want to shut the plant down." The feedback system may be set up to measure both quality and quantity of production, but, to the first-line foreman, the payoff is to keep the line going. Now, if we wish to make that first-line foreman a Self-Starter, we have to make sure that all four arrows in figure 9–5 are pointing in the same direction. Unfortunately, what usually happens is that the plant manager says, "We want high quality production and we want it *fast.*'' The foreman, of course, gets both psychological and economic payoffs just for keeping the line going, often at the expense of quality. The puzzled plant manager then says, ''I wish we could develop more Self-Starters in those first-line supervisors. They just don't seem to have what it takes to grab the job and run with it.''

Of course, the savvy plant manager would be able to grow Self-Starters because he'd know how to point all four arrows in the same direction. That is, he would *mean* what he *says* he wants and needs from his staff. His feedback system would measure the extent to which those wants and needs are being met. And the economic and psychological payoffs he offers would keep his employees moving in the right direction.

## The Feedback System Can't Be Used As a Basis for Punishment

When the feedback system is used as a basis for punishment, employee resentment can take curious forms, most of which are extremely undesirable. If a department head pounds his desk and shouts, ''I don't ever want to catch you with a scrap rate above 2%,'' he probably won't ever *catch* an employee with a scrap rate above 2%. In reality, of course, scrap rate will be running at 2.5 or 2.8%, but our bombastic department head won't be able to single out the employee whose scrap rate is that high. When the feedback system is used as a basis for punishment, people quickly learn that it doesn't pay to tell the truth.

Self-Starters aren't people who don't make mistakes. In fact, they are people who do so many things that they frequently make mistakes—and then they do something about rectifying those mistakes. If you want to develop this Self-Starting trait in all your employees, it's necessary to use a behavioral approach. Remember, we're concerned here with two behaviors: bringing a mistake to somebody's attention and then taking the action to correct it. Therefore, you have to use the feedback system in two ways. If somebody detects a mistake and brings it to your attention, you must both discuss the fact that the mistake was made and then reinforce the mistake maker for leveling with you. The key is to keep these behaviors separate; if they're indistinguishable, people learn that it doesn't pay to report their mistakes to their supervisors. The behavioral approach to developing Self-Starters allows us to deal with each specific behavior we want to develop and increase the frequency of desired behaviors.

## The Feedback System Must Be Simple to Use

Here again, sports provide an appropriate analogy. It's not too difficult to record the total yardage gained by the halfback, divide that by the number of times he carries the ball, and come up with an average of yards per carry. This information is readily available within the ''system,'' and it's easy to compute and record. Consider, however, the difficulty of determining the average number of *steps* per carry. Someone would first have to count how many steps each person took in carrying the ball. But how? Do you count only whole steps or half steps as well? Does a step forward count the same as a step backward? How about a step sideways? Moreover, it would be extremely difficult to see all the steps a football player takes, particularly when a swarm of tacklers surrounds him. Is he taking one step or four? Needless to say, the chore of counting a player's steps would be disagreeable and frustrating, and the results would probably be questionable at best.

One company I worked with provided an interesting example of the perils of a feedback system that was just plain awkward to use. In an effort to get people to check quality rate within their groups, we made up 8½″ x 11″ sheets that listed the quality items each group should check. But we couldn't get people to use the sheets. Finally, a foreman pointed out to me that he and his colleagues weren't used to carrying 8½″ X 11″ sheets. They were, however, used to carrying note cards approximately the size of a computer card. Knowing that, we were able to reduce the information slightly so it would fit onto a computer card. Then we had it printed on a batch of these cards and distributed them to everybody in the various work groups. Because this new format was so convenient, the employees accepted it readily and, more important, used it religiously to check their work quality. See what a big difference a seemingly small change made? Once the mechanics of the system were simplified, employees accepted it wholeheartedly.

In this chapter you've learned how information about performance can be a motivating factor in developing Self-Starters *if* that information is used as part of a performance feedback system. The better the feedback someone receives about his or her performance, the greater the likelihood that he or she will take self-correcting action and, sooner or later, become a true Self-Starter.

To help you evaluate your performance feedback system, the diagram on page 164 is for you to copy and use as a worksheet. Here's what to do.

1. Make a copy for you and anyone else who will be doing the evaluating.

2. In the blank spaces across the top, fill in the performance indicators that you want to evaluate. These should be measures that you are currently using. Attendance, yield, receivables, average order size, production, cost/budget, and accuracy are just a few examples of potential indicators to evaluate.

3. For each indicator, decide how well it measures up as a performance feedback tool against the seven points in this chapter. Do this by scoring it from one to ten, with one being poor and ten being outstanding. Then decide how your performance feedback system measures up. Chances are it doesn't do too well. But don't be too upset. Most feedback systems don't do too well.

The time to be upset is when you evaluate the same variables 90 days from now and there hasn't been much of an improvement.

| List Indicators Here → | | | | | | |
|---|---|---|---|---|---|---|
| 1. Goal Related | | | | | | |
| 2. Self-Administered | | | | | | |
| 3. Positive Measurement | | | | | | |
| 4. Immediate | | | | | | |
| 5. Relevant | | | | | | |
| 6. Not a Basis for Punishment | | | | | | |
| 7. Simple to Use | | | | | | |

## SCORE      WHAT IT MEANS

7-17      Your performance feedback is almost non-existent. You have a lot of work to do.

18-30     Either by design or accident, some things are being done at least a little. Keep working at it.

31-40     Good solid job. Find out what needs improvement and get it improved.

47-59     You're either incredibly lucky or you've been working very hard at building a good performance feedback system.

60-70     Wow! Are you sure you didn't cheat. If your score is up in this range, you've been working very hard for some period of time AND you've been doing the right things while building your performance feedback system.

As you continue to implement the techniques described in this, come back to this evaluation tool from time to time. It'll help you keep your performance feedback system on track.

# Graphing Techniques

Try to recall the last meal you ate. Now, what comes to mind? The names of particular foods or mental pictures of what you'd eaten? Chances are, a series of pictures, a visual representation of the meal, flashed across your cerebral screen.

Information is always more readily grasped when it can be represented pictorially. One reason people enjoy movies, television, and live theater is that they can see exactly what's going on. Even when we're listening to the radio, we recreate in our minds a mental picture of the dialog as the story unfolds. Good radio announcers, who are aware of the importance of vivid imagery, describe scenes in terms of pictures. They are able to take bald facts and create a memorable scene for our mind's eye. The good announcer describes a sports play so that we can mentally recreate the action. We can almost "see" the play—with our minds, if not our eyes.

Researchers who have studied people's ability to remember things have found that when people both see *and* hear information, they remember substantially more after three days than when they either see *or* hear it. After three days, people remember 10% of what they were told and 20% of what they were shown. However, if they *both* heard and saw something, they remember 65% of that information. In other words, there is almost six times as much retention when people both hear and see. Obviously, the old saying that one picture is worth a thousand words is true.

|  | After 3 Hours | After 3 Days |
|---|---|---|
| Hear | 70% | 10% |
| See | 72% | 20% |
| Hear and See | 85% | 65% |

So what does all this have to do with the Self-Starting Mechanism in general and the design of effective feedback systems in particular? Plenty, because a pictorial representation of performance information is one of the most important parts of an effective feedback system. And that pictorial representation is further enhanced when combined with explanatory words. That's why I emphasize the importance of using graphs when installing the Self-Starting Mechanism in your organization.

What I'm suggesting is that this:

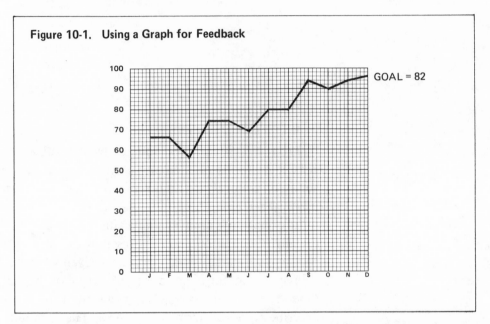

Figure 10-1. Using a Graph for Feedback

has much more of an impact on person's behavior and motivation than this:

| | | | |
|---|---|---|---|
| January | 66 | July | 80 |
| February | 66 | August | 80 |
| March | 56 | September | 94 |
| April | 74 | October | 90 |
| May | 74 | November | 94 |
| June | 69 | December | 96 |

**The Simpler the Better** To be most effective, a graph should be as simple as possible, and it should depict as closely as possible what is actually taking place—either within the organization as a whole or within an area that is under a particular employee's control. The measurement unit should be indicated on the left-hand side of the column on the vertical axis; this unit might be attendance, yield, scrap, overtime, unit sales, dollar sales, new accounts, percent of satisfied customers, or whatever the variable is that we want to measure. The dimension of the time—hourly, daily, weekly, monthly, quarterly, or yearly—should appear across the bottom axis. As a general rule, the further

down you go in the organization, the shorter the time period you want to measure. For a maximum motivational effect, you want something between a daily and a monthly measurement. Although you might occasionally want something graphed on a quarterly or yearly basis, this would be for general trends or control purposes and would probably not have any significant motivational effect on the behavior of people within the organization. Of course, those occupying the top two or three positions might be motivated when they see, on a quarterly basis, the fruits of their labors, but quarterly or yearly graphing of results wouldn't have much impact on the majority of employees.

As a general rule, it also makes sense to measure only one variable on a graph. Traditionally, graph users have been involved in technical fields such as engineering, and they frequently chart four or five variables on a single graph, using dotted lines, solid lines, thick lines, and thin lines. I've found that most people are better able to understand, both conceptually and practically, one variable per graph. Figures 10–2 and 10–3 illustrate the dif-

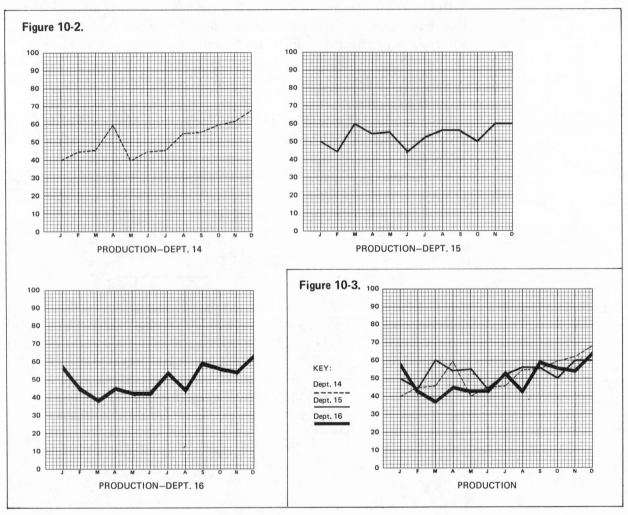

Figure 10-2.

PRODUCTION—DEPT. 14

PRODUCTION—DEPT. 15

PRODUCTION—DEPT. 16

Figure 10-3.

KEY:

Dept. 14

Dept. 15

Dept. 16

PRODUCTION

ferences in clarity and psychological impact between several variables on one graph and one variable on several graphs. Figure 10-2 contains three small graphs; this format is preferable to the one in figure 10-3 (several variables/one graph) in terms of comprehension.

It's also helpful to use different colors on the graph to chart progress toward the goal because they indicate more clearly what employees are doing. If you have white graph paper and if the time, numbers, and goal line are all in black, then use a bright color to track the actual performance. This way, if the performance line is very close to the goal line, people won't confuse the two lines and will be able to relate where they are to where they want to be.

**Graph Goals and Goal Areas**

It's important to include the goal line on the graph. Although a graph always has more impact than a computer printout, a column of numbers, or a written report, some graphs are more impressive than others. And the best graphs are those that clearly define the goal to be reached.

But what about a situation in which somebody is so far from his goal that it appears out of reach? Won't graphing such discouraging information have a demotivating effect? Possibly. But, fortunately, you can arrange a graph in such a way as to give that employee incentive to get up into the *goal area* which we described in chapter 9; the implicit understanding is that beyond this goal area lies the ultimate target.

Let's say, for example, that you want an employee who is averaging 55 to hit a target of 90. That would give us a graph that looks something like figure 10-4.

In the chapter on establishing goals, I pointed out that a goal that's too far

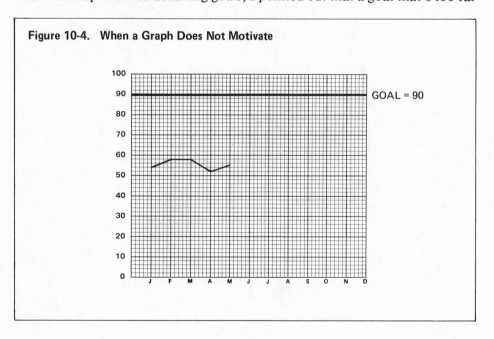

Figure 10-4. When a Graph Does Not Motivate

out of reach actually leads to a decrease in motivation. And that's exactly what a graph like this might do, too. However, it's possible to bracket the goal and explain the goal area to the employee this way: "The target we want to end up at is 90. We're at 55 right now. In the next three months, I'd like to get us up above 65. That is, I'd like to get us somewhere in the goal area between 65 and 90."

With a graph that looks like figure 10-5, the employee begins to feel the motivation that comes with accomplishment as soon as he surpasses 65. At this point, you can and should reinforce the individual by noting that he has improved and made good progress. The individual can also see that there is still room for further improvement. Thus, the employee experiences a feeling of accomplishment and, at the same time, recognizes an opportunity to stretch and grow.

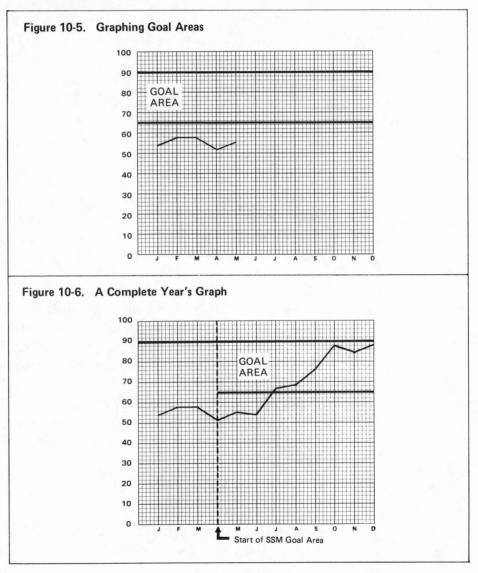

Figure 10-5. Graphing Goal Areas

Figure 10-6. A Complete Year's Graph

Let's say that, at the end of the year, the graph looks something like figure 10-6. At this point, it is reasonable to expect the individual to tighten the goal area up a little bit. You might say so in these words: "We seem to be hitting 80 to 90 pretty consistently now, so I'd like to place the goal area somewhere between 80 and 90, which would give us a target that looks something like this" (figure 10-7):

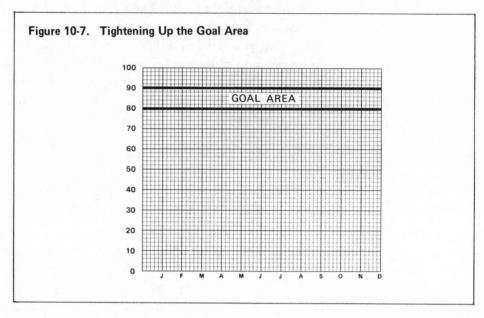

Figure 10-7.  Tightening Up the Goal Area

GOAL AREA

In advancing the bottom of the goal area, you mustn't draw it to exactly where the person was the last time performance was measured. If you do, you impose an uncomfortable constraint. If as soon as the person hits a target, that becomes the new acceptable minimum; and, as soon as he takes another step, that minimum standard snaps up behind again, that is moving the standard up too quickly. People subjected to this disconcerting rubber-band effect begin to take smaller and smaller steps to prevent the minimum standard line from snapping up too quickly behind them. I suggest that after somebody has been at, say, 75 for a while, you move the minimum acceptable line up to 70, letting him know, of course, that the ultimate target you're shooting for is 85-90.

It's possible to change the scale on the graph so that people can see more clearly how their performance affects overall production. Let's go back to our original example. Someone was averaging 55 to 57, and we wanted him to get up to 90; let's suppose that not only did he hit 90, but he's now averaging 91 to 91.5, depending upon the month. To get performance up from 91 in January to 92 in February might require a lot of effort. On our original graph, it would look something like figure 10-8.

The problem here is that you can hardly see that barely perceptible—but crucial—progress. That's because the scale on the graph has not been ad-

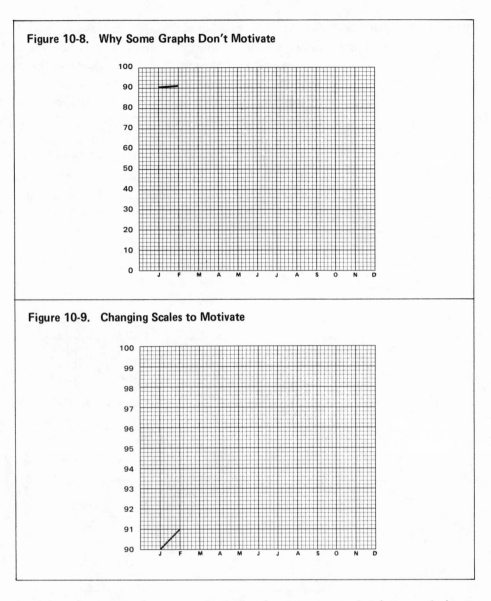

Figure 10-8. Why Some Graphs Don't Motivate

Figure 10-9. Changing Scales to Motivate

justed to the point where a performance improvement of .3 is very obvious. But for the individual in control of that variable, that .3 probably represents considerable effort.

The solution would be to rescale the graph so that it runs not from 0 to 100 but from 90 to 100. A graph scaled this way would look something like figure 10-9. Notice how impressive an improvement of 1% appears on such a graph.

People respond positively when they can *see* how their contribution makes a difference. Sometimes people lose their motivation to be Self-Starters when they work hard but are barely able to see the result of that effort. However, when the graph is rescaled to show more exactly how their contribution affects improvement, they are inspired to put more into the job.

**Bar and Cumulative Graphs**

So far, I've emphasized only line graphs, and I haven't even mentioned either bar or cumulative graphs. That's because we're concerned here with movement, and bar graphs tend to illustrate the status quo, focusing on the absolute level rather than a change in performance. Although we're interested in absolute levels, we're generally more interested in what's happening in terms of improvement. The other problem with a bar graph is that it is time-consuming to maintain; we want something that's easy for people to update, and time graphs meet that criterion. However, if you want a graph that's colorful, has lots of visual impact, is easy to see from a distance, then a bar graph might be the thing to use. Just make sure the bars are wide enough to be meaningful and the colors selected bold. Figure 10–10 illustrates a bar graph.

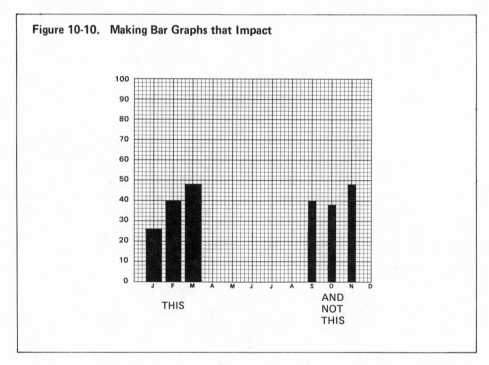

Figure 10-10. Making Bar Graphs that Impact

On a cumulative graph, we might cumulatively add up sales. While it's often useful to do so, it can also engender a false sense of security. That is, the graph may indicate upward movement, but we may still be behind where we would like to be. Even if we add to the graph a goal line that shows on a cumulative basis where we want to be each month, there is still potential for a demotivating effect. If sales are considerably behind target five or six months into the year, people generally see no way of hitting that year-end goal. But if monthly goals are charted, they can still hit each of those six remaining goals, even if they're behind at the mid-year point. The probability in this situation of higher motivation and performance during the last six months is greater when progress is measured on a monthly basis rather than on a cumulative basis.

**Graphs + Positive Reinforcement = Progress**

"Hey, wait a minute," you say. "We tried putting up graphs and nothing really happened. Oh, I guess they worked for a while—but not for long." If that's been your experience with graphs, don't worry; you're not alone. Many people have found that graphs, by themselves, are virtually meaningless. Only when an organization incorporates its graphs into other aspects of the feedback system can it expect them to be useful.

The graph merely represents a sort of football field. Now, in order for the players on that field to succeed, you must give them applause. It's that applause, or positive reinforcement, aspect that makes the charted information meaningful. Too often, we put up graphs, people see them, and performance improves a little bit—but nobody reinforces that improvement. Because the improvement was not reinforced, performance quickly returns to its old level, and the graphs are chucked away as another "idea that didn't pan out." Thus, if you have doubts at this point about the impact of graphs, know that those are natural doubts. But don't give up on the idea of graphs. They, combined with reinforcement, *do* work. I suggest you review chapters 7, 8, and 9 carefully and then put up the graphs. Knowing what you do now, you'll be better able to nurture Self-Starters.

**Good Graphs Foster Healthy Competition**

What kinds of graphs do you put up and where? It's best to display a departmental graph that represents the performance of the entire team, work group, or department. If you want to measure individual performance, do so on an individual basis. Frequently, managers will put up a graph that shows how each salesman is doing in terms of unit sales; the rationale is to "foster competition." The problem is, such a graph often fosters the wrong kind of competition. It focuses on the competition among individuals, but we want the focus to be on each person competing against himself or herself. We also want the whole sales team to compete against a team goal. It's only natural, of course, that each of the individuals on the team is going to compete against the others. But their fiercest competition should be against the goal line. When salespeople aren't competing solely against each other, individuals feel free to help one another. Team competition also prevents the top one or two salespeople from feeling exempt from the "game" because they are so much better than everybody else. A well-designed graph on the wall that charts team performance and individual graphs that serve as "contracts" between manager and subordinate encourage the most important kind of competition there is: the team tries to beat the team goal, and each individual tries to beat his or her *own* record.

**Explanations Are in Order**

As more and more graphs begin to appear around the work place, people will start to wonder what's happening. The best way to allay their apprehension is to explain exactly what the graphs are all about. To do so, you might say something like this:

"As you probably know, we did very well in sales over the last three months. We'd like not only to maintain our position but to move to the head of the list because we know we can do it. Our overall target is to continue building account volume. You people are the key individuals in helping us build this, and we'd like to keep you informed as to how we're doing. As part of our communication effort, we're going to put up charts in each work group so we can keep track of our progress. Here's what these charts will look like.

"The charts will have the months of the year numbered across the bottom. Going up the left-hand side of the chart will be the item that we're going to keep track of. This first chart, for example, shows overall sales. This next chart will show us how we're doing on developing new accounts. As you can see, our new account goal for the office is fourteen a month. Each of you has made individual commitments to me, and I'll be talking with each of you about these commitments.

"This next chart shows us what unit volume is so we can compare dollar volume with unit volume. This last chart shows how we're doing on average order size. That affects our shipping costs; the larger our average order size, the lower the overall shipping costs."

You might conclude by explaining the role of the people you're talking to in building the sales. Ask them for suggestions and ideas, not only now but on a continuing basis. Be sure to reinforce the suggestions, even those that don't work out.

Graphs, then, are an important part of a feedback system. And because they are the most visual part of that system, they must be designed and constructed carefully and explained honestly and thoroughly. Done properly, they will help you immensely in developing Self-Starters. With a graph or, preferably, graphs in front of them that measure and monitor their own individual, team, and departmental performance, people become more committed to improvement and progress. And they are willing to spend more time in self-corrective, self-management efforts than they would if their feedback system lacked visual proof of achievement.

# 11 Counseling Techniques

What if, after you've applied all the techniques I've outlined so far, things still aren't where they should be in your organization? Before we discuss your next steps, let's take a quick look at the guidelines I've set forth to help you initiate the Self-Starting Mechanism. Are you sure that you have:

- Communicated high expectations to those people whose Self-Starter potential you wish to develop?

- Communicated those messages both verbally and nonverbally?

- Delivered your messages with an awareness that what you said, when you said it, why you said it, and how you said it were all targeted toward high expectations?

- Negotiated clear-cut goals that are specific and realistic under the control and influence of the particular employees?

- Developed action plans that help reach that target?

- Designed an immediate, timely, relevant feedback system based upon a positive measurement unit?

- Positively reinforced subordinates for the right behaviors in a timely fashion and with specific comments?

- Reinforced progress as well as excellence?

If you can honestly say you've adhered to each of these guidelines and things *still* aren't where they should be, you're ready to sit down with those employees you wish to see become Self-Starters. This chapter is basically about that crucial conversation. It consists of the prediscussion—things to do before you have the heart-to-heart talk, the actual discussion, and the follow-up to that discussion.

**Prediscussion**    Prior to talking with an employee whose Self-Starting potential you wish to develop, you must do three things. Only if you take the time to lay a solid prediscussion foundation can you hope to achieve success during the actual discussion.

1. First of all, *review everything in the preceding chapters to make sure that expectations, goals, action steps, feedback, and reinforcement are all in place.* Additionally, make sure that nothing else is blocking your accomplishment of the task. Sometimes, an unexpected factor thwarts our efforts.

    One company, for example, was trying to increase productivity in its warehouse. In different sections of the warehouse, management was measuring cases picked per hour, bins picked per hour, and units picked per hour. Managers worked hard to create a climate of high expectations in which employees could perform. They set up specific targets for each work area and developed action plans to help people reach those targets. They provided daily feedback on how employees were progressing toward the target. Whenever there was any progress, no matter how slight, employees were reinforced and thanked for their effort in making that improvement.

    Unfortunately, however, productivity did not increase. When management looked more closely at the situation, they found out why: not enough sales were coming in to sustain any increase in productivity. The warehouse employees really couldn't operate at their maximum, because there weren't enough orders to push them to the limits of their productivity. As soon as the company realized this, it turned its efforts toward the sales area and used the Self-Starting Mechanism to improve sales. As sales went up, so did warehouse productivity, and the same warehouse force was able to handle an additional 14% in sales.

    In this instance, the Self-Starting Mechanism was stymied because not enough line items were being ordered or processed through the warehouse to improve productivity. Before management scheduled heart-to-heart talks with key personnel, it looked hard to find out what was blocking the completion of the task. You should do the same. Perhaps an employee doesn't have enough time to complete the task, or perhaps the task is competing with something else. As manager, you must function rather like a guard on a football team, clearing out some of the opposing tacklers so that the player holding the ball can really run with it. Before you sit down and discuss performance problems with an employee, you should make sure that you've cleared away any impediments to the employee's progress.

2. *Decide how you're going to handle steps 3 through 12.* To really maximize your return on the time you'll spend reading this chapter, you

should make a commitment to yourself to write a "script" for the up-coming discussion. How? Simple. Before you have a heart-to-heart talk with an employee, read the suggestions in step 3. Then put down on paper *exactly* how you're going to handle step 3 in the actual conversation. Do the same thing for steps 4 through 12. For step 4, for example, decide what you're going to do and say to put the individual at ease and reduce the tension of the encounter. For step 5, write down the exact words you're going to use to describe the performance problem. And, for step 6, write down the exact question you intend to ask after you finish describing a performance problem. Then put the notepad aside for a couple of days. After you re-read your notes, see if there are ways you could sharpen your approach a bit. Now you're ready to rehearse it. Your best bet is to role play the anticipated scenario with your spouse, somebody in employee relations, or a colleague from another organization. Explain the situation to whomever you select and ask for his or her candid evaluations. Once you've done all this, you're ready to have the heart-to-heart discussion.

It never ceases to amaze me that professional sales managers, for example, who wouldn't dream of sending their salespeople out on a call without some call planning, will talk to an individual salesman about job performance without planning for that discussion. A plant manager who would chew out a department head mercilessly and articulately for not planning a line speed change will, nevertheless, sit down with that same department head and launch a heart-to-heart discussion on a performance problem without planning carefully what he's going to say.

Bill, the sales manager for a medium-sized manufacturing company, was often guilty of this haphazard approach. Bill was a good sales manager and performed well in his role. From time to time, however, he had problems with the performance of different salesmen. Generally, these problems concerned such things as decreased call activity, calls on the wrong kinds of accounts, drops in dollar volume, and lack of new accounts. Before he'd heard about the Self-Starting Mechanism, Bill found it difficult to sit down and discuss nonperformance with individual staff members. "The problem," he told me, "is that things always seem to get off on the wrong foot. As soon as the salesman becomes hostile and defensive, I, too, become defensive. The harder I come down during the discussion, the more defensive the salesman gets. We really end up getting nowhere except angry and hostile toward one another."

After I told Bill about prediscussion planning here, he decided to give it a try. First, he wrote out exactly *what* he was going to say and do and *how* for steps 3 through 12. Then he rehearsed it. He rehearsed it with his wife, and he tried it out with a friend of his who was a real estate broker. He even decided to go one step further: he asked another friend of his to reverse roles, with the friend pretending he was Bill and Bill playing the role of the subordinate. Bill's friend, with the script in front of him, did the appropriate things and asked the right kinds of questions. Finally, Bill role played the upcoming encounter with his wife one more time and recorded their dialogue on a small cassette. He listened to the cassette a couple of times on the way to work in the morning, noting where he could strengthen his presentation. At last, he was ready to sit down and confront a salesman who was having problems.

Later, Bill told me that, while it wasn't a perfect discussion, it was the best one he had had to date, and both he and the salesman ended up in a win-win situation. Both felt the discussion had been positive, that good things had been accomplished, and that they were making progress in the right direction. Furthermore, Bill found that each time he held such a discussion, it took less and less preparation.

My point is, don't go in cold; don't fly blind. Sit down and figure out what you're going to do for each of steps 3 through 12. Write out a rough sort of script upon which to base your discussion. Don't take the script into the actual discussion with you (unless your handwriting is so poor that nobody else could read it), but consider making some notes on just one or two questions you're going to ask. This sort of thoughtful preparation will ensure that you'll at least get off on the right foot and will increase the probability that the discussion will be successful.

3. *Position the discussion properly.* Let the subordinate know that you would like to talk to him or her about a specific issue. If you want to talk to Mary, for example, about the number of new accounts she has opened, tell her that. Say something like this: "Mary, sometime in the next few days, I'd like to sit down and talk with you about how we're progressing toward our goal of four new accounts every month. I noticed from the field sales-call reports that we're not hitting that target, and I'd like to work with you on finding ways we can get back on target. When would be a good time to talk about it?"

An opening like this gives Mary a fair indication of the situation. First of all, because you're concerned about the rate at which new accounts are being opened, she knows that between now and the time you have the actual discussion, she should think about what she's doing, what she's not doing, and what she should be doing differently to increase the number of new accounts. By saying that you'd like to look at some way you and she could get closer to target, you're also letting Mary know that the discussion will be a positive one, that you're not going to chew her out or castigate or berate her for not "measuring up." Finally, because you've asked her for a specific time to discuss the issue, she realizes that it's not just a general concern that you'd like to talk about "sometime" but a specific problem that you want to get under control soon.

Make sure that the issues you're going to discuss concern timely events. Don't plan to talk about scrap problems from three or four months ago or sales problems from last quarter. Talk about what's going on *right now*. If the matter you want to discuss is something that's been going on for several months and is still going on, it's certainly all right to talk about that. However, if an issue wasn't important enough to talk about three or four months ago when it happened, it's probably not worth talking about now. Or, if it is, there's not much sense in talking about it now because the discussion won't have much effect so long after the fact. You're better off waiting until the problem recurs and then talking about it immediately.

It's best to have the discussion soon after you've asked the subordinate to think about the particular problem. If a week or two elapse, the person might begin to worry excessively about what you're thinking or doing in the meantime. Schedule the discussion for no more than three days after you mention it. During that brief interim, both you and, especially, the employee will have time to formulate some ideas on how things could be brought back on track.

**Discussion**  4. *Put the individual at ease.* In other words, create an atmosphere that permits him to devote all his energies to the task at hand. People can spend their energy on different things. Let's suppose an individual has 100 units of energy that he can devote to any particular situation, and let's say that we want that individual to devote all 100 units of energy to the resolution of a particular performance problem. Unfortunately, when employees are summoned to the boss's office for a "little talk," they generally expend all their available energy on the stress inherent in the relationship part of the discussion. So until the employee in question has a comfort-

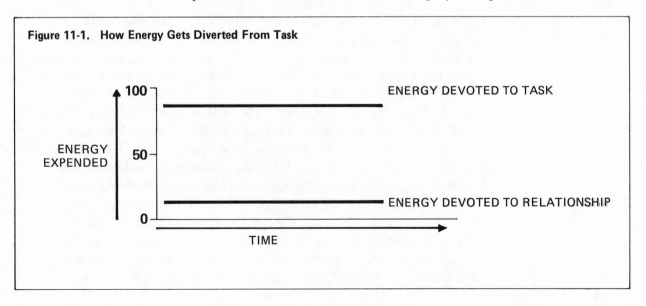

**Figure 11-1.  How Energy Gets Diverted From Task**

ENERGY EXPENDED — 100, 50, 0

ENERGY DEVOTED TO TASK

ENERGY DEVOTED TO RELATIONSHIP

TIME

able relationship with you, he won't be able to devote all 100 units of energy to the task of resolving the performance problem.

As you can see in figure 11-1, as long as the relationship tension remains high, the individual will be expending his 100 units of energy on tension and stress. It's up to you to try to reduce the amount of relationship tension and, in turn, free the individual's energy so that it can go toward accomplishing the task at hand (figure 11-2). Spend a few minutes discussing general issues, such as the weather, a recent vacation, or a son's or daughter's graduation from high school. This simple technique reduces relationship tension and prepares the individual to devote all his energy to more important concerns, specifically, how to improve his questionable performance.

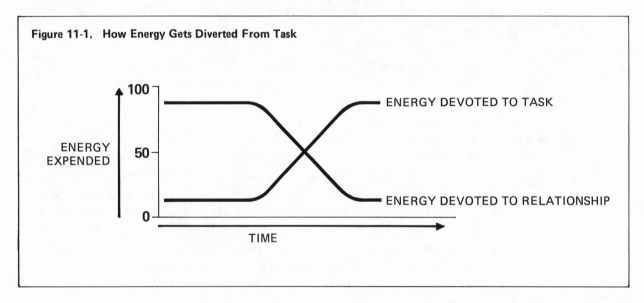

**Figure 11-1. How Energy Gets Diverted From Task**

While the process of putting the individual at ease should not be artificial and contrived, it can, nonetheless, be planned. But if it's planned in such a way that it seems insincere, it's not worth much. How relaxed would an employee be whose boss blurted out, in rapid-fire delivery, the following monolog? "Well, Joe, come on in, sit down, have a cigar. Nice day, huh? How're the kids doing? The little woman? Had a good vacation? You know, Joe, I noticed the sales are down, and I think we ought to talk about it." Joe wouldn't have to be very sensitive to be offended by this distasteful opener. But he would probably appreciate and benefit from a casual and relaxed discussion for a couple of moments about his kids or a trip he and his family took recently. Once he's at ease, he's ready to talk seriously about the perplexing performance problem.

Once you've put the employee at ease, make sure he stays there. How? By refusing to take all phone calls or see any visitors for the duration of the discussion. After all, you're going to be discussing something that's important to both you and your subordinate—the latter's performance. Nothing ruins the flow of a discussion more than somebody bursting in to "just have three things signed," to "get an okay on something," or to "check out the final specs." Nothing, that is, except the telephone.

As I said in chapter 4, interruptions of any kind can communicate to the individual with whom you're meeting that you don't consider this discussion very important. Additionally, interruptions can hamper and even prevent the give-and-take that must flow back and forth in a discussion like this. So tell your secretary, "No calls, no visitors." Now you're ready to *talk*.

5. *Describe the performance problem*. And be sure that you do so *factually*. This is not a time to be subjectively critical. Statements that are judgmental, blaming, and evaluative often are perceived as some form of personal attack, and the individual at whom they're directed responds accordingly. The subordinate, believing that the best defense is a good offense, often tries to attack verbally himself. Obviously, nobody wins in these situations. And all available energy is drained as both "sides" fight with one another about something that may well be totally irrelevant.

*Describing* the behavior and performance rather than *evaluating* or *judging* it is what Carol Goldthorpe, vice president of MICA, a Toronto-based communications consulting firm, calls the "mirror approach." "The best thing to do," she says, "is simply to hold up a mirror to that individual and describe the behaviors that you saw take place. Tell the individual that you saw this, this, and this take place, and then ask him how it looks. It's like the difference between telling somebody that she has a really ugly hat on and asking her to look in the mirror and see for herself how the hat looks. If she herself can see that the hat is ugly, she's much more likely to stop wearing it."

The same is true of subordinates. You don't have to criticize them for making mistakes. If you hold up a figurative mirror so the subordinates can see themselves clearly, they'll realize that they've made mistakes, and they'll take it upon themselves to change those patterns of behavior. The message underlying the description of the performance problem should be, "I love you but not your behavior." Subordinates should realize that you're not personally attacking them; instead, you're describing a behavior or performance problem that can be tackled and solved.

Here, for example, are some differences between descriptive and evaluative statements. Each one says essentially the same thing but in a slightly different way.

| | |
|---|---|
| *Descriptive*: | I see from the reports that sales have dropped. |
| *Evaluative*: | Aren't you concerned about your sales reports? |

| | |
|---|---|
| *Descriptive*: | This is the third month in a row the modular report has been late. |
| *Evaluative*: | You'd think I was asking for the moon if I asked you to get this thing in on time. |

| | |
|---|---|
| *Descriptive*: | You've been absent every Monday for the past five weeks. |
| *Evaluative*: | Don't you want your job? |

| | |
|---|---|
| *Descriptive*: | Our market share is dropping. |
| *Evaluative*: | It would seem that your vaunted sales team isn't doing a very good job. |

| | |
|---|---|
| *Descriptive*: | We haven't had any new accounts in the last six months. |
| *Evaluative*: | Don't those clowns know how important new accounts are? |

| | |
|---|---|
| *Descriptive*: | I noticed you only asked for the order once during the sales call. |
| *Evaluative*: | I think you're afraid to ask for the order more than once. |

The descriptive approach is not designed to let people off the hook. Quite the contrary, it's designed to put them *on* the hook and make them account for their own performance. Evaluative or judgmental statements trigger defensiveness, while descriptive statements generally do not.

In describing the performance discrepancy, you can also state the general goal you have in mind and any parameters within which you have to operate. If, for example, you want to see what steps you and the subordinate can outline that will get sales back to 110, state that as a goal. If you're looking for ideas on how absenteeism can be reduced, state that as a goal. The following are a couple of appropriate goal-related statements. "Bill, I noticed that sales have dropped over the last couple of months. Let's see how we can increase them." "Mary, our turn-around time has increased from two working days to three and a half working days. I'd like to see what we can do to reverse that trend."

6. *Follow the identification of a problem with a future-oriented neutral question*. Different types of questions will elicit different types of responses, so it's important that you ask the right questions. Try to avoid questions that are "historical" in nature, that can be answered yes or no, and that begin with why or who. Instead, ask questions that are future-oriented, open-ended, and neutral.

Questions that are historical in nature go back in time: "Why did this drop so much? and "Who caused this problem?" are two examples. For years, we've been told that a good manager gets to the heart of the problem by finding out *why* something went wrong. And while it is indeed important to find out why something went wrong, there are better ways to do it than to ask point-blank for the reason. When a subordinate attempts to answer questions that are historical in nature, we too often get angry and accuse the individual of "giving us excuses rather than solutions." Yet, the fault lies with us, not with the other person. By phrasing our question in the historical mode, we force the subordinate to become slightly defensive. Then our anger at this defensiveness escalates the antagonism, and the conversation deteriorates completely.

Instead, we should ask future-oriented questions. These focus on how we can improve something in the future rather than on what went wrong in the past. Questions such as "How could this be corrected?" or "What could we do to reverse this trend?" elicit not excuses but positive statements about how something could be improved. It's interesting to note that, by asking this type of question, we usually can find out what went wrong. If a subordinate can tell you how something can be corrected or improved in the future, he's already performed the mental gymnastics necessary to determine why it went wrong in the first place. Once a subordinate has acknowledged to himself that something has gone wrong and has figured out how to improve in the future, there's no reason to demand a verbal confession as well. To do so only increases defensiveness.

Closed questions, those that could be answered with yes or no, should also be avoided. Questions such as "Do you think you can do this?" or "Is it possible to reverse this trend?" fall into this category. When the only answer you receive is a yes or a no, the communication channel closes, and you have to begin all over again. Instead, ask open-ended questions, those that require some sort of *active* response. A question like "Which of these solutions are you recommending?" demands such a response from the listener. Thus, the conversation continues, and, as it does, both participants can build the positive steps that will lead to a solution of the problem.

It's also important to avoid questions that begin with *why* or *who*. When we ask somebody, "Who said to do that?" or "Why did the drop occur?," it sounds as though we're trying to blame someone. And, quite naturally, the person who senses he's being blamed becomes defensive. If it's important to find out, for example, who is accountable for something, start by posing neutral kinds of questions, those that ask *what, when, where, how,* and *which.* Because neutral questions rarely trigger a defensive reaction, they keep the discussion on a more positive note.

The two best words to begin questions of this type are *what* and *how*. "What can we do to counter the slowdown in the economy?" and "How can we overcome the effects of the competition?" are both future-oriented, open-ended, and neutral questions. They ask the person to look ahead to the future to see how something can be improved. They require an active response on the part of the listener. And they're neutral.

Note, too, that these questions both have the word we in them. There are several reasons for this deliberate use of *we*. First of all, it promotes the idea of a team. After all, you and your subordinate are in this thing together, and it's up to the two of you to help the subordinate out of the pickle. Additionally, there might be something you could do differently that would help the subordinate straighten out the situation, and, unless you phrase the question to include yourself, the subordinate might be reluctant to tell you exactly what you could do to help alleviate the problem.

It's also important at this point to specify any limitations or parameters within which you have to operate, such as a budget, company policies, or union contracts. You might want to define these limitations before you ask the future-oriented, open-ended, neutral question. Here are two ways to do so: "Within the pricing policy we presently have, how can we counter the slowdown in the economy?" or "What can we do to overcome the effects of the competition and still stay within our credit guidelines and new account policy?"

7. *Reinforce the subordinate's positive statements with either a specific reinforcing statement or a nonverbal reinforcement*. This will increase the probability that the individual will continue to come up with good ideas, both in this and future discussions.

| Surbordinate Says | Manager Says |
|---|---|
| We could try a new point-of-purchase advertising approach. I've been noticing that the materials we're presently using get bent out of shape easily. | Mary, that's an excellent suggestion. This is the type of thing that's going to improve our sales right where the rubber meets the road. |
| If we made up one scrap bin for the first shift and a separate one for the second shift, we would eliminate some of the bickering between shifts about who's responsible for scrap. | Bill, that's the kind of thinking that will not only reduce scrap but will help us improve teamwork and communication. Those are the types of things we need to work on continuously, no matter how good they are now. |
| I'm pretty sure that this new promotion will help improve dealer relations. | Nancy, I like that sort of enthusiasm for a new project. Commitment and creativity like that really make sense. |

If we changed the form so we could gather information for the report on Friday, it could be processed over the weekend and be ready for everyone on Monday morning.

Sam, creative thinking like that is important in a position of responsibility like yours.

Nonverbal reinforcements, such as nodding at the appropriate times, smiling when somebody suggests something possible, increasing eye contact, and leaning forward slightly toward the speaker, all serve to bolster confidence and encourage creativity. Too many managers overlook the importance of reinforcing their subordinates nonverbally, yet it's a very powerful technique. [A psychologist once asked participants in a research project to call out two-digit numbers—22, 13, 47, 92, and so on—at random. Every time someone called out a number that ended in 9 (such as 19, 29, 39), he nodded and smiled slightly. Before long, he was able to double the frequency that participants called out double-digit numbers ending in 9!]

Just as nonverbal cues can be used to indicate positive expectations, they can also be used for positive reinforcement. Positive expectations increase the probability that somebody will engage in a behavior the first time. And positive reinforcement increases the probability that the person will engage in that same desired behavior again. Thus, by using nonverbal signals as a basis for reinforcement, you increase the probability that an individual will continue to come up with ideas on how the performance problem can be resolved.

8. *Consider any solution that meets the criteria.* This is not the time to evaluate each solution. Just write down all the subordinate's suggestions, using the original wording when possible. This is perhaps one of the more difficult steps for a manager to complete successfully. The tendency is to jump in and explain why particular ideas the subordinate offers won't work. The wackier the subordinate's idea is, the more tempted the manager is to declare, in no uncertain terms, that they couldn't possibly work.

Now's the time to formulate specific steps or behaviors the subordinate can undertake to get performance back on track. If the person you're talking to offers only vague, generalized responses and perhaps even blames somebody else for the existing problems, try posing neutral questions beginning with *what* or *how* to pin down specifically what he's talking about. Remember, when people are under stress, their ideas may reflect some of that stress and frustration. That's okay. Just respond as neutrally as possible, get the ideas down on paper, then go back and decide which ones you'll be able to implement. No doubt your questions and the subordinate's answers will resemble somewhat the following examples.

| | |
|---|---|
| *Manager*: | How can we improve customer relations? |
| *Subordinate*: | We can try to get the sons of bitches in shipping to do their job. [general blame] |
| *Manager*: | What specifically did you have in mind for them to do? |
| *Subordinate*: | They don't send us shipping notices in time. [specific behavior] |
| *Manager*: | Okay, that's a possibility; we could get them to give us more lead time when they send us shipping notices. |

| | |
|---|---|
| *Manager*: | How could we increase the sales volume measured on a unit basis? |
| *Subordinate*: | We could drop the price by 20%. That should really increase sales. |
| *Manager*: | One possibility then is to reduce the price. What else? |

| | |
|---|---|
| *Manager*: | How could we get turn-around time back to where it was? |
| *Subordinate*: | We could hire more people to handle the work load. |
| *Manager*: | That's at least an option. Let's put it down. |

| | |
|---|---|
| *Manager*: | What could we do to reduce the absenteeism on the second shift? |
| *Subordinate*: | We could double the shift premium. |
| *Manager*: | That might not be possible under present policies. But since we didn't set that as a parameter, we'll put it down as a possible option. |

Notice that, in each of these situations, the emphasis is on keeping the ideas flowing. We're not trying to evaluate the ideas or suggestions or even obtain a commitment to them at this point. All we're trying to do is get the subordinate talking about options and alternatives that will get things back on track. The more that individual talks and the less you talk, the greater the number of ideas that the employee will offer. That's a significant plus because the individual who comes up with an idea has a sense of "owning" it. By feeling this sense of ownership, the person who originally formulated the idea will work harder to get the idea adopted and put into effect. That's one reason it's important to put the ideas down in the subordinate's own words. The closer you come to using the exact words the subordinate uses, the more ownership the subordinate will have in an idea and the greater the likelihood for its success.

9. *When excuses are offered, respond with a neutral question*. Excuses generally appear in one of the three situations:

- An uncontrollable variable is blocking success

- We slip and ask the wrong kind of question

- The person responds defensively

In each situation, your response should be the same: you should come back with another open-ended, future-oriented, neutral question. This kind of response puts the conversation back on a positive track, and soon you are once again both looking for constructive ideas rather than concentrating upon faults, deficiencies, weaknesses, and past history. Here are some examples of less-than-desirable subordinate comments followed by neutral questions designed to get the conversation moving forward again.

---

*Manager*: How can we get sales back up to where they should be?

*Subordinate*: Well, I don't know what we could do. Sales are down everywhere.

*Manager*: I've noticed that too, but how can *we* counter the effect of dropping sales here at the Modular Corporation?

---

*Manager*: How can we improve our turn-around time?

*Subordinate*: Damned if I know. No one else seems to care.

*Manager*: Well, how can we get them to *start* caring?

---

*Manager*: What can we do to improve quality in department 14?

*Subordinate*: We can't. It's the supplier's fault that quality's no good.

*Manager*: Well, how can we get the *supplier* to improve his quality?

---

*Manager*: What can be done to get more geophysicists on board here?

*Subordinate*: Geophysicists are scarcer than hen's teeth. Everybody's having trouble finding geophysicists.

*Manager*: Well, what can we do to get more than our share in *our* company?

---

You should keep three goals in mind during this part of the discussion. Your first goal is to encourage the subordinate to come up with ideas. Initially, you don't care whether the ideas are really great, just okay, or completely screwball; the key thing is to start and maintain a flow of ideas. If enough ideas are generated, chances are good that at least one or two of them can be used as the basis for solving performance and/or production problems.

Secondly, you want to concentrate on those ideas that show some promise. Once these ideas are flowing, you'll have to start steering the subordinate in a more practical direction. Your goal here is the articulation of ideas that have a real possibility of paying off, and you reach it by strongly reinforcing those ideas that seem to have more merit than others. All ideas, however, should be reinforced both with positive statements and nonverbal body language, such as eye contact, smiles, nods, and other conciliatory gestures.

Finally, you want to obtain the subordinate's commitment to the best of these ideas. That's what step 10 is all about.

10. *Obtain commitment to the target*. What you're really doing here is "closing the sale": you're getting the individual to commit to accomplish a certain task or reach a certain level by an agreed-upon date. By this time, you should have been able to outline five or six possible ideas for resolving the subordinate's problems. When you feel you've got most of the alternatives out on the table, you can work to obtain the subordinate's commitment to reaching a particular goal and getting things back on target. Here, again, you may have to ask several future-oriented, open-ended, neutral questions to obtain that final commitment.

Let's assume that sales are averaging 80, and you'd like them back up to 110. There are several ways the ensuing question-and-answer dialogue might go. Here, for instance, would be an ideal:

| *Manager*: | Which of the steps or combination of steps you've suggested would move us from 80 to 110 the quickest? |
|---|---|
| *Subordinate*: | Well, I think that, by combining the idea of point-of-purchase materials with the one about selecting five or six high potential accounts where we don't have much penetration, we would reach our target in a hurry. |
| *Manager*: | Those both sound good, Mary. How long would it take us to get to 110 if we put those into effect right away? |
| *Subordinate*: | I think we could get there in three months. |
| *Manager*: | That sounds like a realistic target date to me. Let me just see if I can summarize what we've talked about here. [Summarize the conversation.] |

Clearly, this exchange illustrates an ideal way to get the commitment. Mary has readily agreed to the target and the date by which you wanted to reach it. Note how the first question was phrased: "Which of the steps or combination of steps you've suggested would move us from 80 to 110 in the least amount of time?" As soon as Mary answers that question, she is already committed to the target of 110. The question then is not *whether* to reach 110 but *how long* it's going to take to get there. The only item left to discuss is a realistic target date. The issue of the target itself has been settled.

Let's look now at another way of getting almost as good a commitment, using a different type of response.

| | |
|---|---|
| *Manager*: | Which of the steps or combination of steps you've suggested would move us from 80 to 110 in the least amount of time? |
| *Subordinate*: | We can't get to 110. |
| *Manager*: | Well, how close do you think we can get? |
| *Subordinate*: | I think we can get to 100. |
| *Manager*: | Which of your suggested solutions do you think will get us there the fastest? |
| *Subordinate*: | Well, I think using new point-of-purchase material and looking at the five or six high-potential accounts where we don't have the penetration would be best. |
| *Manager*: | If we put those two ideas into effect, Mary, how long do you think it will take us to reach 100? |
| *Subordinate*: | Probably somewhere between three and four months. |
| *Manager*: | Okay, let's say that we'll get to 100 in three or four months. Just so we have an exact date to live with, do you think it would be closer to three, three and a half, or four months? |
| *Subordinate*: | I think I feel more comfortable with four months. |
| *Manager*: | Okay, good. Let's agree that we'll get back up to the level of 100 four months from now. |

Notice that, in this situation, we didn't get quite such an enthusiastic commitment as we did in the previous one. Nonetheless, it's clear that the subordinate is involved in the issue and committed to solving the problem. Once somebody commits himself to accomplishing something by a certain time, the momentum to do so starts to build. As soon as Mary makes a little bit of progress and is subsequently reinforced for it (chapter 7), she will continue to do an even better job of selling. In the majority of cases, both Mary 1 and Mary 2 will end up at about the same point and after about the same amount of time, even though Mary 2 was a little hesitant to make a commitment to her boss.

11. *Summarize and express confidence in the subordinate's ability to handle the situation*. In this step, you will briefly reiterate the key points you and the subordinate agreed upon and express your positive expectations. You might say, ''Well, Mary, I think we've agreed that the new point-of-purchase materials and the targeting of five or six key accounts will get us back up to 110 in four months. I know you have the skills to do this, and I'm confident in your ability to use them in the field.'' Your concluding statement doesn't have to be long, but it should be positive and it should indicate to the subordinate that you have confidence in his or her ability to hit the target and hit it on time.

12. *Set a date to meet again*. Frequently, both manager and subordinate will forget to get back together again to discuss where they've been, where they are going, and how things are progressing. This lapse is unfortunate because the individual whose performance was lagging probably needs more immediate feedback than he's been receiving in the past, at least until things get back on target. It's also important for you to remind the subordinate that the issue you've just discussed isn't something to be taken lightly. The best way to make sure that both these things take place is to agree upon a specific date to get together and talk about progress.

**After the Discussion**

13. *Make sure you keep any promises you make*. During the course of the heart-to-heart conversation, you probably asked if there was anything you could do to help get things back on target. If the subordinate comes up with some reasonable suggestions and if you agreed to provide some help, make sure that you follow up on that. This isn't to suggest that you should do the subordinate's job for him but that you should hold up your end of any bargain you made. Your conscientious effort to do what you said you would will help strengthen the subordinate's resolve to do the same.

14. *Check milestone dates and progress*. This includes meeting at the time agreed upon at the close of the original discussion. Just as in the goal-setting and action-planning process, the heart-to-heart talk should include agreement on specific dates and milestones that are to be reached by those dates. Subordinates are quick to suspect that what they are working on isn't really very important if no one seems interested in it or them. And if you fail to meet with them at the agreed-upon time or fail to check with them about their progress on the scheduled milestone dates, they are bound to interpret your forgetfulness as indifference.

15. ***Finally, reinforce any and all improvements on the part of the subordinate.***
Even after a poorly prepared and executed heart-to-heart discussion, a subordinate's performance will improve just slightly because of the increased pressure from above. However, if that improvement in performance isn't reinforced, it quickly dissipates. A good heart-to-heart talk, one based on the principles and techniques in this chapter, almost always leads to an immediate improvement. As soon as this improvement is apparent, reinforce it. When you do, the improvement will continue and often even accelerate. And, before you know it, your "problem" employee is back on track.

Even after a poorly prepared and poorly executed heart-to-heart discussion, a subordinate's performance will improve just because of the pressure. There may not be much of a change, but it will occur.

After a well prepared and well executed heart-to-heart discussion, there is usually an immediate improvement of some substance. If you study and apply the techniques in this chapter, you'll find that most of your coaching and counselling sessions will go quite well.

But keep in mind that whether the session is poorly done or well done, it is only the "antecedent" to a new behavior pattern. While the session probably occurred as the consequence of a previous behavior that was not so desirable, it is more importantly designed to generate new behavior. In terms of the ABCs of behavior described on page 106 in chapter six, steps three, four, and five (pages 178-182) are consequences of the previous behavior. Step five, in particular, is a consequence.

But steps six through twelve (pages 182-190) are the *antecedents* to the new behavior that you're seeking. The ABC model from page 106 can be linked together as a series of ABC models. In terms of the counselling techniques we're examining here, it would look something like this *without the consequence for the new behavior*.

| FIRST ANTECEDENT | OLD BEHAVIOR | FIRST CONSEQUENCE/ANTECEDENT | SECOND | NEW BEHAVIOR |
|---|---|---|---|---|
| *Doesn't matter for this example* | *Late reports* | *Counselling session* | | *Timely reports* |

If there is no positive consequence for the change in behavior, it won't last. Go back and review the diagrams on page 130. If we put counselling into the model as the antecedent, assume a new behavior, and leave off any reinforcement for the new behavior, we'd get something like this.

| ANTECEDENT | BEHAVIOR | CONSEQUENCE | PROBABLE OUTCOME |
|---|---|---|---|
| *Employee is counselled about timely reports.* | *Reports come in on time.* | *Nothing* | *Employee will revert to old behavior of submitting late reports* |

What's being suggested is that counselling sessions are more than important — they're necessary. Doing them well involves planning. Doing them well also involves the use of certain behavioral skills which can be learned. One of those skills is the use of reinforcement during the counselling session.

But the counselling session is only a short term shot in the arm. Without the proper followup reinforcement, the new behavior will be extinguished and the old behavior will reappear.

# 12 | What to Do Now

Well, there they are—the tools, techniques, and concepts you can use to grow people into Self-Starters. So what do you do now? What do you do tomorrow that you didn't do yesterday? Ideas, after all, are of little value in and of themselves. They become useful only when they're implemented and acted upon. That's why, in this last chapter, I want to help you implement the ideas I've put forth so they'll pay off for you and your organization.

**Commitment Is Key**    There are several things you can do to make sure you get off on the right foot. First, commit yourself to the idea that the Self-Starting Mechanism is going to work for you. The most visible type of commitment you can make is simply to start practicing some of the techniques of the Self-Starting Mechanism *yourself*. Few things seal the doom of a new project more surely than a boss who says, "I want everybody to practice what we learned from this seminar [course, book, manual, or whatever]," and who then obviously disregards the new material himself. Actions speak louder than words, and if you want your staff to employ the techniques that compose the Self-Starting Mechanism with *their* subordinates, then you'd better use them yourself—visibly and enthusiastically.

Next, obtain commitments from those around you who can affect the ultimate success you enjoy in using the Self-Starting Mechanism. If you have a boss, seek some type of commitment from him or her. While it's important that your *own* commitment be wholehearted, it's not necessary to get as firm a commitment from your superior. Chances are, your boss will respond in one of five ways to your request to install the Self-Starting Mechanism.

1. This sounds like a good idea. I like it. I'll buy my own manual, read it, and practice the techniques myself. I want to be involved.

2. It sounds like a good idea. Go ahead and try it and let's see how it works. If you need anything from me, just let me know.

3. It seems like something that *might* work. Try it and we'll see what happens.

4. I think you're crazy, but you can try it by yourself if you want.

5. No.

The amount of commitment and support you need depends upon the degree of autonomy you enjoy within your work environment. If you are quite autonomous, all you need is one of the first four levels of commitment. You might be able to introduce certain Self-Starting techniques even if your boss flatly refuses to support you, but it would be difficult, and it could strain your relations with him or her irreparably.

You might also want to obtain the support of a union organization, especially if you're going to use these techniques in a union environment. It's helpful to explain to representatives of the union what you plan to do in order to involve members in the practical application of the techniques. These techniques have been used in organizations involving most major unions, and the response has always been positive or, at least, neutral. The weakest commitment we ever obtained was from a local that said, "We won't interfere with what you're doing." Granted, that's not a very strong commitment, but at least it was a commitment not to sabotage our efforts.

**You Set the Tone**    Look at your organization, company, or department as a pond. Whatever you drop into that pond is going to spread and affect the entire microcosm. If you're surly, think everyone else is dumb, assign conflicting responsibilities, fail to clarify authority, and give inadequate or only negative feedback, then your disagreeable attitude is going to permeate your entire work unit. If, by contrast, you communicate positive expectations to people and about people, establish clear-cut goals and creative action plans, assign authority to go with responsibility, establish feedback systems so people quickly know how they are doing, applaud their efforts, and use appropriate counseling techniques when performance problems arise, then your subordinates will follow suit. Others in the department will likewise have positive expectations. They'll make sure that responsibilities are identified; they'll work toward goals with clear-cut action plans; and they'll applaud each other. As a result, your team will be a winning one.

It's up to you to set the tone. As managers, we frequently underestimate the impact we have upon the rest of the organization. We're unaware of the fact that much of what we say or do is watched and frequently emulated by others within our unit. The performance of people in any individual work group closely reflects that of the person in charge. So decide what type of climate you want and then go about creating it.

**Not a Program**    Think of the Self-Starting Mechanism as a way of life, not a temporary program, and use it to obtain what I call SSP, or sustained superior performance. If you use the Self-Starting Mechanism to achieve SSP, then those programs that you do introduce will work more successfully.

**5-90-5** Remember 5-90-5. Out of every 100 employees, there's a 5-90-5 ratio. Five percent of your employees are tops. They are Self-Starters in every sense of the word—dependable, responsible, cooperative, and highly motivated *and* motivating. Even if you wanted to, you couldn't do anything to dampen their enthusiasm. Should their momentum ever wane, a judicious application of the Self-Starting Mechanism will revive them fast.

The middle 90% of the employees are the ones we're really trying to touch with the Self-Starting Mechanism. That 90% can be very good, or they can be terrible. It all depends on you. The bulk of all employees makes up this percent, and that's where the most noticeable improvement should take place.

Another 5% of your employees are the drags in the organization. The complete opposite of the Self-Starters, they complain, they cause trouble, they demotivate, and they have a negative effect upon the organization. They shouldn't be there—but they are. The Self-Starting Mechanism will probably change them a little bit, but it may not be worth the effort.

Remember, the Self-Starting Mechanism doesn't always work on all people. Usually, but not always. Some people seem impervious, and even if you hit them over the head, figuratively, they barely respond. My advice is, get rid of those employees if you can. That allows you to concentrate your efforts on the 90%, where the real payoff lies.

**Push versus Pull** A plant manager who had a quality goal of 145 for his plant explained the Self-Starting Mechanism to me this way: "I can *push* this plant from wherever it is to 115, but our goal is 130, and to get the plant to a consistent level of 130, I have to *pull* it. That's where these techniques of yours help enormously. You can only push so far; then you have to start pulling. And your techniques help me do just that."

He was right. You can push a manufacturing, sales, research, branch, distribution, or any other kind of organization only to a certain point; then you have to start pulling. The Self-Starting Mechanism pulls that last little bit out of the organization.

But you can also use the Self-Starting Mechanism in conjunction with push techniques. There's nothing in this manual that says you can't tell somebody to do something. In fact, you can and should. That's part of a manager's job. You might, for example, tell somebody *what* you expected in terms of results (goals) and also tell him or her *how* you wanted the goals to be reached (action plans). That's push. In a number of situations, it's also good common sense. You can increase the probability of people starting off in the right direction by communicating your needs. You can also increase the probability of them moving quickly by communicating positive expectations about their success. Once they start to move, you then reinforce. Positive expectations start progress; positive reinforcement sustains progress. Neither positive expectations or positive reinforcement preclude you from giving somebody a little push in the right direction.

**Right to Fail**   Unless people have a right to fail, they can never be fully accountable for their own actions. And if they're not accountable for their own actions, they lack one of the three elements that distinguishes Self-Starters.

In a misguided effort to help people succeed, we too frequently take away the possibility that they might fail. But if someone never fails, he either isn't trying new things or we are artificially supporting his efforts. Instead, you should let them fall down and scrape their knees once in a while. Only then can they learn which behaviors are inappropriate and which are not. If we remove the potential consequence of failure, we also have taken away crucial learning opportunities. And when we deprive employees of these opportunities to learn, we produce not Self-Starters but individuals whose ability to succeed depends upon our ability to remove at least one negative consequence of their behavior.

I'm not suggesting that you *encourage* people to fail. Nor am I suggesting you knowingly let them fail where the consequences to the individual or the organization are going to be disastrous. However, there are situations where people can learn from small failures and can correct those failures before they hinder the organizations. Let people stub their toes once in a while; they'll learn to tread more carefully in the future.

**Be Prepared for Success**   One of the big dangers in developing Self-Starters is that you'll probably succeed. Normally, success is no problem, but are you ready for someone on your staff to tell you to bug off because he or she can handle a particular problem without any help from you? Perhaps you are. But, nonetheless, you'd better prepare yourself for this eventuality because it's bound to happen once you've successfully developed some true Self-Starters.

Too many of us get considerable satisfaction from solving our subordinates' problems. You know the types of problems; they're the "tough ones that only you or I can really handle"—or so we think. Most people have what George Odiorne, professor of management at the University of Massachusetts, refers to as "occupational hobbies." These are tasks that a manager performs but which, in reality, belong to someone two to three levels below that individual in the organization. Think, for example, of the national sales manager who personally closes sales, the production manager who checks parts, or the head librarian who peruses every card in the file.

The sequence of occupational hobbies usually goes something like this:

1. The manager sees that the subordinate is having a problem.

2. The manager pushes the subordinate aside and solves the problem.

3. The subordinate says, "Thank you. That was a tough problem, and you sure did a good job of solving it."

4. The manager admits that the problem was tough, acknowledges the accolades from the subordinate and others in the area, and proudly strides off.

One of two things usually happens as a result of an encounter like this. For one, the subordinate might be angry that the boss interfered with the completion of the task or the solution of the problem. The subordinate may not articulate these feelings, but they're there. The subordinate, feeling that the boss didn't have confidence in him or her, either consciously or unconsciously begins to react to those negative expectations.

On the other hand, the subordinate might be glad that the boss has undertaken a burdensome chore. The surbordinate who reacts this way has learned the common technique of upward delegation. Every time the subordinate confronts a difficult problem, he or she takes it to the boss to solve. Nobody grows in this situation. Certainly not the subordinate, whose problems are being solved by the boss. And the boss doesn't grow either because he's too busy solving the subordinate's problems and has no time left to learn new skills himself. Never do something for someone they can or should do themselves. (Unless it's just a quick favor like picking up a report on your way over.) If you do, you shrink them and you shrink yourself.

A sure sign of a Self-Starter is that he does his *own* job. You can tell when employees are becoming Self-Starters because they stop thanking you for interfering in the completion of their tasks, and they stop delegating upward. So you'd better be prepared for that initial shock when they first tell you to stay away.

Dick was one manager who wasn't fully prepared. Dick, whose background was in manufacturing, now admits that he probably spent too much time second-guessing his director of manufacturing. Soon after Dick began using the Self-Starting Mechanism, he found that his staff in general and the director of manufacturing in particular were starting to grow. Tim, the manufacturing director, was now performing tasks that were rightfully his but that previously had been Dick's responsibility. Dick could hardly resist offering suggestions and tips, even though Tim was doing a superior job in Dick's former position.

Finally, Tim told Dick that if he, Dick, wanted to be the director of manufacturing, he should fire Tim from that position. Dick was offended by Tim's words. "But, you know," he said later, "Tim was right. Since I've backed off, he's grown even more in the job. He could take over my job right now, and I honestly look forward to the day he does because it'll give me the opportunity to grow on my own."

Not all managers are as malleable as Dick. Some are bothered by strong subordinates, whom they see as potential threats, as people who could push them aside and take over some of their own tasks. If you see subordinates that way, don't try to develop Self-Starters. One of the few "disadvantages" of these techniques is that they *work*. So be sure you're ready for the impact of their success before you start using them.

**Grow Risk Takers**  Use the techniques to encourage risk taking. But know, before you do so, that people who try new things make mistakes. In fact, people who try new things usually make *more* mistakes than people who don't take risks. Organizationally, we tend to punish mistakes, and we seldom reinforce the effort of risk taking.

In some quarters, however, risk taking is encouraged. According to Jesse Phillips, president of Phillips Industries, "We don't criticize people for making the wrong decision; we criticize them for not making a decision. I expect our people to do their homework, to put in the time they need to make the decision, but if the decision turns out to be wrong, we pick up the pieces and continue." A posture such as this, particularly on the part of the company's president, encourages risk taking.

Certain elements of the Self-Starting Mechanism can be used to encourage risk taking.

1. You can communicate positive expectations about success. Remember, of course, that these expectations should be realistic and should not be unduly optimistic about the probability of success.

2. You can assign people specific responsibilities. Reach mutual agreement on goals and ask them to develop *creative* action plans that will help reach those goals.

3. Reinforce any and all reasonable risk taking, even if it leads to an occasional failure. This doesn't mean you want to reinforce failure, but you can say things like, "I'm sorry that idea didn't work out, Mary, but it was a good try. Keep coming up with ideas, and pretty soon we'll find one that will work."

Remember that positive expectations and positive reinforcement are two different things. Sure, both are positive, but positive expectations are expressed *before* somebody does something and positive reinforcement occurs *after* somebody does something. Positive expectations start people off in the right direction, and positive reinforcement strengthens the behavior and ensures that it will take place again.

When you approach risk taking positively and without apprehension, people learn several things.

1. From the feedback and reinforcement you give them, they learn that the boss wants them to try new things.

2. They learn that they are accountable for trying new things in their areas of responsibility. This accountability results from agreeing upon the

goals and then concentrating on creative action plans that will help reach them.

3. People learn that it's better to try new things and fail than not to try at all. They learn that people who never try the new and different aren't growing and that growing is an important part of fulfilling their own job responsibilities.

4. They learn that, by taking steps, professional success can become a reality. As people try new ideas, they'll see that some will work and some won't. If you help them through those situations, they start to identify the factors that led to success and the factors that led to failure. As they become familiar with those factors, they will produce new ideas that will be more likely to succeed because they now know how to separate the good ideas from the impractical ones.

As people learn *how* to take risks, they learn to minimize their losses and maximize the potential of their new ideas. They learn how to capitalize on opportunity. And these are all things that can only be learned by taking some degree of risk.

## Don't Be Afraid to Be Tough

There's nothing wrong with being tough. In fact, it's often appropriate. The Self-Starting Mechanism isn't based on "human relations techniques," although its use does improve relations among humans. The Self-Starting Mechanism is an approach to growing people and that in itself is a tough assignment.

Sometimes we have to push people off dead center to get them moving in new directions. Here's how one manager talked tough and helped his subordinates grow as a result.

*Manager*: That machine's gotta be fixed by tomorrow. I'd like you to get all the crews in so that people are working on it 'til it's repaired. [assignment of responsibilities]

*Response*: I'm not sure we can do it. [questioning reasonableness of target]

*Manager*: Well, I think you can. In fact, I *know* you can. You're smart, you're good, and you've got top-flight crews that you've developed yourself. [communicating high expectations]

At this point, the manager might, if possible, communicate those same positive expectations directly to the crews. Then, after the repair job was successfully completed, he could reinforce their efforts.

*Manager*: I appreciate the effort you put in. You're a top-flight bunch of repairmen, and I knew you could do it. It was tough, but the extra effort you put in really brought it back on line by the time we needed it.

**Remember the Top Performer**

When you use these techniques with people who already are Self-Starters, it will make them even stronger. We sometimes tend to ignore the top performers. After all, they're already Self-Starters, so why bother? But by communicating high expectations and occasionally applauding their efforts, you make sure that they will *stay* top performers and Self-Starters.

**Avoid Culture Shock**

As you start to apply the techniques in this book, some people will be surprised and somewhat disoriented. There are several ways you can avoid or minimize the culture shock that may accompany your introduction of the techniques that make up the Self-Starting Mechanism.

First of all, change slowly. Set some goals for yourself on how you plan to start changing and where you want to end up. Take a few minutes to jot down some behavioral goals for yourself, some ways you'd like to change your own behavior. Remember, the process of shaping requires taking one step at a time. The same thing applies to changing your own behavior. Work conscientiously to change one behavior at a time; then move onto the next area you wish to improve. In the long run, this gradual but steady improvement is far better than a sudden reversal of old behavior patterns.

Second, learn to reinforce people for progress. A systematic way to do so is to keep track of how often you deliver feedback and what kind. On one side of a three-by-five card, put a +, and on the other side, put a −. For a week, keep track of how many times you give positive feedback and how many times you give negative feedback to those around you. If you're like most managers with whom I've worked, you'll find that your ratio is about one + to every three −'s. That is, for every one time you give positive feedback to somebody, you'll give negative feedback three times. Ideally, though, three positives for every one negative is the ratio you should maintain. To attain it, work gradually toward a ratio of one to two; then shoot for a ratio of one to one. Finally, try for a ratio of three positive comments for every one negative. If you're subtle enough, your employees won't be suspicious of the "new you" in terms of positive reinforcement.

The last technique for avoiding culture shock is perhaps the most important. Fortunately, it's quite simple: tell people what you're going to do. I suggest you share with your subordinates the bowling analogy in chapter 9. Explain to them the similarities between job motivation and sports motivation and tell them that you're going to introduce to the work place some of the same things that motivate people in sports. Invariably, this approach disarms people and makes them receptive to the techniques of the Self-Starting Mechanism.

If you take the time to tell people what you plan to do and for how long (indefinitely, in this case), you'll reduce the hazards of skepticism and culture shock, and you'll also lay a solid foundation for success.

**Using SSM with Other Developmental Efforts to Grow People**

Because the Self-Starting Mechanism is a way of doing the job, you can use it with specific developmental techniques. When you do, you will find that people will grow on the job even more rapidly than they would if you used the developmental technique without the help of the Self-Starting Mechanism.

*Training*

Training, of course, is one excellent way to develop people. Courses, seminars, workshops, and self-instructional programs are designed to train people to delegate, communicate, operate machines, sell more, sell better, supervise, interview, or any one of a hundred skills that might be useful within an organization. Unfortunately, training often "doesn't take." People learn the skill they're supposed to learn, but they don't use that same skill when they return to the job. Or if they do behave differently after they've been trained to do so, they behave that way for only a short period of time. Here's how you can use the three factors of the SSM to make sure your training "takes."

1. Call the prospective trainee into your office for a discussion about the upcoming training experience and about what's going to be involved in learning the new skill(s). During the conversation, communicate positive expectations about the learning situation and about his or her ability to learn new skills.

2. Assign the trainee some specific responsibilities in connection with the training. Ask him or her to concentrate on how the new skills will be incorporated into the job and to pick out at least three new ideas or skills he or she plans to bring back to the work place. Urge the individual to specify how each will be used on the job. Stress that this awareness should be one of the goals of the learning process. Then make an appointment to talk with the trainee about these three ideas and about how they'll be applied in a practical, constructive way.

3. After the training program is over, make sure you have the meeting in order to provide the initial feedback and reinforcement. If the trainees have picked out three ideas and developed some valid ways of applying those ideas on the job, reinforce them for their initiative. More important, make sure that, as they display those new behaviors, they are reinforced. Needless to say, you should let *all* employees know that trying out new skills is important.

By combining the three factors of the Self-Starting Mechanism and using them when dealing with trainees, you'll encourage employees to apply their new skills. Thus, you'll also help increase your return investment on training dollars.

*Task Force or Committee Assignments* Many managers assign employees to task forces or committees in order to help them grow and develop on the job. They see these assignments as a way to "cross fertilize" ideas and to encourage different departments to work together for the benefit of all. Should you decide to adopt this method of furthering cooperation among individuals and departments, I suggest you use the Self-Starting Mechanism to increase the probability that the task force or committee will be a productive venture.

1. As you talk to the individuals on the task force and/or committee as a whole, create an atmosphere of success. Let the participants know that you have high expectations for them. Let them know that they have been selected specifically because of their special skills or experiences and encourage them to share those experiences and skills with other members of the group.

2. Make sure that the group has specific goals. Don't make the task force or committee assignment so general that its members can't tell when they've completed whatever they set out to do. Furthermore, break the goals down into specific action plans, and assign the action steps to individual committee members. This encourages the participants to work together as a team to accomplish the overall goal and also ensures that committee members are individually accountable for their assignments.

3. Reinforce both individuals and the committee as a whole. Using two types of "applause," you can reinforce both general group behaviors—teamwork and cooperation—and personal learning growth on the part of each member. You can also reinforce the accomplishment of specific goals. By reinforcing all of these elements, you will positively influence the effect of the task force on both individual and organizational growth.

Remember, the Self-Starting Mechanism is based on three factors—expectations, the assignment of responsibilities, and feedback. When you apply these at both the individual and task-force level, you ensure not only that the task force accomplishes its overall goals but that it becomes a true developmental experience for individuals and the group as a whole.

*New Employee Orientation* New employee orientation is frequently a shambles. Most new employees learn about the job the same way they learned about sex—casually, erroneously, and generally from the wrong source. To make sure that your new employees get oriented properly and off in the right direction, you can again use the Self-Starting Mechanism.

1. Write out a "script" for the new employee orientation that's based on a positive approach—positive in terms of the industry, the organization, the department, and the new employee's responsibilities. If appropriate and feasible, communicate your positive expectations in person. If it's

not possible for you to do so in person, then have an appropriate representative do it, and make sure that the new staff members know that this person represents you in that particular situation. Neither you nor your chosen representative has to follow the script exactly, but if you prepare a general outline that you or someone else can follow, it increases the probability that positive expectations will be communicated.

2. Assign specific responsibilities for the orientation of the new employee. If a representative is going to introduce new employees to the company, make sure that certain responsibilities are assigned specifically to that person. Also, make sure that supervisors or coworkers responsible for the training communicate specific responsibilities to the employee who is being oriented. Too often, the initial assignment of responsibilities is vague and is communicated in a haphazard way. The more specific the assignment of responsibilities and the more these responsibilities are directed toward definite goals, the quicker the new employee will be able to fulfill those goals and obtain the results we're seeking. If appropriate, clarify the individual's level of authority, which probably will increase as the person gains experience on the job.

3. Make sure new employees have lots of feedback (information) about their job performance during their initial learning time. The more often they receive feedback, the more quickly they can pick up the appropriate job skills. Also, make sure they have lots of reinforcement (applause) during this initial time. This will help cement their newly learned skills and shorten their learning curve. If the newcomer works directly for you, make sure he or she receives both kinds of feedback—information and applause. If he or she works for a member of your staff, encourage that staff member to administer appropriate feedback. You, in turn, should reinforce the staff member for reinforcing the new employee. Thus, you'll be teaching a colleague to use the Self-Starting Mechanism as a tool for new employee orientation.

**Don't Try to Grow People Too Fast**

*Gradient Stress* is a term coined by Eugene E. Jennings, a professor at Michigan State University and an astute observer of the realities of organizational life. Jennings says that different people placed in different situations will be subjected to different amounts of stress.

What this suggests in terms of the Self-Starting Mechanism is that people will grow at different rates and that expecting too much of someone in a short period of time is often inappropriate. Figure 12–1 illustrates this phenomenon.

As you can see from the diagram, taking somebody from zero stress (no stress) to stress 1 or stress 2 helps that individual to stretch. He's growing on the job, and helping him grow is part of *our* job as a manager.

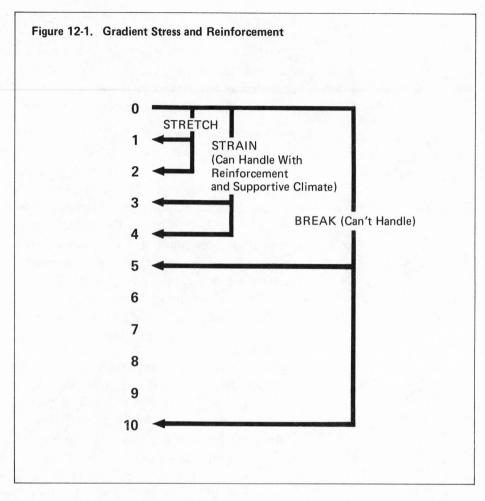

Figure 12-1. Gradient Stress and Reinforcement

If we take somebody from stress 0 to stress 3 or stress 4, the individual experiences a certain amount of strain. However, if the climate we provide is supportive and if we reinforce the individual sufficiently, he'll be able to handle that amount of change. If, however, we take somebody from zero up to 6 or above, that individual will quickly reach the breaking point, no matter how much support and reinforcement we provide.

Interestingly, once somebody becomes accustomed to stress level 4, that area then becomes stress level 1, which he can handle without even stretching. The gradient stress scale is, therefore, a sliding scale, and what would have been stressful to an employee six months before may not be stressful now if the person has consistently received enough support and reinforcement. With the passage of time, what was once stress level 8, 9, or 10 can become stress level 0. But only if we pace the person gradually, one step at a time, and only if we reinforce and support all along the way.

The purpose of this manual has been to show you that there are systematic ways to grow people. Much of what I've offered is based solidly on common sense. By systematically applying the commonsensical techniques I've formulated, you'll be able to grow Self-Starters, those top performers that every organization could use more of. Remember, companies that grow people grow profits. (The reverse, of course, is also true: if you shrink people, you shrink profits.)

Here's a checklist that you can use to review how you're doing. It can also serve as a general review of the entire book. Rank yourself from one to ten on each item with one being low and five being high.

_____ I make it a point to identify small changes in my behavior that produce a big change in job performance.

_____ I do the same for others.

_____ I believe in myself and convey those high expectations to others.

_____ I believe in most other people and communicate those positive expectations to those individuals.

_____ When communicating with people, I avoid comments about others which might be interpreted as having low expectations.

_____ When communicating with people, I make it a point to get everything lined up to have the maximum positive impact.

_____ People who work for me know exactly what their accountabilities are.

_____ Responsibility and authority get matched up well.

_____ I set both low and high targets for myself and for others.

_____ Our targets focus on outputs or results rather than on activities or behaviors.

_____ Goals are always backed up by a well thought out action plan.

_____ We have feedback both in the form of information and in the form of reinforcement.

_____ I make it a point not to ignore good performance.

_____ People who work for me are reinforced for progress as well as for excellence.

_____ When people get to a good solid level of performance I switch from continuous to intermittent reinforcement.

_____ When I do use punishment, it is appropriately used.

_____ I make it a point to check our performance feedback system every six months or so.

_____ Wherever possible, our performance indicators are graphed in an easy to read format.

_____ My counselling sessions are well planned out.

_____ I put to use many of the behavioral techniques described in chapter eleven.

Now total your score. A perfect score would mean that you got 100. It would also probably mean that you cheated. If you found yourself with a low score in one area, create a self development plan to correct it.

Also, remember as you start to grow other people into Self Starters, you'll find yourself growing. And that, after all, is what it's all about — growing ourselves as well as helping others grow. Good luck. And good growing!

**Key Learning Points from Chapter One**

1. People are the largest single controllable variable in virtually every business. Approximately 75% of each gross national product dollar goes to human efforts.

2. People frequently fail to perform up to their potential.

   a. Not everyone can be great, but everybody can be good.

   b. Most people can perform better than they are performing right now.

   c. We should concentrate on helping people improve rather than trying to make them excellent all at once.

3. The work ethic has not necessarily disappeared; rather the work force has changed and organizations have not adapted to that change.

4. The difference between the minor leagues and the major leagues in baseball is the difference between a 200 hitter and a 300 hitter. Self-Starters are not people who get a hit every time at bat, instead Self-Starters are people who hit a little more consistently than others.

5. In some fields, Self-Starters are firstborns.

6. Three factors separate the firstborn from laterborn children:

   a. We have higher expectations for them.

   b. They are given more responsibility.

   c. They receive more feedback and attention about their behavior.

7. The most important thing about the Self-Starting Mechanism is this: it is not whether or not somebody is firstborn that makes them a Self-Starter, it's whether or not the three factors have been, are, or can be put to work to determine the presence of the Self-Starting Mechanism.

8. Other sources for the Self-Starting Mechanism include the following:

a. Where there is an age differential of three or four years.

b. A manager or supervisor creates the environment.

c. An individual creates the environment.

d. A combination of some or all of the above.

9. The Self-Starting Mechanism is readily apparent in sports. People enjoy watching and involving themselves in sports because of the high expectations, the responsibility and the feedback.

   a. Neither professional nor amateur athletes would enjoy participating in sports if there were low levels of expectations.

   b. People would likewise not enjoy sports if sometimes the pitcher pitched the ball, sometimes the catcher pitched, sometimes the first baseman pitched, and sometimes you were out after two strikes and sometimes you were out after three strikes.

   c. Feedback has two aspects: the information aspect which tells people how they are doing and the reinforcement aspect which is the applause. Both of those also apply in sports, where people need information on how they are doing and like some applause to recognize their progress.

**Key Learning Points from Chapter Two**

1. Using the Self-Starting Mechanism is not an addition to the job; it's a way of doing your job.

2. It's an organized approach to common sense that works consistently.

3. The Self-Starting Mechanism focuses on behavior.

   a. General descriptions like "aggressive" or "motivation" are not very useful in helping people become Self-Starters.

   b. What is helpful is to be very specific about the behavior required (what you want somebody to do) to be more of a Self-Starter. The more specific you can be about the behavior you need from an individual, the higher the probability that they will become a Self-Starter.

4. Very small changes in behavior can lead to very large changes in terms of job results. This occurs because of the 20–80 principle. The 20–80 principle suggests that a 20% change in what somebody does might produce an 80% change in their job results.

5. Many of the ways of making people Self-Starters are based upon what good managers do naturally. The purpose of this manual is to help you understand why what you do works so that you can do it more consistently.

6. Self-Starters are consistently high performers who require a minimum amount of supervision, actively seek out growth, like new responsibilities and provide inspiration to others.

**Key Learning Points from Chapter Three**

1. Our expectations influence others—many times in subtle ways. The power of expectations is frequently referred to as the Pygmalion Effect.

2. If we expect something to happen, we tend to behave in a way that brings about that expectation. This influences not only our behavior, but the behavior of others.

3. Some of the things which affect our expectations include history, status or rank, sex, age, race and believability.

4. Placebos are sugar pills in medicine. People can also use "job placebos" to help them do the job.

5. High expectations bring about the beginning of strong performance but low expectations bring about the beginning of low performance.

6. Expectations can affect such personnel policies as testing, selection, performance appraisal and high potential lists.

7. Positive expectations are not the same thing as positive thinking. Positive expectations focus on translating what you think into doing something about it.

**Key Learning Points from Chapter Four**

1. Either high or low expectations can often be communicated inadvertently to people.

2. In terms of the total impact upon another individual, the words you use have an impact value of 5%, your vocal intonations have an impact value of 30%, your body language has an impact value of 45%, amount and type of interruptions have an impact value of 5%, proximity or distance has an impact value of 5% and the setting has an impact value of 10%. Words, vocal intonations and body language constitute the *message*. Interruptions, proximity, and setting constitute the *environment* in which the message is sent.

3. While words are not the most important part (5% impact value), it is nonetheless important to make sure that you say things positively rather than negatively. Because the subconscious mind frequently can't distinguish between positive and negative words, say things like "make sure to be on time" rather than saying "don't be late."

4. Vocal intonations can influence the message with an impact value of 30%. The old saying, "it's not what she said, it's how she said it" is true.

5. Body language is the most important part of the message. It constitutes 45% of the impact value.

6. The five primary body language categories are: a) position of the body itself, b) gestures that are used, c) head movement, d) facial expressions, and e) eyes.

7. Under environment, the primary factors that affect expectations are interruptions, distance and the setting.

8. The items that affect interruptions are: the type of interruptions, the number of interruptions, and the length of the interruptions.

9. Under distance, the four zones in which communications take place, are

   a) the intimate zone (0 to 18 inches), b) the personal zone (18 inches to four feet), c) the social zone (four feet to 12 feet), and d) the public zone (12 feet to infinity).

10. There are styles for communicating each of these zones and it's important to select the communication zone that is appropriate to the type of communication that is being delivered.

11. Developing Self-Starters means taking into account all the different variables that might affect expectations.

**Key Learning Points from Chapter Five**

1. Individual accountability does more to develop Self-Starters than group accountability.

2. Goals should focus on outputs or results rather than activities. Activities are what people do and results are what people accomplish.

3. Interviews show that failure to agree between boss and subordinate averages about 25% on key accountabilities and the results expected in each of those accountabilities.

4. The three steps to better goals are:

   a. Specifying key areas.

   b. Developing performance indicators.

   c. Establishing the goal itself.

5. The four classes of authority that might be delegated to an individual are:

   a. Full authority to take action and carry out the responsibility without consulting or reporting to an immediate supervisor.

   b. Full authority to take action to carry out a responsibility but inform immediate supervisor after the action is taken.

   c. Limited authority. Somebody presents recommendations and does not take action until a decision is reached.

   d. No authority. The individual should be merely familiar with the area of responsibility.

6. Studies show that people seldom agree on levels of authority. Self-Starters should gradually be moved up from the lesser levels of authority to higher levels of authority.

7. The criteria for writing good goals are to have:

   a. Specific end results.

   b. Realistic levels of accomplishment.

   c. Observable accomplishments.

   d. A completion date.

   e. Employee control over goal accomplishment.

8. Standards are minimum acceptable performance standards. Goals are breakthrough targets. Appraisals should be conducted against standards and goals should be used for growth and development.

9. Sometimes employees should be told what their goal is; sometimes they should be asked what their goal is, and sometimes they should be mutually negotiated. No one approach is correct.

**Key Learning Points from Chapter Six**

1. Accountability for goal accomplishment is not enough; there must also be accountability on how to reach the goal. Goals without action planning to reach those goals lead to missed goals.

2. Fifteen steps to better action plans are:

   a. Establish feedback systems.

   b. State each step specifically.

   c. Specify who is responsible.

   d. Identify communication and collaboration needs.

   e. Allow for involvement and initiative.

   f. Build stretch into the plan.

   g. Make sure the steps help your team tackle future problems.

   h. Encourage both individual and group action.

   i. Involve those who carry out the steps in developing the steps.

   j. Make sure the plan fosters creativity by Self-Starters.

   k. Don't take can't for an answer.

   l. Write down all the action steps.

   m. Develop a contingency action plan in case something goes wrong.

   n. Avoid killer phrases that stifle creativity and throw cold water on ideas.

   o. Use booster phrases that foster creative action planning.

**Key Learning Points from Chapter Seven**

1. Feedback consists of two elements:

   a. The informational aspect tells somebody how they are doing.

   b. The positive or negative aspect of feedback might be positive reinforcement for doing the right thing. It might also be negative in form, which would be like "booing" somebody at the game. Or it might be dead silence, which is no feedback at all.

2. We usually punish somebody when they do something wrong and ignore them when they do something right.

3. What we should be doing is punishing somebody when they do something really wrong, extinguishing them when they do something a little wrong and positively reinforcing them when they either do something right or make progress.

4. Reinforcement is something that comes *after* somebody does something. It is not the same as positive expectations. Positive expectations start somebody in the right direction; positive reinforcement makes sure they continue in that direction.

5. The recipient of the reinforcement decides whether it's actually reinforcing or not.

6. Immediacy of reinforcement is more important than intensity. A small amount of reinforcement at the right time has more of an impact in motivating somebody than a lot of reinforcement that is either delayed or comes at the wrong time.

7. We can reinforce either improvement or excellence. Frequently, people reinforce only excellence; however, when you reinforce progress and improvement as well as excellence, you get more progress and improvement. Why? Because *whatever you reinforce, you get more of*.

8. Continuous reinforcement is the best way to get somebody to develop a new skill. Continuous reinforcement is a situation where someone is reinforced virtually every time they do something.

9. Intermittent reinforcement, on the other hand, is like "slot machine" behavior, where people occasionally get reinforced. This is the best way to maintain momentum once somebody is up to a certain level.

10. An advantage of reinforcement is that it has a rippling pond effect within the organization.

11. Comfort zones and roller coaster (up and down) performance occur when somebody gets attention for dropping down to a certain level and no attention when they improve (see the diagrams in Chapter VII for a visual explanation).

12. Reinforcement should be specific. Too frequently we are very general about what is right with something and very specific with what's wrong with it. This helps people learn what's wrong with something, but doesn't help them learn what's right with something.

13. Avoid the "good, but..." syndrome. This is when we say something that's a little bit good and then a number of bad things.

14. The three different ways of delivering psychological income in the form of reinforcement are:

    a. Face to face encounter.

    b. Telephone.

    c. Written word, using either typewriting or handwriting. (A combination of typewriting and handwriting seems to work best.)

15. The ideal reinforcer has five characteristics. It is:

    a. of value to the individual receiving it.

    b. under the manager's control.

    c. immediate.

    d. reusable.

    e. of low cost to the organization.

16. The appearance of sincerity in reinforcement is more important than whether someone is actually sincere or not. Ethically or philosophically that has little appeal for most people, but as a matter of practicality, that's the way it works.

**Key Learning Points from Chapter Eight**

1. There are two primary ways of getting people to stop doing something.

    a. Tell them not to do it again, perhaps even tell them that with a large dose of punishment.

    b. Stop reinforcing the behavior you don't want.

2. Punishment has several advantages:

    a. It works at least in the short run.

    b. In situations where it is necessary to stop a behavior very quickly, punishment will work.

    c. It's useful when it's necessary to get somebody's attention.

3. The disadvantages of punishment are:

    a. Although it frequently works in the short run, it almost never works in the long run. People habituate to the level of punishment and it has no effect.

    b. It doesn't teach somebody what to do that's right.

    c. It frequently eliminates not only the behavior that we want to stop, but a number of associated and closely related behaviors as well.

    d. People will try to escape or avoid the source of punishment.

e. Too frequently, we set out to punish somebody but end up reinforcing them by paying attention to their undesirable behavior.

4. The guidelines for using punishment:

a. Make sure that it's immediate.

b. Make sure it follows every instance of the behavior that you don't want.

c. If you point the gun, be prepared to pull the trigger.

d. Try to keep a ratio of at least three positives to every negative.

e. Do it in private.

f. Talk about the behavior and job performance rather than the individual.

g. If punishment does work and the person's performance improves, reinforce the improvement.

5. Extinction works better than we imagine it would. Extinction is the same thing as not laughing at somebody when they tell a joke. It's ignoring the individual altogether. Unfortunately, one of the problems with extinction is that we usually ignore people when they do something right, rather than when they do something wrong.

**Key Learning Points from Chapter Nine**

1. The second aspect of feedback is the informational aspect. In a sports analogy, the informational aspect would be the yardline markers on a football field or the service line on a tennis court.

2. The seven check points for changing just information into a high impact performance feedback system are:

a. It should be related to a goal.

b. Make it self-administered.

c. Use a positive measurement unit.

d. Make the feedback immediate.

e. Make it relevant.

f. Don't use it as a basis for punishment.

g. Make it simple to use.

**Key Learning Points from Chapter Ten**

1. Graphing is a very important way of providing feedback. After three days, people remember 10% of what they hear, 20% of what they see and 65% of what they hear and see.

2. The simpler a graph is, the more useful it's going to be.

3. Goal areas can be built into graphs to encourage people to move from a low level to a high level while keeping their motivation up.

4. Just putting up graphs, however, has little long-term impact. Putting up the graph is merely providing information and unless progress is reinforced, on the basis of that information, people lose their motivation.

5. Graphs should foster a situation where people compete against themselves rather than compete against each other.

**Key Learning Points from Chapter Eleven**

1. If you have tried everything else in the manual, and performance is still not where you'd like it to be, a counseling session is in order.

2. There are three things to do before you have a counseling session with somebody:

   a. Make sure you've done everything in the preceding chapters to put the Self-Starting Mechanism in place.

   b. Decide how you're going to handle steps three through 12 of the counseling process.

   c. Position the discussion properly with the person that you are going to counsel.

3. The steps in the actual discussion are:

   a. Put the individual at ease.

   b. Describe the performance problem or deficiency factually using descriptive rather than evaluative statements.

   c. Use future-oriented neutral questions that begin with what or how.

   d. Reinforce any positive statements made by the subordinate with either verbal reinforcement or nonverbal reinforcement.

   e. Initially consider any soluton that meets the general criteria you've outlined for the solutions to the situation.

   f. When excuses are offered, respond with a neutral question and then move the employee in the proper direction.

   g. Obtain a commitment to the target.

   h. Summarize your discussion and express a high level of confidence in your subordinate's ability to handle the situation you discussed.

4. After the discussion:

   a. Make sure you keep any promises you make.

   b. Check milestone dates and progress against those milestones.

   c. Reinforce any or all improvements on the part of the subordinate.

   (This is the key to making the discussion pay off because, too frequently, we have such a discussion, the employee improves and we forget to reinforce the improvement.)

1. The four primary levels of commitment to using the Self-Starting Mechanism are:

   a. Actual involvement and support.

   b. Support but no involvement.

   c. Acknowledgement that the idea might work and encouragement to try.

   d. Permission to try the idea even though the person thinks it won't work.

2. You set the tone for your entire organization.

3. The Self-Starting Mechanism is a way of life rather than a program that comes to an end.

4. Remember the 5–90–5 rule.

5. Keep in touch with the push versus pull approach.

6. Give people the right to fail. People who have never failed usually haven't learned very much.

7. Be prepared for the situation arising after you've developed a Self-Starter, when they decide that they don't need you quite as much as they used to.

8. Watch out for your own "personal occupational hobbies."

9. Remember that appropriately using the Self-Starting Mechanism can help you grow risk-takers. Helping people to be risk-takers involves:

   a. Communicating positive expectations about success.

   b. Assigning specific responsibilties and creative action plans.

   c. Reinforcing any or all reasonable risk-taking even if it leads to failure.

10. People learning to be risk-takers go through five stages. These stages are:

    a. They learn you want them to try new approaches.

    b. They learn they are accountable for new ideas in their area of responsibility.

    c. They learn they shouldn't set out to make mistakes.

    d. They learn it's better to try new things and fail, than not to try at all.

    e. They learn that certain steps lead to a higher probability of success.

11. The Self-Starting Mechanism requires you to be tough from time to time. However, it's a mental toughness more than it's a physical toughness.

12. Remember to use the three factors of the Self-Starting Mechanism on people who are already Self-Starters. Sometimes we let them down by ignoring them altogether.

13. Use the 3 by 5 card approach to avoid cultural shock in your own organization.

14. Tell people what changes they can expect from you as a result of reading this manual. Don't be secretive; instead be open.

15. Use the Self-Starting Mechanism to maximize your developmental efforts from training, from task force or committee assignment and for new employee orientation.

16. Remember the rule of gradient stress in moving people one step at a time. Moving people one step at a time grows more people more quickly than trying to take people too far, too fast, and too soon.

17. Companies that grow people grow profits. Companies that shrink people shrink profits.

**Chapter 1**
1. How much does absenteeism cost American industry?
2. What percent of wage earners say they can accomplish more each day if they really tried?
3. What percent of our gross national product goes to some form of worker compensation?
4. What does every manager say at least once a day?
5. How do potential and performance match up in most organizations?
6. Has the work ethic really disappeared?
7. Are most Self-Starters firstborn?
8. What are the factors that lead people to be Self-Starters?
9. What are the sources that can activate the Self-Starting Mechanism?

**Chapter 2**
1. How much of the Self-Starting Mechanism is common sense?
2. How does the Self-Starting Mechanism affect attitude?
3. What is the relationship between the Self-Starting Mechanism and motivation?
4. How does the Self-Starting Mechanism meet both company needs and individual needs?
5. Why are some people who are Self-Starters not good at developing other people into Self-Starters?
6. How does the Self-Starting Mechanism relate to sustained superior performance?
7. What are the characteristics of Self-Starters?
8. What people who are highly motivated are a danger to their organization?

**Chapter 3**
1. How does the Self-Starting Mechanism work with underprivileged workers?
2. What impact did the first element of the Self-Starting Mechanism have upon the performance of an insurance company?
3. How does sex affect job performance?
4. How do subordinates respond to you?
5. How can placebos overcome a slump in sales?
6. Can people really change?
7. How does the Self-Starting Mechanism affect team performance?
8. What are the implications of the Self-Starting Mechanism for testing, selection, performance appraisal and high potential lists?
9. How do you affect others' behavior and job performance?

**Chapter 4**
1. Why are the words you say only 5% of the total message you send?
2. How can you take a positive approach when communicating with somebody?
3. How can you turn somebody off without intending to?
4. What effect do interruptions have on helping people grow?
5. What are the four primary zones people have for communication and how do you maximize the use of each?
6. How can you seat people so that team spirit is maximized?
7. To have a positive impact, where should you sit when communicating with subordinates?
8. How can you rate your own communication style?

**Chapter 5**
1. Why doesn't making everybody responsible for quality work?
2. How do people get so involved in getting there that they forget where "there" is?
3. What are the elements of a performance system?
4. How can the ball park be translated into business?
5. Why don't people seem to want to accept the responsibility they have been given?
6. How do you get people to use the authority they have been given?
7. How do you develop measurements for the unmeasurable?
8. What impact does the probability of success have on an individual's motivation level?
9. Do you set goals too high, too low, or just right?

3. Do you ever hit somebody over the head with a 2 x 4 to get their attention? If so, how?

4. Why don't people own up to their mistakes?

5. How do you get people to own up to their mistakes?

6. Why do people "filter" the information they give us?

7. How do you get people to give you unfiltered information?

8. How can sales awards sometimes backfire?

9. Why does trying to embarrass somebody into performing a task frequently not work?

10. What is even more punishing than punishment?

11. When should you use this interesting technique?

12. What is one condition that will cause this technique not to work?

**Chapter 9**

1. What is the relationship between bowling and job performance?

2. What are five elements that make a system complete?

3. How did a restaurant reduce its cutting yield from 33.5% to 31.5%?

4. How can you get people to begin to accept responsibility for their own performance?

5. How important is the timing of feedback?

6. How do you keep salesmen motivated and calling on accounts when it might be several months before those calls begin to pay off on the bottom line?

7. How can the Self-Starting Mechanism encourage scientific creativity?

8. What are four ways in which an organization gets pulled apart?

**Chapter 10**

1. Is the old saying that "one picture is worth a thousand words" really true?

2. Why do graphs work so well in motivating people?

3. What are two situations where graphs don't work?

4. What is the best type of graph to use?

5. How can the Self-Starting Mechanism foster healthy competition?

**Chapter 11**

1. How do you counsel somebody you want to make a Self-Starter?

2. What is the first thing you do during such a counseling session?

3. What is the difference between descriptive and evaluative counseling statements?

4. What type of question works best in obtaining a positive response from subordinates?

5. What are four responses you can make to a positive response of a subordinate?

6. What are the three situations that cause excuses to arise during counseling?

7. What are four ways to handle excuses when they do arise?

8. What are three things you can do after a counseling session to make sure that it takes hold?

**Chapter 12**
1. What are the five levels of commitment that people can make to the Self-Starting Mechanism?

2. What is Connellan's Rule of 5–90–5?

3. How can you get people to where you want them by pulling rather than pushing?

4. Should people be allowed to fail?

5. How do you develop risk-taking in subordinates?

6. Can you be tough and still develop Self-Starters?

7. How do you handle people who already are Self-Starters?

8. How can the Self-Starting Mechanism be used in conjunction with training, task forces and new employee orientation?

9. What happens when you try to develop people too quickly?

10. How can you make sure that you're not developing somebody too quickly?

# APPENDIX III
## Using the Self-Starting Mechanism to Improve Grades

Billy was flunking out of school. It was the third school he had been in in the last two years. He had been in a public school, a private school, and this was the second private school.

I had been doing some consulting work for his father, who was the president of a $60 million manufacturing firm.

Needless to say, Billy had a scholastic problem. Over dinner one night, Billy's father asked me if the Self-Starting Mechanism could be used to help keep Billy in school and improve his grade average.

While I'm not a child psychologist, I felt that the Self-Starting Mechanism could help Billy's situation. However, we did not have much time, for the next week was the beginning of the last marking period in the school year. Billy and his parents had been warned that if his grades did not show a significant improvement, he would not be readmitted in the fall. That evening, Billy's parents and myself sat down and mapped out a program to keep Billy in school.

Seven weeks later was the end of the marking period. Billy was still in school and had been readmitted for the fall. He was certainly not an all-A student. (In fact, he was only a weak D average student.) His marks were D-, D-, D and a C-, but that was a significant improvement over what he had been averaging the previous five marking periods and the school readmitted him. Here is what was done to keep Billy in school.

1. Billy's parents used the counseling techniques described in Chapter 11 to obtain from Billy a commitment to try and improve his grades. What they obtained was not a particularly strong commitment. However, in view of his past record, any commitment at all on his part was a big step in the right direction.

   During these discussions, they focused on behavior, rather than on Billy himself. Instead of saying, "Billy, how come you're so dumb in math?," they used future-oriented, open-ended questions that focused on grades such as, "How could we get the math grades up?"

2. They communicated positive expectations to Billy. Statements they used were, "I know you're better than you're doing." This separates Billy from his scholastic performance. He was, of course, still held accountable for his grades, but any negative communications focused upon his grades rather than himself. In addition, his parents made sure that all the nonverbal things they did matched the verbal positive expectations that were being communicated.

3. Billy and his parents started setting weekly goals. Billy had five classes in which he received grades. Every week, they set a goal for what his grade (on a scale from 0 to 100) would be at the end of that particular week. Notice that this is shortening the goal-setting cycle considerably from the normal six to seven-week interval that is used in grades. I decided that just as shorter goal-setting cycles are helpful for employees who are in trouble, shorter goal-setting cycles would make sense for kids who have trouble in school.

Weekly goals, however, do no good if the feedback is still received only every seven weeks. What was needed was a feedback cycle that matched the goal-setting cycle. So with the help of Billy's teachers, the feedback cycle (information) was shortened to weekly. Because weeks can be a long time away, teachers were asked to give Billy grades on a weekly basis.

Even if there was no homework or test given that week, teachers were asked to give Billy a grade based upon his responses in class and comments that he made. To make sure that this was easy for the teachers to do, they were all given postcards that were addressed and had typed on them "grade for (Spanish, math, etc.) for the week of _____." This gave immediate feedback in the form of information to both Billy and his parents on how he was doing.

4. Every positive step or action in the right direction or improvement was reinforced. If Billy was averaging 40 in math and set a goal for 50, he was reinforced for setting a stretch goal that required him to improve. If in this situation, he hit 44, he was reinforced for improving. If he hit 50, he was reinforced for both improving and hitting the goal. If he hit 52, he was reinforced for improving and for surpassing the goal. These are all short-term results. Of course, they focus on grades and improved grades is what we were after.

What is also important is *reinforcing behaviors* that we know are going to help achieve the results we are after. In Billy's case, these were study behaviors, so some weeks when he might have been at 40, set a goal for 50, and hit 38, he was reinforced for trying even if he missed his grade goal for that week. He was also reinforced if he was studying his homework upstairs or if he took time out on Saturday morning to check some homework. By reinforcing both results (grades on a weekly basis), and specific study behaviors (such as study in math or science), Billy was receiving reinforcement (applause) for both results and behavior.

I'd like to be able to tell you that Billy is now a straight-A student, but he's not. He is, however, a good, solid-C student and has recently entered his senior year in a public high school.

Nancy and Peter have spent more of their share of time fighting. Some fighting and bickering is normal among siblings, but over the past year or so, the amount of fighting by Nancy and Peter seemed to have increased to the point where it was quite irritating to their parents.

Their mother, Ruth, had attended a workshop for department heads that I conducted for one company. She approached me at coffee break and we talked about the three elements of the Self-Starting Mechanism. Curious if the same techniques applied in child management, she described the situation to me and asked if the Self-Starting Mechanism might be used to reduce the fighting and bickering between her children.

If you remember the description earlier in the manual about the Self-Starting Mechanism, we used the analogy of the three-legged stool. Each of the three traits of the Self-Starting Mechanism—expectations, goals and feedback (both information and reinforcement)—has to be present. Ruth's situation was an example where just one of the three legs was missing. That is, feedback was missing, and particularly the reinforcement aspect of feedback.

A simple question led to insight on her part. "When do the kids get more attention, when they fight or when they're good?" Her answer, of course, was that the children received more attention when they were fighting. As long as they were behaving, both Ruth and her husband tended to ignore the kids. However, when they fought, they received a great deal of attention from both the parents. Inadvertently, Ruth and her husband were reinforcing (by paying more attention) the bad behavior rather than the good behavior.

What Ruth and Jack did was to still speak to the children when they were fighting and state that fighting was not an acceptable type of behavior in their household. However, let's say this equals one unit of attention. Jack and Ruth made sure that when the children were not fighting, they received two to three units of attention. They were reinforced for playing well together. Specific comments such as, ''I'm glad to see the two of you getting along so well,'' were made and occasionally a tangible reinforcer was tied in.

An example of this might be, ''Say, the two of you are really getting along well this morning, let's go get an ice cream cone down at the corner.'' The behavior was significantly better inside of three weeks. Inside of two months, it was not only good, but was better than it had ever been since the children were old enough to interact with one another.

Phil was a branch manager for a wholesaler. Although the company was doing pretty well, Phil decided there were some areas in which the firm could improve its performance. He decided to use the Self-Starting Mechanism to tackle the sales area. In particular, he wanted to focus first on the inside salesmen, since approximately 60% of the company's busines came through the five inside salesmen.

Using the Achievement Climate Survey, he found out the following information:

1. The inside salesmen felt themselves to be the recipients of high expectations. Phil and others expected a great deal from the inside salesmen in the way of performance. Their expectations were not too high, but certainly involved some stretch.

2. Goals were unclear. Specific targets to hit were not negotiated nor were they communicated to the inside salesmen. There was generalized pressure from time to time to improve sales, but specific targets to hit on a daily, weekly, monthly basis were not articulated.

3. Feedback in the form of information was not as good as it could have been. There was little feedback in the form of information on the performance measures that really counted within the inside sales area.

   Feedback in the form of applause existed but only for outstanding performance. There was not reinforcement for improvement and there was no reinforcement for effort. This meant that the inside salesmen were receiving reinforcement only for excellence and not for improvement toward excellence.

With this information in hand, Phil was ready to make sure that all three elements of the Self-Starting Mechanism were in place. As you can see, the expectations were there in this situation, but goals could be improved, feedback in the form of information about goal progress could be improved and feedback in the form of applause and reinforcement could be improved.

Phil specified three goals that he wanted to reach. The first key area was cost control, and the indicator he selected was phone expense. The goal was "to reduce the phone expense from $3600 to $2700 a month by March 1."

The second key area that Phil selected was customer relations. The indicator that was selected was percent of time the phone was picked up by the third ring. Phil wasn't sure where he was on this, but a week of checking showed it to be about 21% to 22% of the time. The goal then became "to improve the percent of time the phone was picked up by the third ring from 21% to 65% of the time."

The third key area that was selected was sales volume. The indicator was average number of line items per order. The goal here was "to increase the average number of line items per order from six to 11."

Graphs were established tracking each of these items. The phone expense was tracked on a monthly basis, the percent of time that the phone was picked up on the third ring was tracked on a daily basis and average number of line items was tracked on a daily basis. Any time there was any improvement, it was reinforced. Phil made sure that he was timely and specific in his reinforcement of progress.

Phone expense the first month dropped from $3600 to $3300. Percentage of time the phone got picked up by the third ring went from 21% to 55%. At the end of a month, line items per order had gone from 6 to 8.2. At the end of the second month, phone expense had further dropped to $2700. The phone was now getting picked up by the third ring 88% of the time and average number of line items per order had climbed to 11.2.

At this point in time, Phil and the five inside salesmen decided to drop the measure of the phone being picked up by the third ring except for occasional checking. The reasoning was that the 25% reduction in phone expense meant a 25% reduction in phone time. Therefore, picking up the phone by the third ring was almost automatic.

The net impact thus was a reduction in phone expense from $3600 to $2700 a month and an increase in the average number of line items per order from 6 to 11.2. There was also an initial increase in the percent of time the phone was answered by the third ring from 21% to 88% and a presumed maintenance of that level.

# APPENDIX VI
## Using the Self-Starting Mechanism to Improve Quality

Jack was faced with a problem. Quality defects in his department were running at an alarmingly high rate. Quality defects were 50% higher than the targeted amount and even the targeted amount yielded an overall quality rate of only 89%. (Jack's plant, including his department, also suffered from poor labor relations, excessive absenteeism and high costs.

An Achievement Climate Survey was taken throughout the plant. The results were similar for most departments, but for the purposes of this brief history, we'll just use Jack's department. The survey showed that in Jack's department, there were some steps that could be taken to improve performance. Based upon the three factors of the Self-Starting Mechanism, the survey showed that:

1. Employees felt that supervisors did not think very much of the employees. Low communications were being communicated and employees felt that although they were unable to articulate specifically why, that the supervisors had relatively low expectations for performance.

2. These low expectations were in sharp contrast to expressed goals. Goals were set at reasonably high levels that involved stretch. Although the goals were not "mission impossible," they clearly indicated that a great deal was expected. (This is a common pattern in many organizations where an Achievement Climate Survey will show that even though high goals have been set, people are communicating low expectations in other ways such as intonations, nonverbal language and general environment, as is mentioned in Chapter 5.)

3. Feedback in the form of information was in moderately good shape although it was haphazardly distributed and was frequently too late to allow people to do much to change their operations.

4. Feedback in the form of applause was almost nonexistent. As one employee penciled on his survey, "they're pretty damn quick around here to tell you when you do something wrong, but you almost never hear from them when you do something right."

Based upon the results of the survey, training in the use of the Self-Starting Mechanism factors was given. Additionally, follow-up implementation help was provided to Jack and his staff. The two target performance areas were absenteeism and quality.

The three traits of the Self-Starting Mechanism were organized into a coherent approach focusing on attendance and quality. Since graphs were going to go up in the work groups, some sort of explanation was in order. The supervisors got their work groups together and explained that "because we know we are better than our results, we want to set up some goals to try and improve." During these discussions, supervisors made it a point to be positive.

To emphasize the fact that they wanted to take a positive approach, they pointed out to members of the work group that they wanted to measure attendance rather than absenteeism. Goals were established for both quality and attendance. Graphs for each of these were placed on the walls in each work group. Because performance was so far below where it should be, goal areas were established for both quality and attendance. Sensitive to what they were "saying" both verbally and nonverbally, supervisors did their best to communicate positive expectations to employees about the potential for improvement and the probability of reaching the targeted level of performance.

Most importantly, careful attention was paid to reinforcement of any or all improvements. Employees who came to work on time were thanked for being there promptly and their contribution to the improved levels of performance was noted. A typical reinforcing statement for a situation like this would be, "Mike, glad to see you here before the line gets going. As you can see from the graph there, that not only helps our attendance, but most importantly, helps improve the quality of our work group. You're an important member of our team and the effort you're making to be here every morning when the line starts up is appreciated not only by me, but by others in the department. It makes everybody's job a little easier to do."

On those days when quality improved, supervisors made a point of pointing it out to individuals. Occasionally, they would put a short handwritten note over the clock perhaps saying, "today, we beat our quality goal again—thanks very much for your help. Pretty soon, we'll be the best department in the plant."

If quality didn't improve, but the supervisor felt everybody had really made an all-out effort to work on quality that day, they were still reinforced for trying hard, even though the quality goal was not met for that particular day. (Reinforcing the desired behavior even though the results aren't good.) A typical statement used in a situation like this was:

*Employee:*     Well, we missed the damn quality goal today.

*Supervisor:*   Yes, I see that we did, but I also noticed that you were really in there pitching, Mike. I appreciate the effort you put in. With conscientious effort like that, we'll pretty soon be hitting or beating it every single day.

Notice that supervisors are again reinforcing both behavior and results as a way of getting quality to an acceptable level. This particular department, as well as this particular plant, was in severe difficulties. Improvement did not come quickly, nor did it come easily, but nine months after installing the techniques of the Self-Starting Mechanism, Jack's department was hitting their quality target every single day. In addition, attendance was 37% better.

# APPENDIX VII
## Using the Self-Starting Mechanism to Improve Productivity

John was the Shift Superintendent in a warehouse. In fact, a large warehouse. It was the Master Distribution Center of an auto manufacturer's parts division. The center covers over 1 million square feet of warehouse space, contains 105,000 different automotive parts, ships between 40,000 and 60,000 line orders a week, and moves 600,000 pounds of materials in and out every day. Inventory runs around $50,000,000.

Over a four month period of time, John reduced absenteeism from 9% to 3.5%, reduced the incoming loads unplaced at the end of the shift from an average of 70 a day to an average of 1 a day, and reduced the tickets bounced due to misplaced parts from an average of 45 a day to an average of 5 a day.

Here's how John did it. An admitted "hard-nose" when it came to chewing people out for things that they did wrong, he attended a workshop involving the techniques described in this book. He then returned to the plant to put them to work.

He explained his new approach to the employees, telling them, for example, that he was going to start measuring attendance rather than absenteeism. That teamwork was important and everyone needed to be there to get the job done well.

He posted graphs in the appropriate work areas that measured attendance, incoming loads unplaced at the end of the shift, and tickets bounced due to misplaced parts. As he did so, he did several things:

1. He explained the importance of each measurement to the employees and how what they did tied into that measurement.

2. He showed them where present performance was, stated that he'd like to see an improvement, was confident that they had ability to get there, and that he wanted to set an improvement goal with them.

3. They then discussed steps that could be taken, job related tasks that were critical to goal attainment, and possible support that might be needed to reach the goal.

4. Based upon that information, they set two targets — a standard that they would continue to meet and a goal that they would work hard to achieve.

With the positive expectations and goals in place, John then began reinforcing any progress that was made. If incoming loads unplaced at the end of the shift went from 70 to 66, he reinforced that improvement, saying something like ''Gang, I see we've gone from an average of 70 down to 66 today. I appreciated the effort that's gone into that improvement. We're making good progress in the right direction.''

John admitted that such an approach was considerably at odds with his past behavior. There was also no small amount of ''How long will this last?'' on the part of the employees. However, he persevered and within three months, had achieved the results described earlier in this appendix.

Today, John runs two warehouses for the same company.

# APPENDIX VIII
## Using the Self-Starting Mechanism to Reduce Errors

Mary was the accounting supervisor in a $35,000,000 firm. However, she had one major problem that she needed to solve. There were too many errors on invoices.

As you might well imagine, the errors caused a variety of problems. Accounts receivable were never accurate. Income was either overstated or understated. Customers were irritated. Getting the errors corrected was time consuming. And during the time that the errors were getting corrected, customers didn't pay with the result that cash flow was impaired.

Mary took a very simple and straight forward approach. She explained the nature of the problem and all of its ramifications to the people responsible for invoicing, expressed her confidence in their ability, said that she'd like to try to get it below an average of 8 in 60 days.

Mary then placed a graph on the wall of the department and reinforced anyone who caught an error before the invoice went out, any day with no complaints about invoicing errors, and any downward movement from the average of 17 a week.

In three weeks, she had it down to 5 errors per week. It's fluctuated between 3 and 5 since then.

| KEY AREA | INDICATOR | STANDARD | GOAL |
|---|---|---|---|
| Business Department | No. new accounts | 2/month | To increase new accounts from 2.2/month to 3/month by January 1. |
| | No. cold calls | 5/week | — |
| Sales | $ volume | $80,000/month | To increase $ volume from $81,000 to $87,000 by May 15. |
| | Unit volume | 500/month | To increase unit volume from an average of 507 to an average of 540/month by May 15. |
| Profitability | Average order size | 2,600 | To increase average order size from 2,400 to 2,600 by August 10. |
| | Total gross margin dollars/month | $31,000 | — |
| Cost Control | T & E/Sales | 1% | To reduce T & E expense from 1.0%/month to 0.9%/month (hold dollars constant on increased sales). |

| KEY AREA | INDICATOR | STANDARD | GOAL |
|---|---|---|---|
| Productivity | Line items/hour | 12 | To improve line items/hour from 13 to 14 by August 1. |
| Quality | Errors/lines picked | 2% | To reduce error rate from 2.2% to 2.0% by May 10. |
|  | Damage and breakage/ dollar volume shipped | 1.3% | — |
| Cost Control | Delivery expense/ sales | 2.5% | To reduce delivery expense from 4.0% to 2.7% by June 1 |
| Profitability | Inventory turns | 5 | — |

| KEY AREA | INDICATOR | STANDARD | GOAL |
|---|---|---|---|
| Production | Units/shift | 1,125 | To improve production from 1,120 to 1,130/shift by May 15. |
| Labor Relations | No. of grievances/week | 8 | — |
| | % of disciplinary actions that "stick" | 95% | — |
| | Absenteeism | 9% | — |
| Quality | Scrap rate | 1.2% | To reduce scrap rate from 1.2% to 1.0% by March 1. |
| | Rework as a % of direct labor dollars | 3.5% | To reduce rework from 3.5% to 2.8% of direct labor dollars by April 10. |
| Safety | Frequency rate | 1/thousand hours worked | — |
| | Severity rate | Average of 2.1—nothing above 7 | — |
| Housekeeping | Score on form | 85 points | — |
| Cost Control | Disposal item dollars as a % of direct labor dollars | 0.75% | To reduce disposable item dollar % from 1% to 0.75%. |

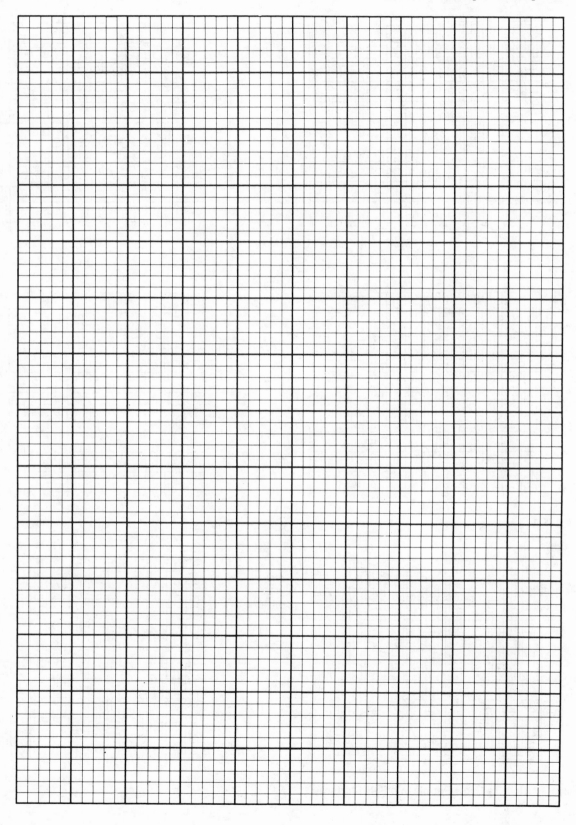

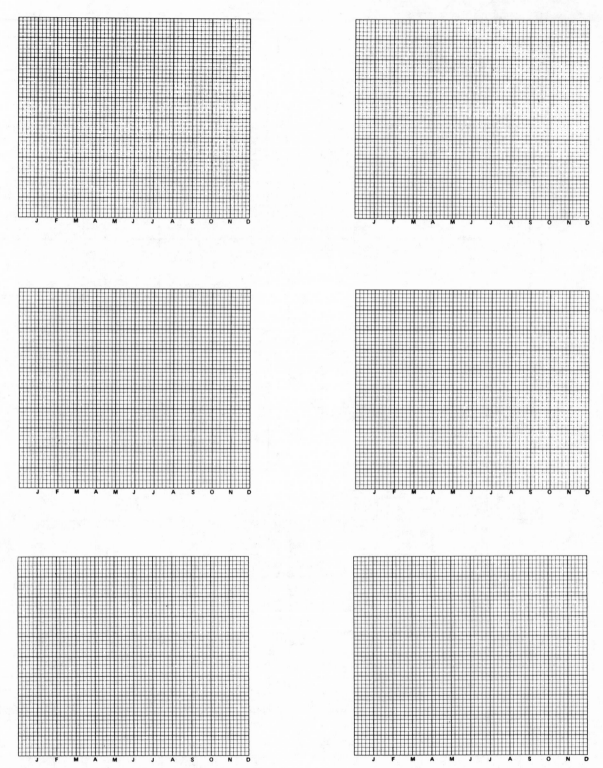

# Special Notes: Creating a High Performance Climate in Your Organization

The techniques described in this book have been used by many individuals to improve performance in a wide range of settings. They've been applied to particular individuals, at the departmental level, at worksites, on a divisional basis, and even corporate wide-basis.

Many organizations find that to reach everyone in the organization, they need other options than just a book. Here are some that are available:

- A twelve program cassette series that explains the concepts contained in the book for those who learn better by listening than reading or for those who like to have tapes to reinforce what they've read.

- Discounts for bulk purchases of the book.

- Executive briefing sessions for organizations holding management conferences.

- Two and three day seminars for employee training purposes.

- Consulting for analysis and implementation of these techniques.

- Designing learning systems for those performance problems that require learning new skills on the part of the employees.

- Presentations before industry groups on improving employee productivity with these techniques.

For details on any of these approaches write Program Director, Performance Research Associates, 2 Northwick, Ann Arbor, Michigan 48105.

# Footnotes

### Chapter 1
1. This diagram was first brought to my attention by Dr. David Whittset.

### Chapter 2
1. Robert Rosenthal. "On the Social Psychology of the Self-Fulfilling Prophecy: Further Evidence for Pygmalion Effects and Their Mediating Mechanisms," *MSS Modular Publications, Inc.,* New York, New York (1974) Module 53, p. 1-28.
2. Albert S. King, "Self-Fulfilling Prophecies in Training the Hard-Core: Supervisors' Expectations and the Underprivileged Workers' Performance," *Social Science Quarterly* (September 1971), pp. 369-378.

3. J. Sterling Livingston, "Pygmalion in Management," *Harvard Business Review,* July-August 1969.

### Chapter 5
1. See Appendix for a sample "goals contract" involving key areas, indicators, and goals.
2. This information is based upon informal conversations with Kenneth H. Blanchard. The basic Situational Leadership Model is more fully described in *Management of Organizational Behavior, Third Edition,* Prentice Hall, Englewood Cliffs, New Jersey. Authored by Paul Hersey and Kenneth H. Blanchard.

### Chapter 10
1. See the Appendix for sample graphs you can copy.